Transforming Our Nation

Empowering the Church for a Greater Harvest

Jacqueline Dugas   James Montgomery

Murray Jarman   Murray Moerman

Wesley Peach   Reginald Bibby

Lorne Hunter   Glenn Smith

Arnell Motz   Brian Seim

Gary Walsh   Gerry Kraft

Church Leadership Library

Richmond, B.C.

Church Planting Canada

is a ministry of *Outreach Canada*

which serves as the Church Planting Track of *Vision Canada*

and as national expression of the international *AD2000 and Beyond* movement

and *DAWN Ministries.*

Dawn Ministries

Canadian Cataloguing in Publication Data

Main entry under title:

Transforming our nation

Includes bibliographical references.
Includes material from the conference,
Canadian Church Planting Congress,
held in Bramalea, Ont., Oct. 27-30, 1997.
ISBN 0-9694564-2-5
1. Church development, New. 2. Church growth-Canada.
I. Moerman, Murray, 1949-
II. Title: Canadian Church Planting Congress (1997 : Bramalea, Ont.).
BV652.24.T72 1998   254'.1   C98-910737-X
Printed in Canada by
West Coast Reproduction Centres, Vancouver, B.C.

Published by *Church Leadership Library*
#16-12240 Horseshoe Way,
Richmond, B.C. V7A 4X9

In memory of

Susie Kraft, wife and ministry partner of Outreach Canada's Executive Director, Dr. Gerry Kraft. Her years of faithful service to OC and her cheerfulness, dedication and courage in the service of our Lord Jesus Christ was an inspiration to all who knew her.

Acknowledgments

Project Manager: Clarence Henderson

Editing and Proofing: Clarence Henderson, Jan Henderson, staff of Outreach Canada

Technical Support: Murray Jarman, Lorne Hunter

Research: Lorne Hunter, Murray Jarman, Brian Seim

Prayer: Jacqueline Dugas, Carol Moerman, Susie Kraft and many others who invested hours praying for the project and for God's ongoing use of the prophetic call of the book.

Cover Design: Cathy Chan

Chapter Contributors

Reginald Bibby—Sociologist of Religion with the University of Lethbridge and author of many studies and books analyzing Canadian religious trends.

Jacqueline Dugas—Director of the Centre for Prayer Mobilization with *Every Home International*, Canada.

Lorne Hunter—Researcher and Demographer with *Outreach Canada*.

Murray Jarman—Research and Systems Coordinator with *Outreach Canada*.

Gerry Kraft—Executive Director of *Outreach Canada*.

Murray Moerman—Coordinator for *Church Planting Canada* with *Outreach Canada*.

James Montgomery—President of *DAWN Ministries* and innovator in the mission strategy of national saturation church planting.

Arnell Motz—President of *SIM Canada* and founding coordinator of *Vision Canada*.

Wesley Peach—Church planter in Québec with the *Associated Gospel Churches* and *UFM International*.

Brian Seim—Missionary with *SIM Canada and* researcher with the *Unreached Peoples Track* of the *AD2000 and Beyond* movement.

Glenn Smith—Executive Director of *Direction Chrétienne* and Chair of *Urbanus*, an international evangelical francophone urban partnership for training practitioners.

Gary Walsh—President of the *Evangelical Fellowship of Canada*.

Preface

Much of the material in this book first appeared in the conference notebook distributed to the 279 registrants at the *Canadian Church Planting Congress '97* held in Bramalea, Ontario, October 27-30, 1997. The conference theme was "Pray, Plan, Plant"—themes also reflected in the sections of these eleven chapters.

This revision has the benefit of recently released components of the 1996 Canadian census, an overview of the first *Canadian Church Planting Congress*, a new chapter by Dr. Gary Walsh and further reflection by the authors after interaction with congress delegates.

Church Planting Canada, sponsor of the congress, is a broadly based ad hoc association of denominations and ministries. Our desire is to work cooperatively to disciple the whole nation and all its people groups through evangelistic church planting, saturating our mission field with the Gospel. *Church Planting Canada* in this way serves as the Canadian church planting track of *Vision Canada* and the international *AD2000 and Beyond* movement and *DAWN Ministries*.

Vision Canada is the result of an affiliation agreement between the *Evangelical Fellowship of Canada's Vision 2000* and several Canadian tracks of the *AD2000 and Beyond* movement. Dr. Arnell Motz served as *Vision Canada's* first coordinator. Administrative support for *Church Planting Canada* is provided by *Outreach Canada*.

The research team, seeking to supply current information on the harvest force and harvest field in Canada, recognizes the need for consistency when measuring either reality. This is particularly important over time, as those committed to working toward the discipling of our nation wish to evaluate progress in the task. We also recognize the valuable discussion that inevitably accompanies any such definition.

For these reasons we believe it important to share the rationale for definitions used in this study. There are two primary issues to be addressed:

1. Definition of the *harvest force*.

In the first half of the century, those who held to Biblical basics such as the deity of Christ, authority of Scripture and unique sufficiency of the cross were termed "fundamentalists." During the second half of the century, the term "evangelicals" came to be preferred by those who held these same truths but emphasized equally the implications of these truths in ministries of compassion in their communities and the world. The development of the *Evangelical Fellowship of Canada* and its relief and development partner, *World Relief Canada*, testifies to the strength of this movement in Canada.

Dr. George Rawlyk emphasized the presence and work of evangelicals within mainline Protestant and Roman Catholic congregations, suggesting approximately one-seventh of those worshipping within these traditions hold to evangelical beliefs.

Many within these historic movements of Christendom are quite comfortable with the term "evangelical," identifying wholly with the "evangel" proclaimed classically by the apostle Peter in Acts 10:34-43. Some in these movements, wishing to distance themselves from the political views of other evangelicals, prefer the term "Biblically orthodox." Others prefer various other terms or none at all.

Recognizing the history of the discussion, the research team compiling the work underlying several of the following chapters continue to use the term "evangelical" (as expressing the Gospel message summarized in Acts 10:34-43) until a broad consensus regarding language use develops otherwise.

2. What should be measured to evaluate progress in the discipling of our nation?

It is broadly recognized that the reason definitions of evangelical strength in Canada vary to the degree they do is that different things are measured.

Current definitions of evangelical strength, depending on criterion chosen, include:

- *Religious affiliation*—currently 10.8% in response to a question asked at the beginning of each decade by Census Canada,

- *Church membership*—9.5% according to evangelical denominational records and Rawlyk's findings of one seventh of evangelicals within historic traditions,

- *Church attendance*—5.2% by the records of the evangelical denominations and Rawlyk's findings of one-seventh of evangelicals worshipping in historic traditions, or

- *Christian beliefs*—16% or higher depending on which beliefs are measured in a given poll.

In 1990 Dr. Arnell Motz, editor of *Reclaiming a Nation,* used a combination of evangelical worship attendance, adherants and evangelicals in mainline churches to come to the conclusion that Canada was 7.6% evangelical in 1989. By this criteria the evangelical movement grew slightly to between 8 and 10% in 1997.

The higher percentages found by polls of individual beliefs are legitimately used to lobby Ottawa for legislation reflecting Biblical values. However, our concern is ultimately for Biblical discipleship in this life and preparation, in Biblical terms, for the day of accountability and the life to come (most evangelicals recognize polled beliefs in an undefined god to be of comparatively little help in understanding the degree to which Canadians have become devoted followers of Jesus Christ).

Furthermore, how are we to respond to those who claim to be born again but hold non-Biblical views on theology (e.g., reincarnation) and/or morality? It is difficult to count such persons as members of the harvest force.

The research and editorial team has chosen to measure the strength of the evangelical movement and its progress in discipling the nation in relatively simple terms: Canadians holding to the evangel (Acts 10:34-43) in the context of redemptive worshipping communities giving priority to evangelizing the world. Our figures are based on a ratio of congregations in which this evangel is proclaimed, to the number of persons yet unconnected to this redemptive community.

Biblical theology does not permit the separation of an individual's theoretical belief system from participation in the nurturing life of the local church. "Unchurched Christians" are a New Testament oxymoron (which we may measure but not define as accomplishing the goal). The same is true of those who believe the Gospel to be true "for them," but who are embarrassed by the absolute claims of the Gospel on the allegiance of those yet uncommitted to Christ.

We recognize some readers will hold other views. However, we believe the most honest gift we can offer is that which makes its working assumptions clear at the beginning of the research study.

May the Lord of the harvest use this book to bring greater prayer and purposeful focus to His Church and His glory as we join hearts and focus our resources in *transforming our nation*.

Murray Moerman

July 1998

Foreword

It is a DAWN Strategy if. . .

The Great Commission to us literally is to make disciples of *nations*. God's interest in nations is made abundantly clear throughout the whole Bible. The current reality is that there is a stirring in nations all over the world.

One of the means God is using to maximize these opportunities is what we call a DAWN (Discipling a Whole Nation) or DAWN-type strategy. A true DAWN project is a saturation church planting process carried out at a national level, and includes eight steps and ingredients.

1. It is a DAWN project if there is a national leader and committee with a firm resolve and commitment to work at mobilizing the whole Body of Christ in a whole nation in a long-term repeating strategy that leads most directly to the discipling of the nation including all the people groups within it. Such a leader, along with the national committee, is sometimes referred to as a "John Knoxer," a man, woman or small group who embody the prayer of the reformer in Scotland whose life-long cry was, "Give me my country or I die."

This leader must not only have the passion and calling but also the spiritual gifts, the experience, the respect of national Church leaders and, significantly, the organizational structure necessary for mobilizing the Church of a nation in a DAWN project.

As DAWN has developed around the world, we have seen an honor roll of such godly men and women rise to the occasion. At least one DAWN project leader has been martyred as a direct result of his role in the growth of the evangelical Church in his nation. Others have risked jail, sold their homes, left their jobs and otherwise sacrificed their security and tranquillity in order to be involved at some level in the process of filling their country with congregations of new converts.

These godly men and women have emerged to take up the cause of the discipling of their nation under a great range of circumstances. The size, strength and spiritual dynamic of the Church varies from place to place. Likewise, the receptivity to the Gospel or the degree of repression and persecution is different in each situation. For these creative and persistent leaders, however, a way is usually found to keep the movement alive.

2. It is a DAWN project if it is built on the premise that the most direct way to work at the discipling of a whole nation is to fill it with evangelical congregations so there is one within easy access, both practically and culturally, of every person of every class, kind and condition of mankind in that nation. This includes all "reached" and "unreached" people groups.

As explained in detail in the book, *DAWN 2000: 7 Million Churches To Go*, the core idea of the DAWN strategy for world evangelization goes like this:

DAWN aims at mobilizing the whole Body of Christ in whole countries in a determined effort to complete the Great Commission in that country by working toward the goal of providing an evangelical congregation for every village and neighbourhood of every class, kind and condition of people in the whole country.

It is concerned that Jesus Christ become incarnate in all His beauty, compassion, power and message in the midst of every small group of people—400 or so to 1,000 or more in number—in a whole country, including all its "reached" and "unreached" people groups.

When this is accomplished, it is not assumed the Great Commission for a country has been completed, but that a practical and measurable goal has been reached toward making a disciple of that country and all the "nations" within it.

With a witnessing congregation in every small community of people, it is now possible to communicate the Gospel in the most direct, contextualized and productive way to every person in that land.

Every person now has a reasonable opportunity to make an informed, intelligent decision for or against Jesus Christ.

Everyone now has a church within easy access both in a practical as well as cultural sense where he or she can attend and be further trained in discipleship should he or she become a Believer.

The penultimate (next to last) step for making a disciple of every "nation" in a country has been reached.

When this happens in *every* country in the world, we can almost hear the trumpet sound. The primary task the Lord gave His Church is close to completion and the Lord can soon return for His bride.

Of all the many affirmations of this DAWN strategy we have heard from around the world, I still like best the comment of a former Methodist bishop in Zimbabwe. "DAWN is a one-word summary of the Great Commission," he said to DAWN missionary Ted Olsen. "Jesus told His followers to make disciples of all nations. DAWN is the essence of our Lord's command."

3. It is a DAWN project if there has been adequate research that determines:

a) the number of denominations in a country,

b) their respective number of local churches and members and/or average attendance,

c) the average annual growth rates (AAGR's) of each denomination,

d) the methodologies being used by various groups that are producing the best growth,

e) the ratio of churches to population for the whole nation and for every sub-group of the nation, and

f) such contextual factors as the history, economy, religion, culture, politics, natural disasters and other societal forces that tend to indicate the relative responsiveness of the population and the methodologies and themes that might best see a response to the Gospel.

Xolisani Dlamini of Zimbabwe is representative of that special breed that, in some circumstances at least, risks life and limb to get the data needed for a successful DAWN project. In completing the research for one region of Zimbabwe, Xolisani hiked hundreds of kilometers, wore out five pair of shoes, interviewed scores of church leaders and spoke with dozens of government officials. In the process he encountered lions, deadly cobras, angry elephants and even killers wielding machetes and witches breathing satanic curses.

But even more important, Xolisani helped gather the data that led the participants in a DAWN Congress to set a goal of planting 10,000 more churches, a goal that many are successfully working toward. On completion of his first round of data gathering, Xolisani said, "Now I know that the research I undertook was a divine appointment. Research is a most important thing! Without it we simply will not know how strong or how weak the Church is or where we need to plant new churches."

Or, as Ross Campbell, now with the *AD2000 and Beyond* movement, said after their first round of research in Ghana, "Nothing was the way we imagined it. We have had to change our whole strategy for 'churching' this country."

4. It is a DAWN project if a national congress is held where the primary leaders of all denominations and other parachurch organizations, along with leading pastors, gather to consider the discipling of their whole nation and analyze the data that has been collected.

This is, obviously, the most visible aspect of a DAWN-type project. It is the event where anywhere from 50 to 1,500 delegates, representing every stripe of evangelical, are gathered in unity and commitment to a long-range strategy of working toward a common goal.

Putting together such a congress requires great persistence in finding and gathering just the right mix of leaders, brilliance and spiritual insight in developing the prophetic message and a program to communicate it, skill in gathering and supervising a strong team of workers, ability to cut costs and raise large amounts of money—and much more! Committees are needed for selection of delegates, finances, site selection and arrangements, housing of delegates, congress program, communications and so on.

Tom Houston, International Director for the Lausanne Committee on World Evangelization, warns that it will be disastrous "...to move ahead before the whole Body is ready." The unity of the Church in some countries makes it possible to start a project almost as soon as it is presented. In Finland it took eight years before such unity came. In Japan, at this writing, there is such division between Pentecostals and non-Pentecostals that the time is still not ripe for a true DAWN project.

Sometimes there is the need for a major spiritual breakthrough. Such was the case in Argentina in September 1994, when leaders were gathered for an initial meeting to consider whether to proceed with a DAWN project or not. Bob Smart, who first experienced DAWN in his native England, broke down all barriers with his humble approach. "I come in the name of the English Church to apologize for what my country did in the Falklands war," he said. "I confess also the pride that we as a Church felt."

At this point, DAWN missionary Berna Salcedo heard someone cry. It turned out to be one of the pastors who had participated in that hostility. Soon other pastors were weeping all around the room. Someone asked Alberto De Luca, leader of the meeting, to give brother Smart a hug as a sign of forgiveness. From that point on, it was not difficult for the Church to come together for a DAWN Congress and national strategy.

5. It is a DAWN project if the delegation gathered at the national congress collectively commits itself to a specific number of churches to be planted by a specific date. This goal can either be suggested by the national committee based on the research done or can be the collective goal of all the denominations, missions and other parachurch organizations.

One of the best ways to set a national church planting goal—and get commitment to it by all denominations in a country—is the way it was done in England. There, the national Challenge 2000 (DAWN) committee spent many hours praying and poring over the data that had been gathered through their research project. They concluded that a goal of 20,000 new churches by the year 2000 seemed to be what the Holy Spirit was saying.

But they shared this goal with no one. Instead, they had each denomination set its own goals at the congress held in February 1993. When these individual goals were added together, the total came to about 20,000!

It was great confirmation to all that this represented the mind of Christ. With this conviction, the multiplication of churches throughout England is overcoming many years of decline.

6. It is a DAWN project if each evangelical denomination, mission agency and other group sets its own goals for number of churches to be planted by a certain date and develops and implements plans to reach that goal. It is expected that all parachurch organizations that do not plant churches themselves will so orient their ministries that they truly work "alongside" churches and denominations in their church-multiplication projects. All the activities of a DAWN process are useless if the participants do not make specific commitments to national and organizational goals for massive church planting efforts

In Guatemala, for example, 15 individual denominations set goals and developed plans for church-multiplication efforts. Under such names as *"Vision 90," "Faith Projection," "Advance," "One by One by One"* and so on, goals were set to double or triple their number of churches, have each church start a new church or reach a total of 1,000 churches. Most of these were five-year goals.

These individual denominational efforts kept a growth movement alive without a national focus and strong committee. Effective denominational projects of this nature include the same components as the national DAWN project.

7. It is a DAWN project if there is a national committee formed to keep the movement alive. One of the most crucial tasks of a DAWN committee is the continual communication of the vision to saturate a nation with churches. This committee sees that the research process continues, helps denomination leaders develop their plans for church multiplication, sees that regional DAWN seminars are held throughout the nation, encourages continued prayer for the movement, plans for the second DAWN Congress and in general keeps the vision alive.

Many committees are finding they can keep in contact with large numbers of Christian leaders through the regular distribution of a publication. Through this they are able to foster interest in and commitment to the national church planting strategy in all its many facets.

A good communication model is the newspaper-style publication called the *Philippine Challenge*, published by *Philippine Challenge*. With a circulation of 9,000 going to pastors and lay leaders throughout the Philippines, it has been chronicling the development and growth of the Philippine DAWN movement begun in 1974.

This publication is full of good news—churches being planted, new strategies being tried and denominational growth programs that are underway. You catch the encouraging flavor when you read some of the headlines: "Local church plants 13 churches in 1992," "Foursquare plants 126 churches in '88," "Mindanao owns half of DAWN 2000 goals," "Cebu church sends missionaries to Thailand," "23,000 churches found," "Church planting institute opens in '92."

This kind of reporting gives readers a bigger picture of what's going on in their nations. As they read issue after issue about what God is accomplishing through the Church, it also becomes a source of vision and creative thinking. People have models to follow and adapt to their situation.

8. It will be a truly powerful DAWN project if it is undergirded by effective prayer movements on national, regional, denominational and local church levels. As the current proliferation of books on world revival emphasize, prayer is the key. "The evangelical scholar J. Edwin Orr," writes David Bryant, "summarized into one simple statement his sixty years of historical study on great prayer movements preceding major spiritual awakenings: *'Whenever God is ready to do something new with His people, He always sets them to praying'*."

If God indeed is "about to do something new" in mobilizing His Body in nation after nation and the whole world to complete His 2,000-year-old command, surely this also will come about as He sets us to praying. Where would we be without intercessors like Jean Lim? God raised her up from a family of idol worshippers in Indonesia and from a life of gambling and greed. She came through a series of deaths of loved ones, attempted suicides, enslavement to Japanese Buddhism and attendance with mediums and witch doctors.

"Now," she says, "I just love to pray and wait upon the Lord in His presence for hours and hours." God has also used her to lead one of the most powerful prayer ministries connected with any DAWN project in the world. Her extended times of intercession, her small prayer group, her constant travels around the nation to organize prayer cells and her organizing of special seasons of prayer all mightily empower the Malaysia DAWN vision of planting 4,000 new churches.

I think there are two sides of the prayer coin that need equal emphasis. One is the spiritual warfare aspect of breaking down strongholds of the enemy in individuals, in cities, in people groups, in nations or wherever they occur. When satanic forces are bound or scattered, there is then entrance for the Gospel. This, rightfully, is receiving a lot of attention and is another indication of the worldwide revival we are in. It is a significant factor in being able to complete the Great Commission in our time.

Jim Montgomery
October 30, 1997

Table of Contents

Section One
Our Foundation: Prayer

The Priority and Power of Prayer
Jacqueline Dugas

Section Two
Our Method: Planting

Can Canada Be Discipled?
Dr. Murray Moerman

Church Planting: Key to Discipling Our Nation
Dr. Murray Moerman and Lorne Hunter

Section Three
Our Focus: Unreached People

Section Four
Our Mission Context

Epilogue

Appendices

Tables and Figures

Chapter Four

Chapter Five

Chapter Six

Chapter Seven

Chapter Ten

Epilogue

Section One

Our Foundation: Prayer

"*Ask and it will be given to you; seek and you will find; knock and the door will be opened to you. For everyone who asks receives; he who seeks finds; and to him who knocks, the door will be opened*" (Matthew 7:7).

Chapter One

The Priority and Power of Prayer

Jacqueline Dugas

As you think of our mission as Christians to take the Gospel to everyone, everywhere, do you ever feel "caught" in a terrifying obligation rather than "called" to a thrilling opportunity?

Many Canadian Christians today wonder if it is possible to effectively reach their new Canadian neighbours with the good news of Jesus Christ. They struggle to believe that people of drastically different cultures and religions would actually accept the radical claims of Christ. Indeed, this is difficult to comprehend with the natural mind. But the witness of Scripture and the stream of testimonies pouring in from around the world give us incontrovertible reason to take on Christ's challenge with joy and assurance. Lives can be transformed here as well!

1 - Prayer is the Key to Fruitful Evangelism

The evangelization of every ethnic group is doable. Also, current reports on the global advance of the Gospel indicate that one factor in particular is making a measurable difference—focused, intercessory prayer. Regions receiving such attention in prayer are experiencing an increase in conversion rates and in successful church planting initiatives.

"Neglect of Prayer is a Willful Limitation of Success"

This is not a new phenomenon. Similar experiences have marked the history of the Church for 2,000 years, and today's harvest of spiritual fruit attests to the fact that determined intercession results in divine intervention. Aware of the relationship between prayer and evangelism, Robert Speer once argued that a neglect of prayer is actually a denial that God is leading. He added, "Neglect of prayer is a willful limitation of success."[1]

In October 1993, nearly 21 million intercessors worldwide participated in history's largest prayer meeting ever—30 days of focused intercession for 64 nations. From every continent, prayer ascended to God for the 64 nations within the 10/40 Window (an area of the world stretching from 10 degrees to 40 degrees north of the equator, from the west of Africa to the east of Asia). One nation located in that region of the world, India, was profoundly affected by the innumerable hours of prayer offered on its behalf. At the international headquarters of *Every Home for Christ* (EHC), harvest reports from India have since indicated that responses to the Gospel presentations increased from 1% to 10% in the months immediately following the first global prayer thrust. In addition, the formation of Christ Groups (church plants) by EHC's ministry in India have soared to more than 150 per month! This is record-breaking church planting in a predominantly Hindu nation.

That God answers prayer is a recognized and accepted fact in the Church worldwide, including Canada. But it appears that the practice of prayer may not be as popular. The astounding difference between church growth in Canada and that experienced on other continents raises the question of whether we are really praying.

For those who may doubt the critical contribution of prayer to the forward movement of the Church, consider the words of Dr. A. T. Pierson..."Every step in the progress of missions is directly traceable to prayer. It has been the preparation for every new triumph and the secret of all success."[2]

Whether we long for personal growth or hope to touch our world and affect the course of history, we must view prayer as both the starting point and goal of every movement in which are the elements of permanent progress.

The Power of Prayer in Russia and the CIS

Recently the pastor of a Presbyterian church in Denver, Colorado, was speaking with Paul Ilyin, Every Home for Christ's Regional Director for the CIS. "Where can we plant a church?" he asked. "Our congregation would like to do something that will bear lasting fruit in your region of the world."

Pointing to a world map near him, Paul replied, "Just pick a town, any town! Everywhere people are hungry and waiting."

Inspired by the abundance of opportunities, the pastor walked up to the map and focusing his attention on the central region asked, "How about here, right in the middle?" That was the town of Tumen, located in the centre of Siberia. Immediately plans were put into motion to begin the planting of a church in a community with no Christian witness.

Upon his return to Russia, Paul sent a team of three men to the town of Tumen (one of them named Peter Stalin!). Their chief purpose was to pray for every home and distribute Gospel literature to each one.

Meanwhile, back in Denver, the Presbyterian congregation began praying and preparing a team who would join the three men and labour with them for some time.

Through many months of preparation, the congregation in the United States was trained in evangelism praying and organized prayer teams that would cover the entire project with intercession before, during and following the launching of the new church. In 1997, barely a year after the initial vision, the town of Tumen had a church of 354 members led by a pastor trained at St. James Bible College in Kiev, and was already sponsoring a second church plant in a neighbouring community!

The plan was so simple. First, prayer. Second, a Gospel presentation to every home, with prayer. Third, an invitation to a public meeting where the Gospel was preached and for which there was much prayer. Fourth, careful follow-up, with discipleship training and more prayer.

This scenario is a familiar one in Russia and the surrounding Republics. Over the last seven years 54 churches have been planted following this simple yet focused strategy. And some of these 54 churches now have up to 10 other church plants under their care.

In June 1997 another pastor from an Assembly of God church in Denver led his congregation to plant a church in Slavutich, the town that was built to replace Chernobyl in Ukraine. They followed the same straightforward plan of prayer, proclamation and follow-up. By April 1998 a congregation of over 150 members was worshiping in Slavutich!

2 - Prayer is the Starting Point and the Sustaining Force

History and current testimonies deliver abundant proof that God works profoundly, effectively and completely in answer to believing prayer.

Prayer must not be seen as a ritual, but rather as an essential tool that God gave us to build His kingdom in our lives and in the world.

As Canadians, we do have good reasons to be very concerned about the spiritual condition and destiny of our country and its people. Is it reasonable then to dare to believe that we can evangelize our Hindu, Buddhist, Muslim, materialistic or secular humanist neighbour here in Canada? The incredible progress of the Church in nations where countless believers are at work in prayer should convince the most skeptical that everyone, everywhere can be transformed by the power of the Gospel.

God Can Do Amazing Things in Canada

A.W. Tozer left us this encouraging thought: "Anything that God has ever done, *He can do now.* Anything that God has ever done anywhere, *He can do here.* Anything that God has ever done for anyone, *He can do for you.*"

Today the great and rapid progress of world evangelization on other continents and in spiritually dark regions of the world serves as an up-to-date testimony of what God will do when His people pray. It is also a strong reminder for us that the evangelization of our multi-cultural and multi-faith nation is achievable.

As we ponder the recent testimonies from Siberia and Ukraine shared earlier, we cannot help but note the dramatic answers that followed prayer offered on behalf of a spiritually thirsty people. If spiritual thirst is a qualifier for receptivity to the Gospel, then Canadians are ripe for harvest!

Various sources and reliable research indicate that Canadians are searching for inner peace and meaningful relationships.

In *A Matter of the Heart,* published in early 1998, Rudy and Marny Pohl share their perspective on God's vision for Canada. They confidently affirm that our multi-cultural and multi-faith nation must be viewed through a Christian-Biblical world view which states that God is the Lord of history and Jesus is the King of the nations. In A *Matter of the Heart* we are encouraged to consider all the peoples of this great country as being here by God's sovereign choice and for His purpose. Here, amidst the nations, the Church of Jesus Christ has the opportunity to be light and consolation. Those who embrace God's vision for Canada will cease to fear for the future of this country and be free to love their neighbour as themselves. Consequently, all who seek to minister to this nation must prayerfully and thoughtfully address divisive issues and past sins in light of the mercy and grace which govern the Kingdom of God.[3]

Unshakable Confidence in God

As we plan and develop strategies to engage our resources, time and energy to evangelize Canada, perhaps one the first questions we should ask ourselves is simply, "What do I believe and expect from God?"

In *Knowledge of the Holy*, A.W. Tozer makes these insightful comments:

> *What comes into our minds when we think about God is the most important thing about us. ...the gravest question before the Church is always God Himself, and the most portentous fact about any man is not what he at a given time may say or do, but what he in his deep heart conceives God to be like. ...Always the most revealing thing about the Church is her idea of God, just as her most significant message is what she says about him or leaves unsaid... Were we able to extract from any man a complete answer to the question, "What comes into your mind when you think about God?" We*

might predict with certainty the spiritual future of that man. Were we able to know exactly what our most influential religious leaders think of God today, we might be able with some precision to foretell where the Church will stand tomorrow.[4]

Without an unshakable confidence in the ability and willingness of God to bring everyone to the new birth experience, it will be difficult to pray effectively for the conversion and spiritual development of people with cultural and religious experience foreign to the Christian tradition.

In Matthew 9:35-38, Jesus assures us that God Himself is Lord of the harvest. Christ affirms with certainty that God is able to subdue everything that would seek to dominate the harvest. "...*Ask the Lord of the harvest, therefore, to send out workers into his harvest field*" (Matthew 9:38). Implied in the word harvest is the promise of bounty, of fruitfulness and of hard work well rewarded.

3 - Prayer is the God Tool Against Resistance

But there is another reality about the harvest that cannot be overlooked. It is the *resistance* factor. In order to bring in the harvest, workers need to exert some measure of effort and careful planning. In the same way we need to be aware of the resistance factor working against the Gospel and determine to address it.

The Struggle Against Powers of Darkness

The apostle Paul wrote, "*For our struggle is not **against** flesh and blood, but **against** the rulers, **against** the authorities, **against** the powers of this dark world and **against** the spiritual forces of evil in the heavenly realms*" (Ephesians 6:12, emphasis Dugas).

This "against" dynamic that operates behind the scenes is the resistance to the Gospel we so often encounter.

9

In his second letter to the Church at Corinth, Paul writes about the presence of strongholds in the world. He immediately defines these as arguments and pretensions exalted *against* the knowledge of God. In the same passage he assures the reader that the Church is well equipped to demolish them.

> *"The tools of our trade aren't for marketing or manipulation, but they are for demolishing that entire massively corrupt culture. We use our **powerful God-tools** for smashing warped philosophies, tearing down barriers erected against the truth of God, fitting every loose thought and emotion and impulse into the structure of life shaped by Christ. Our tools are ready at hand for clearing the ground of every obstruction and building lives of obedience into maturity"*[5] (2 Corinthians 10:3-5, emphasis Dugas).

The phrase, "powerful God-tools," so aptly describes what God has ordained prayer and proclamation of the Scriptures to be able to do. In some of the darkest regions of the globe these "powerful God-tools" are changing the face of the religious world.

For instance, India, the birthplace of two of the world's great religions, Hinduism and Buddhism, represents a formidable stronghold of resistance to the Gospel. With a population of well over 900 million, this vast nation's ethnic diversity is also one of the most complex in Asia.[6]

How can we ever hope to penetrate such a nation and see its people transformed? To those who believe that God is Lord of the harvest, India's people are a part of God's promised harvest. And the recent advancement of the Gospel we described earlier in that culturally and religiously complex land is staggering.

The prayers of the Saints are effective to push back the canopy of oppression over people groups and nations so that the light of the Gospel may penetrate deep into people's hearts.[7] The "powerful God-tools" at the disposal of the Church do have divine power to subdue every dark kingdom to the Lordship of Christ.

4 - Prayer Guidelines for Church Planting

In Matthew 9:35-38 Jesus addresses a number of issues related to the harvest. He clearly links prayer to the harvest. But the harvest is not released and brought in only by prayer. Much work is involved. And in this brief passage the Lord also links prayer to work.

No one who has been directly or indirectly involved in evangelism and church planting will take lightly the human responsibility that is required to do the work. And for each phase of evangelism and church planting initiative there must be a thoughtful prayer support. Here are several basic areas to consider.

The Need for Divine Guidance

The zeal and commitment of the great missionary apostle Paul had no bounds. His commitment to Jesus Christ, the Kingdom of God and the Gospel took him into situations where most of us (if not all of us), hope we will never have to face. His zeal and commitment were in complete submission to the will and timing of the Lord of the harvest. The Book of Acts leaves no doubt as to the restrictions of God's perfect will and timing: *"...having been kept by the Holy Spirit from preaching the Word in the province of Asia. When they came to the border of Mysia, they tried to enter Bithynia, but the Spirit of Jesus would not allow them to"* (Acts 16:6,7).

Preparation and confirmation are essential before launching into a church planting initiative. In *Church Planting, the Next Generation,* Kevin Mannoia recommends a list of seven steps to consider, the first being personal commitment to a significant season of prayer. It could be a month or perhaps the best part of a year spent in intentional prayer asking the Lord for an open mind and an open heart. His direction could be different from our wishes. Also ask the Lord to place thoughts, Scriptures, books and people in your life who can all influence you in the direction you need to go.[8]

The Need for Discernment

In contemplating a particular community for evangelism and church planting, it is critical to gain an understanding of the hidden things that hold the community captive to darkness and rejecting the Gospel. In Jeremiah 33:3, God reassures us that He can and will reveal hidden things. He alone can reveal the key to Gospel receptivity in a community as well as in the life of a single individual.

In recent years many evangelical leaders have demonstrated the need for what is now known as *"spiritual mapping."* Simply stated, it is the process of gathering critical intelligence (information) of the past and present life of a community, region or nation in order to effectively influence people for Christ through prayer and evangelistic endeavours. The intent of spiritual mapping is to equip the Church in order to enhance its effectiveness in influencing people for Christ. George Otis, Jr., founder and president of Sentinel Group and spiritual mapping specialist, gives the following definition: "Spiritual mapping is a means whereby we can see what is beneath the surface of the material world; but it is not magic. It is subjective in that it is a skill born out of a right relationship with God and a love for His world. It is objective in that it can be verified (or discredited) by history, sociological observation and God's Word."[9]

Case studies, research and guidelines for spiritual mapping are increasingly available in book form in addition to being a focus at various conferences.

The Need for Appropriate Employment of Gifting

God knows exactly how to assemble for Himself an effective labour force! The gifts He has invested in each of us are to serve His great purposes.

When the time came to build the Tabernacle in the wilderness, He carefully chose, gifted and appointed the workers: *"See, I have chosen Bezalel son of Uri, ...and I have filled him with the Spirit of God, with skills, ability and knowledge... Moreover, I have appointed Oholiab ...to help him"* (Exodus 31: 2, 3, 6).

One of the great challenges facing the Canadian Church today is the need to effectively reach and disciple the growing numbers of ethnic peoples within our borders. In *Canada's New Harvest* we read, "Evangelism ...not only involves reclaiming nominal Christians, but compels witnessing to Muslims, Hindus, Buddhists, Jews, Sikhs or Traditional Religionists."[10]

It is critical to ask the Lord to provide workers He has filled with His Spirit, skills, ability and knowledge for the task, whatever region or people group is targeted. If you are launching a church planting initiative, ask the Lord to surround you with individuals who will provide you with strategic guidance and advice. Also pray for team workers with the appropriate gift mix for the job.

The Need for an Available Work Force

One of the first steps in mobilizing individuals is communicating the vision. Personal prayer serves as an effective means to increasing the passion in our own hearts and transfering the vision to more of God's people.

Simply sharing prayer requests for the needs of a particular church planting initiative can awaken unusual interest in someone else. As Romans 12: 6-8 indicates, some are needed to proclaim, others to serve, to teach, to encourage, to give, to lead and to show mercy. Allow this list from the book of Romans to enhance your prayers. The success of many ventures depend on the team that surrounds a leader. In *Missions Within Reach*, T.V. Thomas shares that team ministry is particularly effective in ethnic evangelism and church planting endeavours. Some of the great advantages are found in encouragement, shared insights and wisdom.[11]

5 - An Illustration from Home: Prayer Changes Aboriginal Heart

Stories of God at work among First Nations people from the west coast of Vancouver Island to the northernmost reaches of the continent confirm that God desires to bring every people group in this land to know Him. Billy Arnaquq of Broughton Island knows the power of prayer because not only was he brought to spiritual life through the prayers of his parents, but also the entire church in Broughton Island was birthed through their intercession.

A former drug pusher and heading straight for disaster, Billy committed his life to Christ in 1980 during a house fellowship meeting in Broughton Island that his parents had organized. However, the destructive patterns of his past resulted in the demise of his marriage and the alienation of his children. Billy recognized he still had many strongholds in his life to pull down and territory to possess within his being—his mind, will and emotions. Instead of giving up, Billy decided to start winning this territory back through persistent, prevailing prayer and intercession, beginning with his own soul.

By 1993, Billy was pastoring the little church in Broughton Island, but still living alone. Coffee breaks and lunch hours would be spent in prayer for the restoration of his marriage and family. He also prayed individually for every believer in his community.

By the Spring of 1995, Billy and Daisy were remarried during a conference in Broughton Island, witnessed not only by the whole community but also representatives from at least 19 communities of the Eastern Arctic. Today their home is a sanctuary of peace, his relationship with his children restored, and that same peace is flowing out into many homes of Broughton Island. Healing is taking place within households that once knew abuse and family violence. This peace at the family level is also reflected in greater economic prosperity within the whole community. The entire town is becoming a safer, better, more peaceful community because of what God is doing in more and more households like Billy's.

For Billy, the key to all of this is prayer and fasting. He holds regular prayer times every morning at the church, where the mayor often joins him. The mayor also hosts prayer meetings at least twice a week in the community council chambers.

Prayer Results in Continual Revival

Now God is using Billy in even greater spheres of influence to ignite revival fires in the surrounding communities, among them Pangnirtung, Clyde River, Pond Inlet and Arctic Bay. His local church is a giving church, funneling thousands of dollars to other missionary endeavours every year. Billy leads or joins missionary teams that are reaching out to Arctic Russia and even Greenland.

When Billy first began to pray for the community to the north of him, Clyde River, Northwest Territories several years ago, he knew of no believers there. But about four years ago God linked him with a family in that community who had received Christ and opened their home for a house of prayer. These people longed to see the life of Christ come to their whole community, bringing healing and salvation as it had to Broughton Island.

Over the next couple of years God continued to work through prayer, and by January 1997 there were about 40 believers in a community of 600 people. In one week, in answer to prayer, God moved strongly in healing both hearts and bodies. By the time Billy and visiting pastor Roger Armbruster left, the number of believers in the community had doubled. God continues to draw people. For instance, when God healed the family of the town administrator, the change in his life was so evident that everyone who worked in his office who had family problems began to come to him for prayer. Within a short time everyone who worked for the town, or lived within his sphere of influence, had become a Christian.[12]

Conclusion

When we pray we are confessing confidence in the God who is greater. In response to our prayers He can create new dispositions in the hearts of those who oppose the Gospel. He can create a thirst for Jesus in the hearts of those who once rejected Him. He can create circumstances to override the prevailing circumstances. He can provide all we need, within and without, to make us fruitful and effective evangelists and church planters. And He can do all this because He is greater than all.

Whether the mountains we face are immediately before us or on the distant horizon of world evangelism, let us dare to pray with confidence and expect much in return. Prayer is not limited by our timid hearts nor bound by our feeble voices, for it goes forth to reside in the strong heart of God and is acted upon by His infinite power.

Action Points

✓ Take a few minutes to examine your worldview. Do you believe that prayer's effect on the unseen realm affects what takes place in the physical realm? How would such a worldview affect your ministry approach and lifestyle?

✓ How would you need to reschedule your day to make prayer a priority?

✓ What do you need to understand most about prayer for evangelism and what practical steps can you take in order to gain that understanding?

Chapter Notes

[1] Robert Speer in *Prayer Power Points*, compiled by Randall D. Roth, Wheaton: Victor Books, 1995. p.125.

[2] Dr. A.T. Pierson as quoted in *Change the World School of Prayer*, Dr. Dick Eastman, Published by Every Home for Christ, 1976.

[3] Rudy & Marny Pohl, *A Matter of the Heart: Healing of Canada's Wounds*, Essential Publishing: Belleville ON, 1998. pp.92-100.

[4] A.W. Tozer, *Knowledge of the Holy*, Harper & Row Publisher: San Francisco, 1961. pp.1-2.

[5] *The Message*, Colorado Springs: NavPress, 1994.

[6] *Strongholds of the 10/40 Window*, edited by George Otis, Jr. with Mark Brockman, Seattle: YWAM Publishing, 1995. pp.97-99.

[7] John Dawson in *Light the Window*, Seattle: YWAM, 1995.

[8] Kevin W. Mannoia, *Church Planting, The Next Generation: Introducing the Century 21 Church Planting System*, Light and Life Press: Indianapolis, 1994, 1995, 1996. pp.25-27.

[9] George Otis, Jr. in *Breaking Strongholds in Your City*, edited by C. Peter Wagner, Regal Books: Ventura CA, 1993. p.33.

[10] *Canada's New Harvest: Helping Churches Touch Newcomers*, Edited by Brian Seim, SIM Canada. p.59.

[11] Dr. T.V. Thomas in *Missions Within Reach*, Edited by Dr. Enoch Wan, China Alliance Press: Canada, 1995. pp.22-28.

[12] As recounted by Pastor Roger Armbruster of Harvest Field Ministries, Niverville, Manitoba.

Section Two

Our Method: Planting

"But you will receive power when the Holy Spirit comes on you; and you will be my witnesses in Jerusalem, and in all Judea and Samaria, and to the ends of the earth" (Acts 1:8).

"And this gospel of the kingdom will be preached in the whole world as a testimony to all nations, and then the end will come" (Matthew 24:14).

Chapter Two

Can Canada Be Discipled?

Dr. Murray Moerman

Most Christians are familiar with the authoritative words of Jesus:

"All authority in heaven and on earth has been given to me. Therefore go and make disciples of all nations, baptizing them in the name of the Father and of the Son and of the Holy Spirit, teaching them to obey everything I have commanded you. And surely I will be with you always, to the very end of the age" (Matthew 28:18-20).

Jesus' directive may be almost too familiar. Sometimes we may wish His words were not directed toward us.

Canada is a large, diverse and in many ways challenging collection of people groups, beginning with the aboriginal peoples, her two founding cultures and the many cultures from around the world that have joined themselves to Canada since Confederation.

Does Jesus intend us as His followers to take literally this command "to make disciples of all" and apply it to Canada? What does it mean to "disciple" the "nation" of

Canada? Can it actually be done? These vital questions stand at the heart of this book and its challenge to the whole Church of Canada.

The "Nations"

The word "nations" in the Great Commission, most scholars agree, refers—not to such modern nation-states[1] as fill the current political landscape—but to each of the smaller people groups, castes, tribes, clans and other ethnic units that make up each "country."

Canadian "First Nations" reflect this understanding. All share this great land but retain a clear and often proud sense of individual "nationhood." A similar sense of cultural identity is retained by much of English Canada, Québec and immigrant peoples of various European and Asian lands.

The Canadian government has promoted and funded its policy of multi-culturalism, encouraging each culture to retain its sense of being, building cultural centers and holding festivals honoring a wide variety of Canada's ethnic heritage.

It has been commonly noted that people from logging communities will receive the Gospel most readily from believers who already live and work within their particular sub-culture. The same is true of university students, factory workers, government bureaucrats, trades people, skateboarders and farmers. People most trust people who are viewed as being from within their own group.

"Peoples" or "people groups," as sociologists and missiologists often term them, are those segments of society that tend to marry chiefly within their own group. Such groupings have a distinct consciousness of being unique and different from other groups in ways important to those within the given sub-culture. Usually individual members of a people group do not mix significantly with members of other people groups.

22

Figure 1
Examples of People Groups

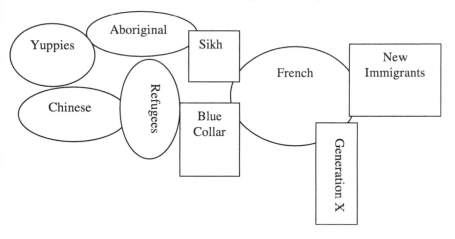

Should this be so? Many, including numerous Christians, think not. Yet the sociological reality cannot be overlooked if we are to effectively disciple the peoples of Canada to the Lord Jesus. In fact, the reality of people groups should be used effectively to bring the Gospel to all peoples. No people group may be ignored or assumed to be a part of another people group.

How many of such sub-cultures and people groups exist within Canada? —Hundreds, probably thousands. The precise number is not known. Whatever the actual number, these are the "nations," or "peoples" (*ta ethne* of Matthew 28:19) that the Lord has commanded us to disciple.

Some Christians are frustrated with the concept of people groups because untrained observers cannot readily observe such groups. Others prefer to ignore the concept, deny its validity or simply declare that all people should see themselves as one.

Yet these self-conscious "people groups" are one of the primary realities of the cultural mosaic called Canada—our mission field. Each *must* be reached for Christ. Each *has* been reached to varying degrees. Each *can* best be reached from within. In those people groups where a church planting movement of adequate strength to disciple the group to its fringes has not yet developed, cross-cultural missionaries are needed to help strengthen and develop such a church planting movement.

What Does it Mean to "Disciple a Nation?"

What does it mean to disciple a nation? What proportion of a nation would need to be devoted followers of Jesus for a nation to be considered discipled?

The Mission Board of the Southern Baptist Church offers definitions for four key terms relevant to this question:

- *A People*: An ethnic or racial group speaking its own language and distinguished by its self-identity with traditions of common descent, history, customs and language. This is the largest group within which communication can take place without encountering barriers of understanding or acceptance.

- *Unreached Peoples*: Are those within which there is no viable indigenous church movement of sufficient strength, resources, and commitment to sustain and ensure the continuous multiplication of churches. The numerical minimum for this degree of strength is frequently viewed as 5% churched evangelicals.

- *Evangelized People*: A people for which the majority of its members have heard the Gospel of Jesus Christ with such cultural and personal relevance that it results in sufficient understanding to accept Christ by faith as a believer (disciple) or to reject Him.

- *Christian People*: A people for which the majority of its members have made a profession of faith in Christ.

One measurement of whether a country is discipled, then, is when a majority of a country's populace professes faith in Christ. But is this the completion of the Great Commission?

A potential difficulty with this view is that "profession of faith in Christ" may permit significant nominalism. Many Canadians at the end of the millenium may profess to be Christian on the 2001 census. However they may not have heard the Gospel of Jesus Christ with sufficient understanding to accept Him by faith and become a believer (disciple).

Jesus sought not professions of faith (cf. Luke 9:57ff) but "fully devoted followers of Christ," to quote a term gaining broad acceptance that may prove better suited to the goal.

A second Biblical reality must come into play in understanding this critically important question. Profession of faith is always expressed Biblically within the community of the redeemed. "Unchurched Christian," in New Testament terms, must be recognized to be an oxymoron. The Church may, of course, take a wide variety of forms (wineskins), but must be characterized by life and service in community.

Finally, it must be clear that the goal of a majority of those professing faith or even "fully devoted followers of Christ" must be applied equally among all people groups within a country or province. The goal may be realized in some people groups to a rate of 70%, raising the national or provincial average to 51%, while other entire people groups within that country or province could remain virtually unevangelized (e.g., under 10%).

A better answer to the question, "What does it mean to disciple a nation?" may be, "Canada will be discipled when each people group within each city, town and community of each province has come to be composed of a majority of fully devoted disciples of Christ."

The goal of discipling the nation, we must remember, is not the discipling of any one of Canada's diverse mosaic of people groups. The goal is nothing less than discipling the *whole* nation.

Is it God's Will?

Donald McGavran, career missionary to India and father of the modern Church growth movement, believed this to be the central question:

The question of whether the discipling of a whole nation is God's will must be answered. For Christians it is supremely important. Unless discipling a whole nation is God's will, Christians will not begin it. If it is, they will spend life and treasure to complete it. Is discipling a whole nation God's will? That is the key consideration.[2]

It is not within the scope of this brief chapter to demonstrate that it is God's will that Canada and the nations be discipled. It is our conviction, however, that what God commands *is* His will, and that God's will is the life-work of those who serve Him.

Further, it is clear from Scripture that God called out of the nations, a people, through Abraham, for the blessing and salvation of *"all the peoples on earth"* (Genesis 12:3).

King Solomon recognized that the ultimate purpose of the temple was that *"all the peoples of the earth may know your (Yahweh's) name and fear you, as do your own people Israel"* (1 Kings 8:43).

The Psalmist anticipated the purpose of God that *"He will rule from sea to sea and from the River to the ends of the earth.... All kings will bow down to him and all the nations will serve him"* (Psalm 72:8, 11).

God said to His servant through Isaiah: *"I will also make you a light for the Gentiles, that you may bring my salvation to the ends of the earth"* (Isaiah 49:6).

In the coming of the Messiah the purpose of God is made yet more explicit. Jesus says: *"I am the light* (not only of Israel but) *of the* (whole) *world"* (John 8:12).

God's purpose to disciple *panta ta ethne* (all the peoples) is the basis of the command to Christ's followers in Matthew 28:19, Mark 16:16 and Romans 16:25ff. *"The Lord is...not wanting anyone to perish, but everyone to come to repentance"* (2 Peter 3:9). The end result—around the throne of God, will be gathered those purchased by Christ's blood *"from every tribe and language and people and nation"* (Revelation 5:9).

The intention of God's gracious heart is clear. We can participate in no higher calling than to fulfill this purpose of God. Those who remain unconvinced will give their lives to other pursuits. Those who believe the discipling of the nations is the purpose of God, revealed and made possible in Christ, will passionately give their lives and resources to this task.

Can the Nations be Discipled?

If it is God's will to redeem and disciple the nations of the world, then the accomplishment of His will must be possible. For we serve not a tribal god or even the chief god of an imagined pantheon, but the only eternal Creator, Redeemer and Ruler of the universe.

It must be possible for those who are His redeemed children to accomplish His will, empowered by His Spirit, for it is to us that the Great Commission has been given.

Some may believe in theory that the nations can be discipled, but doubt whether God's purpose can be accomplished in their lifetime. It is now nearly 2,000 years since Christ issued His Great Commission, and only about

10% of the world's population are now devoted disciples. Twenty percent are nominal Christians, 30% are within cultural or geographic reach of Christ's devoted followers, and 40% remain out of reach of any explicit Christian witness.[3]

Yet, Christianity *has* become the world religion with the greatest number of adherents. The rate at which people have become committed, Bible-believing Christians has escalated during the 20th century, despite great persecution and a spiraling global population growth (see Table 1).

This unprecedented growth provides strong evidence that God is accomplishing His purposes and should greatly encourage those committed to making disciples of all peoples. The completion of the Great Commission in our lifetime, despite the opposition of Satan and the apathy of much of Christ's Church, is an exciting possibility.[5]

Table 1[4]
Increase in Rate of Discipling the Nations

Percentage of Bible Believing Christians	Date	Years to Disciple One Percent of the World
1%	1430 AD	1,400 years
2%	1790 AD	360 years
3%	1940 AD	150 years
4%	1960 AD	20 years
5%	1970 AD	10 years
6%	1980 AD	10 years
7%	1983 AD	3 years
8%	1986 AD	3 years
9%	1989 AD	3 years
10%	1993 AD	4 years
11%	1995 AD	2 years

The question remains: "How can the central purpose of God, the discipling of all nations, best be accomplished?"

The Key to Discipling Nations: the Multiplication of Cells of Believers

Jesus said, "...*I will build my church*" (Matthew 16:18).

The church of which Jesus spoke is not an institution, but simple relational networks of disciples committed to God's life-transforming redemptive purposes. Jesus intended His disciples to multiply cells of believers in every culture and geographic locale. In this way the Church would permeate and transform the world, preparing the redeemed for His return and the age to come.

The discipling of a nation takes place as networks of disciples (churches or congregations) are multiplied within each of that nation's people groups, with each of these networks of disciples in turn forming others.[6]

The case for church multiplication as the foundational missiological building block is well established.[7] In fact, the multiplication of new "cells" or "networks" of many kinds is the heart of building the Body and discipling the nation. For example, as new disciples are touched by Christ and follow Him, new relational networks are formed, and new networks of congregations, denominations and mission agencies are birthed.

All this for one purpose—to see a gathering of devoted followers of Christ within practical and relational distance of every person in every class, kind and culture of people, so that every neighbourhood is penetrated and permeated with the saving love, care, truth and power of Jesus Christ. *"The earth will be filled with the knowledge of the glory of the LORD, as the waters cover the sea"* (Habakkuk 2:14).

Reasons for Church Planting

Roger Forster reports a startling discovery from a study of rapidly growing and declining denominations. Congregations of the most rapidly growing denominations that have not produced new churches, or are not themselves new churches, are declining at exactly the same rate as the fastest declining denomination. He states:

The only reason the (fastest growing) denomination is... growing is because it has churches that are producing churches, producing churches, producing churches, etc. That is where the...numerical growth is taking place. Where a denomination has stopped planting churches it will decline, and it will decline at almost a common regular rate.[8]

The following graphs, prepared and supplied by the Church of the Nazarene in Canada, clearly illustrate the importance of church planting. Critical to the growth of the Church of the Nazarene during the 25-year period studied—whether one examines worship attendance, membership or finances—is the contribution of newly established congregations. Even in declining Sunday School attendance, the rate of decline is significantly moderated by the contribution of new churches.

Many more reasons for church planting may be advanced. Allow me to suggest several.

1. **New churches must be multiplied to advance the Kingdom.**[9] The population of Canada and every major nation of the world continues to grow. In 1960 Canada's population was just under 18 million. Today Canada has approximately 30 million inhabitants. During this same period the majority of established congregations lost members or held their own. Even if all Christian churches grew at the same rate as did

Figure 2
Effect of Church Planting on Nazarene Worship

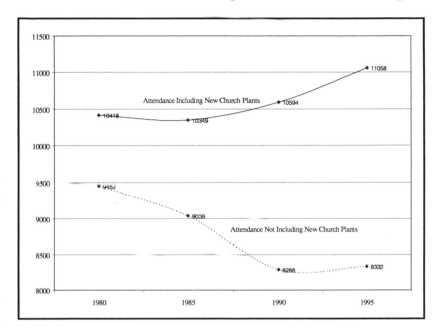

Figure 3
Effect of Church Planting on Nazarene Membership

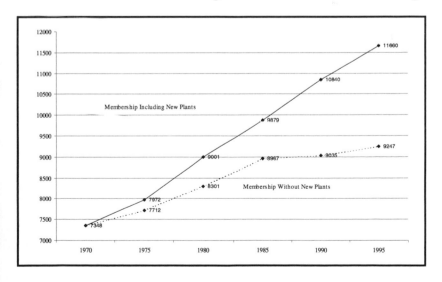

Figure 4
Effect of Church Planting on Nazarene Finances

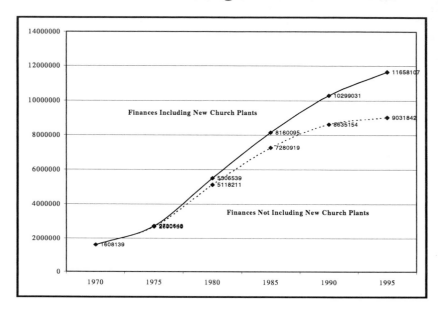

Figure 5
Effect of Church Planting on Nazarene Sunday School

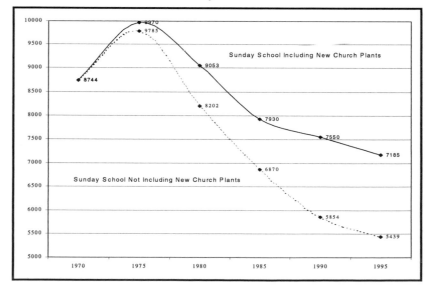

the Canadian population, we would only be holding our own. To advance Christ's Kingdom among Canadians, new networks of believers must be planted.

Established churches alone cannot fulfill the Great Commission. If you add up the number of seats in all existing Christian meeting places, double it (assuming packed multiple worship services), and compare this figure to the population of the region, it becomes clear just how far existing churches are from being able to reach their communities. In addition, of churches 30 years or older, 83% are in decline. Half of these churches did not win a new convert to Christ in the previous year.[10] New churches are therefore needed to assist older churches in fulfilling the Great Commission.

New churches are evangelistically more effective than older churches. Existing churches average four baptisms per year (per 100 members). New churches average 16 baptisms per year (per 100 members).[11]

The individual fruit of evangelism (new believers) is best retained in new churches through discipleship in small groups. However, small groups are generally of limited duration—usually 6 to 12 weeks. Then the hope is the new believer will come to be rooted in the larger congregation. The primary difference between a small group and a new church is the intention of permanence. The small group will end and everyone in the small group knows it. The new church intends to endure, grow and reproduce, and is more effective in the discipling of new believers.

New and different kinds of churches are needed to reach different kinds of people and people groups for Christ. Canada is rapidly becoming a nation of smaller, self-aware ethnic groups. New churches will need to be formed to reach out to "new Canadians," particularly during their more receptive first generation in Canada.

For each kind of person in a community there will need to be several congregations that understand, target and can win and assimilate that kind of person or people group. Yuppies will best be won by churches composed mostly of yuppies seeking to win yuppies. Blue-collar workers will best be won by churches composed mostly of blue-collar families seeking to win them. Canada's Generation X will best be won by churches composed mostly of people targeting that generation. No single church or kind of church is able to win all of the kinds of people within its reach.

Many new churches, with personalities and styles of ministry designed to reach specific groups of people, need therefore to be planted in every community to effectively re-evangelize our great nation.

2. **New churches must be planted because church planting is spiritually healthy.** The laity is spiritually matured and mobilized as new leadership is raised up both for a daughter church and to replace departing leadership in the mother church. In most cases departing leadership and finances in the mother church are replaced within two years, and the mother church can begin planning her next birth.

Church planting refocuses the mother church on her reason for being. Both the mother and daughter congregations become more evangelistic and "purpose driven."[12]

No existing church may allow itself to remain a "dead-end link" in what Christ intended to be an ongoing, reproductive chain. God's intention is that churches plant churches just as normally as young married couples might be expected to have children.

Some churches may find themselves unable to parent a new church due to age, a lack of physical strength, spiritual vitality or leadership resources. In such cases, a local church may need to direct its church planting resources indirectly through parachurch or denominational mission agencies. Sole reliance for church planting on other mission agencies, however, should be used only in extreme cases.

New churches must be planted to replace older churches that die. Churches have natural life cycles just as people do. As congregations age, neighbourhoods change and younger families relocate in large numbers and some older churches die a natural death. A very small percentage of Canadian churches continue to grow for more than a human lifetime.

Statistics indicate that approximately 1% of churches close their doors in a given year. This is not necessarily "bad" or something we should feel guilty about in many cases. The reality is it happens with predictability in the life cycle of many congregations. For this reason, every Canadian denomination or association of churches must plant 1% of its total number of churches each year to hold even, and 2 to 3% or more of its total number of churches annually to move ahead even slowly. Without exception, growing denominations actively plant churches, while static or declining denominations plant very few, if any.

Churches must also be planted to replace the lost capacity of mergers. When two churches merge, the sociological arithmetic is characteristically $1 + 1 = 1.4$. The merging of congregations, denominations or organizations always spells net loss. New churches must be planted elsewhere to replace the loss of each merged church.

3. **All of society benefits when more churches produce more devoted disciples of Jesus Christ.**[13] The best way to invigorate an entire community with the presence of our Risen Lord is to birth new churches.

4. **We must plant new churches to find God's lost sheep and introduce them to the Savior.** This was Jesus' prime purpose. You may wish to review Luke 15. We must remember, *"...the Son of Man came to seek and to save what was lost"* (Luke 19:10). Without Christ people face a frightful destiny, one we prefer not to contemplate, but must because Jesus did. Jesus made this reality clear both in parables (e.g., Matthew 13:24-30, 25, Luke 16:19-31) and direct speech (e.g., Luke 13:1-5, 17:26-35).

We must therefore plant new churches, not with a primary motivation to provide spiritual support for existing Christians, but rather to reach out to those who have not yet become devoted disciples of Jesus Christ. A fundamental shift in thinking is necessary for Canadian congregations to move from a "come to our church" mentality, to a "go and win the unchurched" mentality. Rick Warren points out that a church's health is not measured by its *seating* capacity, but its *sending* capacity.[14] That is to say the onus lies not with the unchurched but with us.

The "Discipling a Whole Nation" (DAWN) Vision

If church multiplication is key to discipling every people group of the nations of the world, including Canada—and we are convinced it is—the question must then be answered, "How can we best multiply congregations to saturate and reach our nation for the Lord Jesus Christ?" The answer lies in the Biblical vision of the unity of the Church expressed in cooperative obedience to the Great Commission.

The whole Church in the nation can reach the whole nation as it prioritizes and sets faith projections for evangelistic church planting—both as individual denominations and as the whole Church in the nation! The Church in Canada, composed of distinct denominations is, like Israel, composed of many tribes and yet essentially one. We must view the task as *our* task and calling *together*.

Either one is a part of the harvest *field*, needing to become a devoted disciple of Jesus Christ, or one is a part of the harvest *force*, needing to engage in the task Jesus has set before us.

One denomination may be able to plant two new congregations a year, another 30 or 50. But as each gives of its *best* to plant as many new cells of witnessing believers[15] as it can—block by block, apartment building by apartment building—the nation is evangelized.

The whole Church sharing in a common commitment to disciple the whole nation through church planting has become known as a DAWN movement. As stated previously in the Preface, Jim Montgomery defines the aim of such a movement as:

Mobilizing the whole Body of Christ in the whole country in a determined effort to complete the Great Commission by working toward the goal of providing an evangelical congregation for every village and neighbourhood of every class, kind and condition of people in the whole country. It is concerned that Jesus Christ become incarnate in all His beauty, compassion, power and message in the midst of every small group of people—400 or so to 1,000 in number—in the whole country including all its people groups.[16]

Roger Greenway puts it this way: "The Church's evangelistic task...demands that every barrio, apartment building and neighbourhood have a church faithful to God's word established in it."[17]

The concept is simple, strategic, Biblical and fundamentally effective.

- DAWN is the best strategy yet developed for world evangelization," says C. Peter Wagner of the *Fuller School of World Mission.*

- Ralph Winter of the Center for World Mission asserts, "DAWN is the most basic strategy of all strategies. There are other things that need to be done besides DAWN, but that is the starting place for the completing of the Great Commission."

This "whole nation" concept has been endorsed as the primary evangelistic strategy for national churches by the *Lausanne Committee, World Evangelical Fellowship* and the *AD2000 and Beyond* movement.

How is it Possible to Rally the Whole Church Around Discipling the Nation While Avoiding the Pitfalls?

Some may object that previous efforts to rally the whole Church in a common cause have fallen prey to theological liberalism, structural ecumenism or questionable political causes. How is discipling the whole nation different?

The "discipling a whole nation" vision avoids these pitfalls by maintaining several clear priorities:

1. The DAWN movement is rooted in the comprehensive purpose and plan of God to turn the hearts of nations and peoples to Him. DAWN is prayer-empowered, Christ-centered and focused squarely on the Great Commission

rather than any worthy or questionable political derivative of Biblical understanding.

2. The DAWN movement respects denominational autonomy and distinctives. Rather than interfere with any denominational task or structure, it focuses on encouraging all in the use of evangelistic church planting to disciple every segment of society and grow Christ's Church. At the same time, the Church works as a whole, setting goals together, growing in faith, raising up leadership—pursuing the heart and purpose of God.

3. DAWN is focused not only on pursuing the Great Commission, but *completing* it in segment after segment of our country. This is our common task. To this end, clear, pertinent information on the current status of the harvest force (growth of the Church) and harvest field (unreached people groups and neighbourhoods) is gathered and updated so that clear understanding of progress may be shared by all.

4. DAWN helps us function as a body. Every part of the body—local churches, denominations, parachurch organizations, missions, individuals—reinforce one another as each plays a role in seeing churches multiplied.

5. DAWN is not a program. Programs hold the interest of participants for a season and new interests are pursued. DAWN, rather, is a long-term vision for cooperatively discipling the nation through saturation church planting without any attempt to centralize or program the process.

6. DAWN is goal oriented as the whole Church, unified in a common goal that leads most directly to the discipling of the nation, evaluates honestly its own progress and contribution to the common task. Each local church, district, denomination and mission agency is invited to seek God's direction reflected in faith projections of what may be accomplished by prayer, faith, obedience and the power of God.

7. In many nations around the world the DAWN vision has unified, mobilized and made the Church more effective in its task.[18]

The Practical Process

How does the DAWN vision work practically?

Details vary in the implementation of DAWN in countries around the world. Common elements, however, suggest the value of the following:

- A person or group of persons earnest for the reaching of their country, as was the reformer, John Knox of Scotland, who cried out to God, "Give me Scotland or I die!"

- A national representative working committee, that shares the vision and is willing to give of personal and organizational resources to guide this relatively simple process.

- The gathering and updating of relevant information regarding the current harvest force and harvest field in the country. From this can be gleaned a "prophetic message", how God sees His Church in the nation and what He is saying to His people.

- Periodic national and regional gatherings of the leadership of the Church to consider what God may be saying and how each denomination may best respond for God's purposes to be accomplished. These gatherings are frequently called "congresses," to emphasize the decision-making element of response. Goals will be set and reviewed, progress celebrated, prayer for revival renewed and fresh commitments made.

- The commitment to continue the process until Jesus returns: mobilizing prayer, monitoring of harvest force and harvest field progress, dissemination of information in publications and congresses and sharing church planting models and resources.

International Case Studies

The Christian Church has experienced measurable results in a wide variety of countries around the world:

- In 1992 **England** held its first congress, attended by 750 leaders from 32 denominations, who committed to plant 20,000 new churches. All major denominations now have church planting goals. By 1995 a national decline in the ratio of population-to-churches had been overcome with the planting of 1,600 new churches.

- In **Ukraine,** a national goal for 50,000 new churches has been set: 303 church planters are being trained in 16 sites, and over 100,000 unchurched people are now attending over 3,800 evangelistic groups that double as embryonic new churches.

- **Japan** has been a culture traditionally resistant to the Gospel since harsh persecution all but wiped out a newly developing Church some centuries ago. During the 30 years from 1960 to 1990, the Church had been growing at a sluggish 1.7% annual average growth rate (AAGR). Between 1990 and 1993, however, 64 denominations together doubled that rate to 3.6%, and 14 of these denominations averaged an amazing 10.3% growth rate.[19]

- **Peru** set a goal of 50,000 new churches by the year 2003 in 1993 (an average of six new churches a day) and has been planting new churches at an incredible 15% during the three years since that DAWN goal was set.

- **Egypt** is the first nation in the Middle East to hold a national church planting congress. In 1996 leaders agreed in a common vision for 10,000 new congregations in this majority Muslim nation.

- In 1992 leaders in **Zimbabwe** set a goal for 10,000 new congregations, and have since seen 3,400 new congregations established with 1.6 million new members. The nation is being discipled.

- **India** represents about 15% of the world's population and 30% of the world's unreached peoples. Is a DAWN project possible in India? Already seven of the states in India have saturation church planting projects underway as part of the national goal of seeing 1,000,000 evangelizing churches reaching the unreached.

- In 1990 there were no indigenous **Malay** churches. There are now 55 known congregations in the country toward a national goal of 4,000 new churches.

- The **Philippines** is home to the first DAWN project. A goal of 50,000 churches by the year 2000 was set in 1975, when only 5,000 evangelical congregations were known in the nation. As of February 1998 close to 40,000 new churches have been established. National leaders are convinced they can reach their goal of 50,000 by the end of 2000.

- **Brazil,** with an evangelical population of 16.5%, growing at an AAGR of 8.3%, set a goal of establishing 150,000 new congregations by 2010.

- **Norway** set goals for 500 new churches in 1996, as the Archbishop of Canterbury offered the keynote congress address. This is significant not for the size of the goal but because the goal was set by a tax-supported "state" church that historically has not seen the need to grow.

- **Finland** in 1994 had 85 leaders from five denominations commit to planting 2,000 new congregations by the year 2000.

- In the **United States**, with approximately one-third of its population evangelical, saturation church planting is being implemented in three networks: by denomination, ethnic group and city-by-city under the auspices of "Mission America," but no national goal has yet been set.

A Strong Step Forward for Canada

In October 1997, leaders representing 39 denominations, 13 mission agencies and four seminaries gathered in Bramalea, Ontario, to pray, consider needs and develop strategy for a cooperative "whole nation" approach. This was the first time such a national church planting congress was convened. Two hundred and seventy-nine delegates participated.

During a closing communion service, delegates affirmed a Congress declaration in which they committed themselves to incarnating Christ through a geographically accessible and culturally relevant evangelical church for every Canadian. A numerical goal of planting 10,000 new congregations by the year 2015 was affirmed.

Denominational leaders also met in their respective denominational families for prayer and planning and to set denominational goals and strategies to contribute toward the national goal. Leaders also met inter-denominationally in regional groupings, representing each of six Canadian regions, to plan how they could cooperatively develop practical strategies and networks to maximize effectiveness.

The **Canadian Church Planting Congress '97** was hosted by *Church Planting Canada*, a track of the Evangelical Fellowship of Canada's *Vision Canada* initiative and the *AD2000 and Beyond* movement. The Church Planting Canada servant-leadership team is composed of seventeen leaders of twelve denominations and two mission agencies. A broader steering committee in which all Canadian denominations and mission agencies are invited to participate gives further guidance.

In order to plant 10,000 new churches by the year 2015, 1,078 new congregations will be needed by December 31, 2000. Before the end of the Congress, 21 denominations indicated their intention to plant 541 new congregations toward this total. Others will indicate their commitment upon consultation with colleagues. Non-attending agencies are invited to inquire or indicate their church planting contributions to this "whole nation" effort by contacting the author at Outreach Canada.[20]

At the time of this writing[21] area gatherings of denominational leaders have been convened in each of Canada's major regions for the purpose of cooperative resourcing. For details on current regional undertakings please consult www.outreach.ca/cpc.htm[22] if you have internet access or see Church Planting Canada's quarterly newsletter.

Can the Great Commission be Accomplished in Canada?

What about Canada? Can Canada be discipled? Some may say, "the setting of national church planting goals is a good step, but can it be done?"

We believe the Lord of the harvest in fact calls each of us from "armchair quarterbacking" to the field. The discipling of the nations is God's will. The clear intention of the Lord Jesus is that the Great Commission not only be pursued but also completed by His disciples before His return.

Saturation church planting is the best means under heaven given for doing so. We believe the whole Church has the resources to establish the presence of the Lord Jesus in every people group and neighbourhood of the whole nation. We have God's promised power and the means of receiving all He has for us to accomplish His glorious purpose.

So we return to the question: "Can Canada be discipled?" Any of us as *individual* churches, denominations or mission agencies would have to say, "No, we are not able to do so." But *together* we **can**, we **must** and we **will,** by God's grace, disciple the peoples within Canada to the Lord Jesus Christ.

We believe the discipling of the nation, by the grace of God and the empowered obedience of his people, can be accomplished to the glory of God.

Is this arrogance? No, rather unified obedience to the long-standing command of Christ motivated by the Great Commandment (Matthew 22:37-40).

Jesus called His followers to disciple all the nations of the world (Matthew 28:18-20) at which time He will return in glory (Matthew 24:14). This task is the heart of the mission of the Church. The Biblical river of redemption flows in the Old Testament from Abraham's call to be a blessing to all the peoples of the earth (Genesis 12:2-3) to the New Testament vision of the consummation of history as peoples of *"...nation, tribe, people and language..."* gather to worship our glorious Redeemer (Revelation 7:9).

Since it is the theme of Scripture, God's will, the purpose of Christ's coming, death and resurrection, and signal of His return, I believe the discipling of the nations, and Canada in particular, is eminently possible. We are called to disciple the nation, and by God's grace and power we can do it. As Christ is made incarnate through cells of His Body in every segment of society, *"...the earth will be filled with the knowledge of the glory of the LORD, as the waters cover the sea"* (Habakkuk 2:14).

Action Points

✓ Do a study of the last 20 years of your denomination, district or movement. Where would your group be in terms of baptisms, worship attendance, finances and membership without the new churches planted during this period?

✓ Some have suggested Christian unity is best expressed in practical action for the sake of the Great Commission. How could your organization experience mutual benefit from working with another denomination in church planter assessment, support groups for church planters or training events for churches planting churches?

✓ As you observe what God has done in other countries in which the Church has worked together in a DAWN-type project, what needs to be done in Canada to mobilize the whole Church to disciple the whole nation? What action may the Lord be calling you to take to bring about this needed step?

Chapter Notes

1. 221 such "countries" currently make up the world political map.

2. James H. Montgomery and Donald A. MacGavran. *The Discipling of a Nation*. Milpitas, CA: *Global Church Growth Bulletin, 1980.* p.17.

3. Whether responsibility for the slowness with which the fulfillment of the Great Commission has progressed over the centuries belongs primarily to the Church or to God is at least in part a theological question we cannot explore in depth, but will recognize in this footnote. Our conviction, based on God's response to Israel's failure to be a light to the Gentiles and upon New Testament texts (e.g., Matthew 24:14) is that the responsibility of the Church cannot be set aside lightly.

4. Ralph Winter. *Mission Frontiers, (Bulletin of the U.S. Center for World Missions)* Jan.-Feb. 1996. Vol. 18, No. 1-2. p.5.

5. Not all will acknowledge Jesus as Lord and become devoted followers before He returns. Jesus' parable of the sower (Matthew 13) and the book of *Revelation* make this clear. But all the nations will have heard the Gospel of Jesus Christ with such personal relevance as results in sufficient understanding to accept Christ as Lord or to reject Him.

6. The essential multiplication of cells for the building of each component of the human body is a helpful analogy.

7. "Planting new churches is the most effective evangelistic method under heaven." For its rationale cf. C. Peter Wagner. *Church Planting for a Greater Harvest*. Regal Books: Ventura, CA, 1990.

8. Roger T. Forster. *Models of Church Planting*. Ichthus Media Services, 107 Stanstead Road, Forest Hill, London, England SE23 1HH. p.6.

9. "Every new church robs Satan of turf. Every new fellowship of believers takes away his power." Elijah Khoza, former witch doctor, Zululand, South Africa.

10. *Leadership* magazine, 1996. A similar figure (85%) is suggested by Dr. Daniel Allen, *A Church of God*, Cleveland TN., church planting coach.

Chapter Notes

[11] C. Peter Wagner, pp.32-33.

[12] Rick Warren. *The Purpose Driven Church*. Zondervan Publishing House: Grand Rapids, Michigan, 1995.

[13] "Through His redeemed (God) causes justice to roll down in families, neighbourhoods, cities and states....Soundly Christian men and women...are powerful instruments of social advance. Evangelization is the best friend of all reformers who desire the reconstruction of the social order along righteous lines....social engineering exercised on pagan societies yields only a trickle of lasting progress. Exercised on nominal Christians it yields a slightly larger trickle. But exercised on committed, illumined Christians it yields a mighty stream of abundant life, righteousness and justice. Do we desire the uplift and transformation of any nation? *Disciple it.* Do we want an end to oppression and exploitation in any segment of society? *In it multiply Christians and churches.* Are we patriots working to bring progress, plenty and peace to our beloved country? *Create in it tens of thousands of cells of* shalom, *units of mercy and peace.*" James H. Montgomery and Donald A. MacGavran, *p.22-23.*

[14] Rick Warren, p.32.

[15] The phrase "cells of witnessing believers" refers, not first of all to the "cell church" model originally popularized by Asian believers, but to the Biblical image of the "Body of Christ" being composed of parts–congregations, small groups and individuals– which together make up the whole.

[16] James H. Montgomery. *DAWN 2000: 7 Million Churches to Go.* Pasadena, CA: William Carey Library, p.12.

[17] Roger Greenway. *"Content and Context: The Whole Christ for the Whole City,"* in *Discipling the City*, ed. Greenway. Grand Rapids, MI: Baker Book House, 1979, p.104.

[18] See the section titled: "International Case Studies." James H. Montgomery, when asked about the failure rate of the application of the DAWN vision, replied: "There have been no failures to date." (Conference in Colorado Springs, June 1997, on the application of DAWN principles to reaching cities.)

Chapter Notes

[19] James H. Montgomery. *Then the End Will Come: Great News About the Great Commission.* Pasadena, CA: William Carey Library, 1997, p.6.

[20] Outreach Canada, #16 - 12240 Horseshoe Way, Richmond, BC V7A 4X9, Phone: (604) 272-0732, Fax: 272-2744, or Email: mmoerman@outreach.ca

[21] The six months since the Congress.

[22] Scroll down to "Regional Networks and Activities" and click on your region of interest.

Chapter Three

Church Planting: Key to Discipling Our Nation

Dr. Murray Moerman and Lorne Hunter

How many new churches will be needed to disciple the nation of Canada, filling every neighborhood, apartment complex and people-group with the grace, presence and power of the Lord Jesus Christ incarnate in His people?

The suggestion of the need for 15,000 new cells of believers by the year 2020 will greatly challenge the vision of many church leaders. Yet such saturation is necessary for the completion of the Great Commission and is possible!

The Lord of the harvest seeks all those for whom He died (Luke 15:1-10) and will give us labourers for the task as we pray (Matthew 9:38).

How Christian is Canada?

Bart could not understand why a new church plant was being proposed. "Canada is already Christian," he protested. "Look at the census statistics. Besides, the way I see it, there are already enough churches in town. I travel in Canada a lot and I have never had any difficulty finding a good church in which to worship."

Some will point to Statistics Canada's census data which indicates a majority of Canadians identify in some way with Christianity. According to 1991[1] census figures, 81.8% of a population of about 27 million identified with Christianity (catagorized as shown in Table 2).

Table 2
Self-Reported Christians by Census (1991)

Catholic	12,335,255
Mainline Prot	6,578,325
Evangelical	2,775,025
Orthodox	387,395
Total	**22,076,000**

If such self-reported identification with Christianity represented an impassioned love for Christ, commitment to the Kingdom of God and responsible membership in Christ's Church, we would be greatly encouraged. But unfortunately this is far from the case. Identification with Christianity by Canadians is nominal by most measurements.[2]

Of Canadians who claim to believe, only 21% participate in worship at least twice a month[3] or read the Bible regularly.[4] Eighty percent of Canadians are not participants in any Christian church, even nominally! The Gospel of Jesus Christ has made some significant inroads, but the discipling of Canada has a long way to go.

Table 3 indicates Census Metropolitan Areas (CMAs) with the largest percentage of non-Christian affiliation.

Table 3[5]
Non-Christian Affiliation by CMAs (1991)

Vancouver	41%
Victoria	34%
Calgary	30%
Toronto	27%
Edmonton	27%
Winnipeg	22%

This table suggests western cities are generally home to the highest percentages of Canadians who share no identification with Biblical Christian beliefs. These are certainly not the only cities where fresh, focused, prayerful evangelism and church planting efforts are needed, but certainly such efforts are greatly needed here.

Further detail of the breakdown of self-reported non-Christian groupings in Canada's 25 CMAs is provided in Appendix 1: "Non-Christian Religious Affiliation (1991)."

Canadian Identification with Christianity is Declining

Not only is Canadian identification with Christianity largely nominal, but it has been declining as cultural support for Christian values wane in government, education and media.

For example, whereas in 1991 approximately 82% of Canadians identified in some fashion with Christianity, this level of identification had fallen to 68% by 1996,[6] a decline of 2.8% annually over that period.

Those not identifying themselves with Christianity thought of themselves as shown in Table 4.

By region, the percentage of Canadians who identify themselves with Christianity are identified in Table 5.

Table 4 Non-Christian Religious Affiliation (1996)[7]	
Nothing in particular	16%
Agnostic	3%
Atheist	3%
Jewish	1%
Muslim	1%
Other non-Christian	1%
Something else	5%
Do not know	1%

Table 5 Self-Reported Christians by Region (1996)	
British Columbia	56%
Manitoba	61%
Saskatchewan & Manitoba	73%
Ontario	64%
Québec	79%
Maritimes	77%

A 14% decline in identification with Christianity over a five-year period is an extremely rapid rate of religious and social change. This turning away from Christianity has resulted in enormous cultural change in the moral values and laws of our land. The resulting cultural changes affect fundamental definitions, such as the value of human life and the nature of the family. The demand for "positive tolerance"[8] now opposes the very notion of the possibility of truth or the legitimacy of evangelism. These changes should drive every committed Christian to earnest prayer and birth in the heart of every believer, a renewed commitment to disciple our nation.

Dr. Brian Stiller, president of *Ontario Theological Seminary*, argues that Canada cannot technically be "reclaimed" for Christ because Canada has never been a Christian nation by the criteria of Scripture.[9]

Large numbers of new cells of believers need to be planted if we are to permeate Canadian culture with the presence of Christ—a culture that no longer understands or relates to the Gospel.

New Canadians

Canadian immigration legislation eliminated race and nationality regulations in 1967 (Bill C-55). In 1997 new refugee legislation (Bill C-84) was introduced. The passing of these Bills has brought the world's mission fields to our land, particularly Canada's port cities. In addition, thousands of international students come annually to Canada's universities from coast to coast. Whereas immigration following World Wars I and II came largely from Europe, current immigration draws a larger proportion of Pacific Rim peoples.

Canada's demographic landscape is rapidly changing. The number, size and variety of ethnic and religious groups in

Canada continue to grow. Canada is becoming a nation of smaller, self-aware ethnic groups—some assimilating, others choosing to hold to their own traditional values.

Further, the percentage of "New Canadians"—those who are first-generation immigrants to Canada—appears to be on the increase. According to the 1986 Canadian census, 3.9 million persons, or 15.4% of the national population, was composed of first-generation immigrants. By 1996 17.2% of the population were first-generation immigrants.

The resulting needs and opportunities for church planting among "new Canadians" are urgent, immense and growing. A 1997 *Vancouver Sun* report called for 300,000 new immigrants to enter Canada annually to finance the ailing Canada Pension Plan.[10] Such an immigration policy would require 300 new churches reaching out to immigrant populations to be planted annually.

The challenge and complexity of cross-cultural bridging into new languages and cultures is great, but the Church must and is rising to the task.[11] For example, the Christian and Missionary Alliance denomination, in the early 1980s planted one non-Anglo ethnic church for every eight Anglo congregations. By the 1990s, the Alliance was planting one non-Anglo ethnic church for each Anglo congregation. Today two non-Anglo ethnic churches are planted for each new Anglo congregation. Nearly 27% of Alliance congregations are non-Anglo, non-Caucasian. Evangelism and worship currently takes place in 13 languages.

Unchurched Christians

Biblically, the concept of "unchurched Christians" is unknown. In the Old Testament, exclusion from the covenant community was viewed as extreme punishment (Deuteronomy 23:1-6). Without being a part of the community, sharing in worship was impossible. In the New Testament those who left the worshipping community were not considered disciples of Christ (1 John 2:19).

Yet masses of Canadians who may remember an aspect of their Christian heritage when the census taker comes to the door, or who may consider themselves nearer to Christianity than any other religion of which they are aware, remain unchurched. Are they Christians? While it is not within the scope of this chapter to explore this vital and urgent theological question, most will recognize Jesus did not seek affirmations of interest but fully devoted followers (Luke 9:57-62).

Nominal Christians are not yet, by Jesus' criteria, part of the harvest force, but rather the harvest field. The number of Canadians who are Christian "in name only" were nearly 7 million at the time of the 1991 census and probably over 7.6 million in 1997.

The good news, as Dr. Reginald Bibby points out,[12] is that unchurched Canadians who continue to see themselves as Christian, at least by their own definitions,[13] may be winnable into the Christian fold by congregations willing to change nonessential methods and styles for the sake of the harvest. New church plants in particular are most able to mold their philosophies of ministry to reach out to nominal Christians.

Unchurched Evangelicals

Nominal Christians are frequently "fuzzy" about the Biblical call and terms of response to the Gospel. Evangelical Christians, in contrast, are considered virtually by definition to understand and hold strong commitment to the authority of Scripture.

While an estimated 3.4 million Canadians were deemed to be evangelical[14] by a George Rawlyk/Angus Reid study,[15] it appears by comparing this figure with actual church attendance that many of these evangelicals remain unchurched.

Two questions are raised by this inconsistency: "How many evangelicals are unchurched?" and "Why are they unchurched?"

If we subtract from a total of 3.4 million estimated evangelicals the 1.16 million members of evangelical denominations, an estimated 483,626 evangelicals worshipping in Roman Catholic congregations[16] and an estimated 105,497 evangelicals worshipping in mainline traditions,[17] 1.65 million "unchurched evangelicals" remain.

Why are these evangelicals unchurched? Additional study is warranted. Disaffected evangelicals may well need new churches with fresh "wineskins" of worship style. Perhaps the evangelistic message to which they initially responded was shallow. Perhaps care for these "new babes in Christ" lacked consistency. "Unchurched evangelicals" may desire congregations exhibiting equal concern for "soul care" and "social care."[18] Or they may need to be challenged with a more Biblical view of discipleship and life in Christ than they now possess.

It must be remembered that God does not seek nominal identification or even church attendance per se (Revelation 2-3), but fully devoted disciples of Christ (Matthew 16:24-25). "Unchurched Christian" is a Biblical oxymoron.

Efforts to enfold "unchurched evangelicals" into Christian communities (i.e., churches) are vitally important both to restoring such persons to growing Biblical relationship with Christ, and to our broader call to disciple our nation. As unchurched evangelicals are re-gathered to a vital relationship with Christ and responsible church membership, a great strengthening comes to the harvest force for the sake of the rest of Canadians and the world.

The Macro: 24 Million Unchurched Canadians to Reach and Enfold

As we surveyed the harvest field in 1997, unchurched Canadians were estimated to total in excess of 24 million persons. These are individuals for whom Christ calls us to *"...leave the ninety-nine... and go after the lost sheep..."* until they are found (Luke 15:4).

In a complex Canadian social system, these 24 million "lost sheep" participate in 100s or 1,000s of "people groups" (social networks), each of whom urgently need, in new and impassioned ways, to be permeated with the love, care, truth and power of our risen Lord.

The Micro: How Many Unchurched Canadians Can One New Congregation Enfold?

In developing a strategy to disciple a whole nation it is important to look at the micro as well as the macro. As new cells of believers are planted in every people group, neighbourhood, city block and apartment building with the presence of our incarnate Lord, we must ask, "How many people can each new church reach and enfold?"

The average size of an evangelical congregation in Canada appears to be approximately 135 persons. Some congregations grow larger, but most remain somewhat smaller.

Several reasons for this plateau in congregational size have been suggested:

- Some congregations lose their vision for local outreach and mission, striving instead for maintenance of existing budget and programs.[19]

- Some congregations inadvertently become "relationally saturated" at that size because they do not provide additional "cells" (Sunday School classes, home groups, ministry teams, etc.) into which to incorporate newcomers.[20]

- The budget is being met and the congregation has lost motivation for reaching out to bring in those outside Christ.

- Many pastors are unaware that adding the next 100 persons to their existing congregation is more difficult than reaching 100 "lost sheep" by daughtering a new congregation and rebuilding the mother congregation.

At an average size of 135 worshippers, each congregation may have existing relational bridges with "lost sheep" to have influence for the Gospel with an average of approximately 500 persons. Some congregations shed the light of the Gospel onto a larger number of persons in their community; others are able to touch fewer persons.

How Many Churches are Needed to Disciple the Nation?

Let us raise the bar considerably by faith and entrust to each congregation the vision and calling to build relational bridges of love and trust to double that amount—1,000 persons—in its community. What a challenge this would be![21] Not all will be enfolded into the active life of the congregation, but each church would maintain personal relational contact with 1,000 people, doing everything it could to influence each person to become a fully devoted follower of Christ. **This is a key element of the strategy God is giving to us to disciple our nation.**

Let us go further. If 1,000 persons could be relationally influenced by the average Canadian congregation and 24 million Canadians remain unchurched, 24,000 additional congregations will need to be planted to give the Canadian Church the potential to disciple the nation. A witnessing cell of believers must exist in every neighbourhood, apartment building, people group and other sub-culture and community of 1,000 persons. Lower goals may be appropriate in the short term as Canadian congregations regain the skill of church planting, but the long-term vision for a nation saturated with cells of believers must remain if we are to disciple the nation.

Some smaller communities, particularly in certain rural Maritime and Prairie areas, already have established an average of one evangelical congregation for every 500 to 1,000 people. Congregations in these communities may be encouraged to renew their efforts to build relational bridges to every unchurched person in their community. They may be encouraged to assist sister congregations in other regions of the nation sponsoring new church plants in areas where they cannot reach out directly. The vast majority of Canada's cities and people groups, however, require many new cells of believers to achieve a ratio of even one congregation for every 2,000 people.

The issue is not whether non-Christians can physically reach a given gathering place of believers, but whether believers are relationally reaching non-Christians with tangible expressions of Christ's love. We cannot assume unchurched people will go to a church. New cells of believers must be established within the networks of those yet unchurched.

What Kinds of Churches Are Needed?

When we speak of a national corporate vision and strategy for the establishment of thousands of new cells of believers among Canada's millions of unchurched people, it will immediately be clear that we are not necessarily talking about the model of a congregation that requires "three acres and a steeple." We may not, in some Christian traditions, even be speaking of seminary-trained leadership.

Church Planting Canada has suggested the following simple but essential definition of a *church* for the purposes of multiplication in discipling the nation: *"Any gathering of Christians meeting regularly for worship celebration, caring, teaching and prayer, and actively engaged in evangelism (with the intention of continuing to meet for these purposes indefinitely)."*

Roger Forster, of *Ichthus Fellowship* in England, emphasizes four essential characteristics for such new churches in our generation. "They must be informal and flexible, based on authentic relationships, culturally sensitive and relevant, purposeful and focused, deliberately yet naturally reproductive."[22] Such a model emphasizes the essential simplicity and organic nature of the Church. Such reproducing cells of new believers must be:

• Committed to Biblical truth.

• Living in dependence on prayer and the empowerment of our supernatural God.

Beyond such basic elements, the Holy Spirit must be given freedom to form the *"wineskins of the new creation"* (cf. Galatians 6:15b). Certainly the Christian Church, in most of its historic traditions, is currently seeking renewal to become more effective in our post-modern era.

Where are Such New Cells of Believers Most Needed?

We must now look at Canada through a series of lenses designed to enable us to see the task before us more clearly. Where specifically are new cells of believers most needed so that Christ's life-giving presence will become incarnate in every segment of Canadian society?

In one sense the answer is, "almost everywhere!" As Roger Forster states: "We need to plant out more and more churches, so that everywhere we go we trip over them. Not just one in a town, but dozens of them all over the place—different shapes, different sizes—but so that wherever people go they find the Church, Jesus' Body and see Jesus."[23]

Canada and its cities and people groups may be viewed somewhat as Rubik's cube—made up of many smaller cubes, each of which contribute to the whole. In this context God's redemptive purpose remains thorough and unchanging. *"Not wanting anyone to perish, but everyone to come to repentance"* (2 Peter 3:9), God desires that all His lost sheep are found!

The purpose of research is to assist the Church in finding God's lost sheep. Research breaks down the nation and its teeming, complicated, multi-faceted cities into their constituent parts, each of which contains many lost sheep.

We must learn to look at discipling a nation from several perspectives:

- **Political boundaries**—national, regional, city, census divisions, census subdivisions and census tracts.

- **Ethno-linguistically**—people groups, as self-defined by language and ethnic distinctives.

- **Demographically**—classes of people, as defined by age, marital status, education, etc.

- **Religious and philosophical worldviews**—world religions and other faith groups.

- **Culturally**—socioeconomic, white and blue collar, etc.

- **Physical geography**—the valley, basin, mountain areas, etc.

We must look for people through each of these templates to ensure that every person of every class and kind has access to the incarnate Christ through a witnessing cell of believers where He is presented in all His love and grace and His message proclaimed in power. Such research is never complete, but must be continually updated and refined to shed the clearest current light upon our task.

Please note: research and the tables which follow in later sections are not finally about numbers, but about perishing people with everlasting souls! Our "search-and-rescue" mission is too important to settle for generalizations about where those we are called to reach are located. We need facts concerning where new evangelizing churches are most needed. God cares about every individual.

The Challenge of Narcissism

Since the idealism of the mid-20th century, North American culture has become increasingly narcissistic. Recent research has suggested that a majority of North Americans are now clinically narcissistic.[24]

This trend poses unique challenges requiring fresh approaches to Biblical evangelism and discipleship. The narcissistic personality is not only self-centered and inclined to interpret the Gospel solely in terms of potential personal benefits, but the narcissistic culture tends not to struggle with issues of guilt or responsibility, or to relate to any conscious sense of sin requiring forgiveness. The post-modern narcissistic personality struggles rather with anxiety, low self-esteem, lack of meaning and hopelessness. Felt needs include issues of acceptance and appreciation, a lack of worthy models and goals to idealize and emulate, and the need for a sense of belonging.

Fruitful pre-evangelism approaches will emphasize the doctrines of acceptance and approval in Christ, the worthiness of Christ as our "hero" and model, belonging to God and the Body of Christ as authentic family and the reality of the resurrection countering hopelessness. Since the inadequate sense of "self" in the narcissistic personality has resulted in large part from the fragmentation of the extended family by mobility and the nuclear family by divorce and temporary common-law relationships, practical restorative pastoral ministry will attempt to resource contemporary marriage and family life as a means of enabling the next generation to be released from narcissistic emptiness.

The Opportunity of Spirituality

An unexpected opportunity is resulting from narcissistic emptiness, namely a renewed popular recognition of the essential spirituality of humans. Canadians frequently write off "institutional religion" as irrelevant, but view themselves as spiritual (in generally undefined ways) and interested in spiritual things. Denominational "brand name" loyalty is generally down, while interest in spiritual reality is up.

In this setting, church planters may choose to emphasize denominational affiliation with those "consumers" of religious rites of passage who value family denominational roots, while exploring growing spiritual interest among those who place no value upon denominational standards and affiliation.

"Hidden" Multi-Family Housing

More than 9.5 million, or 33%, of Canada's residents live in multi-family housing. This designation includes condominiums, apartments, townhouses and mobile-home communities. Figure 6 shows a comparatively high percentage of Québec residents living in apartments, followed by Ontario and British Columbia.

Why Focus on Apartment Dwellers?

Studies in the United States suggest only a small percentage (one-seventh) of apartment dwellers, compared to the national average, are being reached by the Christian community.[26] While we are presently unaware of similar studies in Canada, comparable challenges are likely to face the Canadian Church.

Figure 6[25]
Multi-Family Housing by Province

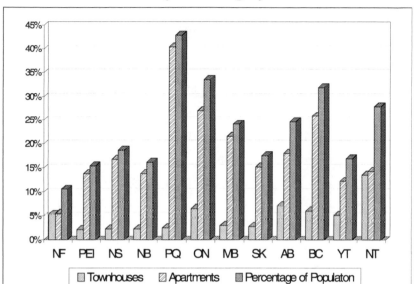

Some Canadians choose apartment living for economic or security reasons. Others prefer to "cocoon" from the outside world. As a result, Canadians living in apartments, remain largely "hidden," and perhaps inadvertently overlooked and unreached by the Church.

Another reason apartment dwellers are only one-seventh as "reached" by the Church compared to those in single-family homes, is the difficulty of outside access and traditional door-to-door efforts within these "gated communities." Church bulk mailings frequently do not find their way into individual resident mailboxes in apartment buildings. For these and other reasons some church planters choose "easier ground."

Yet one-third of all Canadians live in multi-family dwellings! New congregations must be planted in every multi-family complex. We must identify units of 1 to 2,000 persons in high-density housing and establish on- site congregations there. Founding pastors will need to identify with those they are reaching out to by moving into the complexes. The resulting congregations will meet in living rooms, common rooms or other suitable locations.

The vision of "a church in every apartment complex" will require church planters, lay or clergy, to personally move into high-rises, apartments and gated townhouse communities to offer relevant ministries, establish support cells and begin new congregations.[27]

It is vital that we take up this uniquely urban challenge if we are to see "a gathering of Bible-believing Christians within practical, cultural and relational distance of every person in every class and kind of people, penetrating every neighbourhood with the saving love, care, truth and power of Jesus Christ."

Churches for Aging Canadians

Figure 7 shows the largest proportion of Canadians currently in the 30-to-50-year age range. This "bulge" in population will continue to age, with no younger population growth development yet in sight. What does this mean?

It has been recognized for some time that a majority of adult believers have come to faith while in their youth. For this reason most congregations give priority to youth ministries and Sunday School classes. This must continue, particularly as the majority of Canadian youth are growing up without a knowledge of the Gospel adequate to become disciples of the Lord Jesus Christ. Jesus' heart has always been directed toward children and youth. Churches targeting the "Buster" generation must be culturally relevant in styles of music and community.

Yet aging Canadians are generally nearer their time of eternal reckoning than those younger. Aging Canadians are also conscious of needs relating to health issues, peer

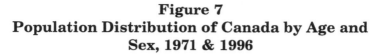

Figure 7
**Population Distribution of Canada by Age and
Sex, 1971 & 1996**

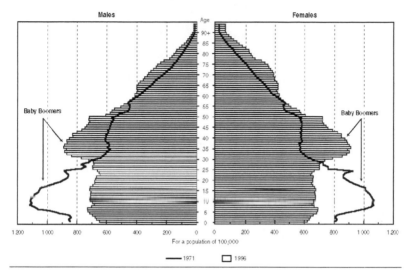

community and the desire to be useful to others in early retirement or their declining years. Many new churches targeting the unique needs of the aging must be formed to reach this growing population with the hope of the Gospel.

First Nations

Long before any Viking foot touched the shore of what has come to be called Canada, the land was settled by First Nation bands who, many years before, had presumably traveled east across the Bering Strait. These aboriginal peoples, comprised of hundreds of tribes, occupied the entire land. Today aboriginal peoples number approximately 2.8% of Canada's population.[28]

Europeans, as the invading peoples, were linked with Christianity which, in turn, was understandably viewed as the "white" religion—resulting, despite some noble efforts and some notable disasters on the part of Christians, in slowed progress of the Gospel among aboriginal peoples.

One all-aboriginal denomination, the *Native Evangelical Fellowship*, is growing well, supported by *Inter-Mission Cooperative Outreach* (IMCO) member mission agencies. The *Pentecostal Assemblies of Canada* and the *Christian and Missionary Alliance* also have strong and growing aboriginal divisions.

Despite these commendable efforts, great needs for the Gospel remain evident in the aboriginal community. Table 6 shows the number of new congregations needed to permeate Canada's aboriginal community with the healing grace of the Lord Jesus. In each of the following tables please compare "Population Per Church" as an indication of the comparative need for new church planting.

The challenge of church planting among Canadians of aboriginal origin is accentuated by a renewal of interest in "native spirituality" in many First Nation bands, as well as recent attention given to the abusive institution of residential schools historically endorsed by church and government.[32] Focused prayer for indigenous leadership as well as cross-cultural mission leaders to establish hundreds of new cells of believers is needed.

Table 6
Aboriginal Canada:
Comparative Church Planting Needs

Home Language	1996 Population	Known Evangelical Churches[29]	Current Pop. per Church	Number of New Congregations Needed 1:2000	1:1000
Aboriginal[30]	103,555	26	3,983	26	78
English or French[31]	695,455	162	4,293	186	533
Composite	799,010	188	4,250	212	611

Founding Partners of Confederation

Following the entry of Canada's First Nation peoples, Canada was settled by French and English peoples. As a modern nation-state, Canada was founded in 1867 by an uneasy partnership of these two language groups.

When *Reclaiming a Nation* was published in 1990, research at that time suggested the net number of new evangelical churches likely to be needed by the year 2000 in order to provide one evangelizing congregation for each 2,000 people of that language group.[33] A summary is reproduced in Table 7.

Table 7
English and French Canada:
Comparative Church Planting Needs – 1989

Language	Evangelical Churches 1989	Projected Population In 2000	Current Pop. per Church	Evangelical Churches Needed
English	6,567	20,649,981	2,694	3,758
French	334	6,811,143	17,470	3,072

While projected population figures for the end of the century have changed since 1989 and are not directly comparable with the following table, it is instructive to compare research results six years later in Table 8.

Table 8
English and French Canada:
Comparative Church Planting Needs – 1995

Language	Evangelical Churches 1995	Projected Population In 2001	Current Pop. per Church	Evangelical Churches Needed
English	7,493	20,202,251	2,540	2,608
French	457	6,611,912	13,916	2,849

The comparison is informative and generally encouraging. Research suggests English language church planting gained a net of 926 congregations (154 congregations per year), reducing the population-to-church ratio (a key indicator as we seek to disciple the nation) modestly from 2,694 to 2,540 persons.

Precise information from Biblically orthodox renewal groups in some mainline denominations is still being sought and will affect the picture further. French language church planting gained a net of 123 congregations across Canada (21 per year), reducing the population-to-church ratio from 17,470 to 13,916 persons.[34]

Significantly, the gap between the evangelization through church planting of English and French Canada remains enormous. Québec remains "culturally Catholic" but is increasingly secular. The need for new church planting in Québec is 555% greater, on a per capita basis, than in English Canada. French Canada is the largest unreached[35] people group in North America, with some six million people.

The Body of Christ must raise the need for new French-speaking churches in our priority for prayer, leadership and resources. Undoubtedly unique challenges face the growth of the Body of Christ in Québec. Yet reasons for encouragement remain. Residents of Québec believe in the existence of God,[36] life after death and the deity of Christ at rates approximately 10% higher than the national average.[37]

European Immigration

In Canada's early years, particularly following World Wars I and II, peoples from many European ethnic backgrounds arrived, frequently from countries in which Christianity was established, at least nominally, as the state-supported religion. Table 9 overviews the comparative need for church planting among these people groups in Canada by

Table 9
Canada's European Roots:
Comparative Church Planting Needs

Usual Home Language	1996 Population	Known Evangelical Churches	Current Pop. per Church	Number of New Congregations Needed 1:2000	1:1000
Polish	119,645	4	29,911	55	99
Croatian	24,200	0	24,200[38]	12	24
Serbian	19,935	0	19,935	10	20
Serbo-Croatian	14,085	0	14,085	7	14
Italian	215,095	18	11,949	90	197
Russian	33,760	4	8,440	13	30
Greek	68,700	9	7,633	25	60
Hungarian	24,640	4	6,160	8	21
Portuguese	123,325	24	5,139	38	99
Armenian	19,530	5	3,906	5	15
Ukrainian	32,015	9	3,557	11	30
Romanian	20,880	6	3,480	4	15
German	114,080	58	1,967	0	56
Dutch	12,910	8	1,614	0	5
Spanish	141,645	132	1,073	0	10

"home language" in descending order of need as measured by "Current Population per Church."

Even where "0" appears in the "Number of New Congregations Needed, 1:2000" column, significant numbers of unchurched individuals of this language group remain for one evangelizing church for each 1,000 persons to be provided. New churches remain the best way to reach these families with the incarnate presence of the risen Lord Jesus Christ.

It is encouraging to note, however, that the "church-to-population" rate of 1:2000 has been reached among three groups of Canadians normally speaking the indicated language at home. Congregations speaking these languages can now turn their energies to additional tasks:

1. *Discipling their own people group to its fringes.* Many unevangelized families and households within their language group, both speaking the language and those being assimilated into Canadian culture, remain to be reached and discipled. New churches may well need to be planted to reach them all. Church-to-population ratios of 1:400 or less are frequently required.

2. *Engaging in church planting ministries in their countries of origin.* "Foreign" missions to their "mother country" will be a natural response to God's call to disciple the nations.

3. *Engaging in church planting ministries among other people groups in Canada.* Church planting may now be initiated among those people groups with which they feel the most natural affinity or cross-culturally to other groups which the Lord of the harvest directs.

Asian Immigration

In more recent years, immigration to Canada has come in greater proportion from Asian nations, particularly Pacific Rim nations, relative to earlier European immigration. Table 10 suggests the comparative need for church planting among Canada's more recent newcomer people groups in descending order of need as measured by "Current Population per Church."

For language groups with stronger "Current Population per Church" rates, review the comments following Table 8.

Church Planting Needs by Province/Territory

When a composite of all languages is considered by total population, the Christian movement in four provinces and the Northwest Territories remains above a 1:2000 church planting ratio, yet no province has reached a 1:1500 church

Table 10
Canadians of Asian Origin:
Comparative Church Planting Needs

Usual Home Language	1996 Population	Known Evangelical Churches	Current Pop. per Church	Number of New Congregations Needed 1:2000	1:1000
Punjabi	154,480	3	51,493	74	151
Urdu	27,085	1	27,085	13	26
Gujarati	26,685	0	26,685	13	27
Bengali	11,820	0	11,820	6	12
Hindi	23,220	3	7,740	9	20
Tamil	55,670	16	3,479	12	40
Vietnames	93,765	28	3,349	19	66
Chinese	586,810	187	3,138	106	400
Khmer	11,305	4	2,826	2	7
Japanese	17,685	10	1,769	0	8
Tagalog	72,490	49	1,479	0	24
Lao	9,500	10	950	0	0
Korean	41,985	46	913	0	0

planting ratio. Table 11 shows the relative degree of discipling by province—both that which has taken place, and the task yet remaining. Particularly striking is the imbalance in "Current Population per Church" between provinces.

We note with gratitude the churches in some provinces and the Yukon have discipled their regions to "church-to-population" ratios below 1:2000. We rejoice greatly in this commendable progress! May the churches in every province and among all people groups come to this place also—and quickly!

Yet masses of unchurched peoples remain. In no province or territory have churches come to provide an evangelizing congregation for every 1,500 people. We must carry the Great Commission further. The average congregation may be able

Table 11
Current Church Planting Needs by Province – 1997

Province	July 1, 1997 Population	Known Evangelical Churches	Current Pop. per Church	Number of New Congregations Needed 1:2000	1:1000	1:500
Newfoundland	563,641	306	1,842	0	258	821
Prince Edward Is.	137,244	73	1,880	0	64	201
Nova Scotia	947,917	503	1,885	0	445	1,393
New Brunswick	762,049	485	1,571	0	277	1,039
Québec	7,419,890	636	11,667	3,074	6,784	14,204
Ontario	11,407,691	2,972	3,838	2,732	8,436	19,843
Manitoba	1,145,242	601	1,906	0	544	1,689
Saskatchewan	1,023,483	611	1,675	0	412	1,436
Alberta	2,847,006	1,211	2,351	213	1,636	4,483
British Columbia	3,933,273	1,439	2,733	528	2,494	6,428
Yukon Territory	31,632	16	1,977	0	16	47
N.W. Territories	67,528	25	2,701	9	43	110

to provide practical relational bridges for the presence of Christ into groups of 500 to perhaps even 1,000 individuals. Therefore we press on in faith—praying, planning and planting—in order to provide an evangelizing congregation for every 500 to 1,000 persons in every region and people group in Canada, so coming to a place where, in our life-time, we may disciple our nation.

Church Planting Needs by Larger Cities

Appendix 2 has been added to direct the discipling efforts of the Canadian Church in cities with populations over 100,000. This table shows the population of the seven largest language groups residing in the city, along with the degree of discipling having been accomplished in the city as measured by the permeation of cells of believers. Finally, the number of new cells of the Body of Christ needed if each church were to develop relational bridges for the Gospel to 2,000 individuals is suggested as a guide for church planting. It must be remembered that most congregations are not strong enough to reach 2,000 people. Therefore many more churches will be needed. In all likelihood we should seek to provide a church for 1,000 or even 500 individuals of any given neighbourhood or language group.

Church Planting Needs by Smaller Cities

Cities and towns with populations of 2,000 or more are listed, by province, in a declining ratio of church planting need in Appendix 3. Please note that while the net number of new cells of believers required to disciple smaller cities to their fringes is usually less, many unchurched people remain unreached in smaller communities. Further, it is worthy to note that the relative ease with which congregations in smaller cities can cooperate in community-wide evangelistic activities is in fact greater.

Church Planting Needs in Canada's Largest Language Groups

After English and French, Table 12 shows the need in descending order as of 1989[39] for new church planting among Canada's 14 largest "unofficial language" groups. The "Evangelical Churches Needed" column is calculated on a 1:2000 church-to-population ratio.

Table 13 updates this picture with the best information we have as of the end of 1995 for purposes of comparison, celebrating progress and planning church planting strategy for the future. Table 13 is also calculated on a 1:2000 church-to-population ratio.

A number of observations are in order:

• Of Canada's 15 largest "unofficial language" groups listed in Table 13, the Portuguese and Greek communities appear to have made the most notable progress in church planting during the six-year period in view. Both population-to-church ratios and the number of evangelical churches needed (to provide a 1:2000 ratio) for these language groups have improved significantly.

- Vietnamese- and Portuguese-speaking congregations have more than tripled between 1989 and 1995. Arabic- and Chinese-speaking congregations have more than doubled in this period. Greek congregations have increased nine times while Polish-speaking churches have increased four times.

Table 12
Fourteen Language Groups Requiring Most New Churches - 1989
(Canada's Largest "Unofficial Language" Groups)

Language	Evangelical Churches 1989	Projected Population 2000	Current Population to Church Ratio	Evangelical Churches Needed
Italian	22	316,373	12,320	136
Chinese	73	267,907	3,144	61
Portuguese	7	122,660	15,011	54
Greek	0	84,250	84,250	42
Polish	0	63,379	63,379	32
Punjabi	3	55,604	15,878	25
German	46	129,255	2,407	19
Vietnamese	8	46,780	5,009	15
Ukrainian	3	27,192	7,765	11
Arabic	4	25,348	5,429	9
Inuktitut	1	20,375	17,455	9
Czech	0	10,179	10,179	5
Lithuanian	0	9,362	9,362	5
Urdu	0	9,478	9,478	5

- Though Italian appears to have dropped between 1989 and 1995 from first to fourth in number of new churches needed, the current Italian population-to-church ratio showed a slight decrease. The number of Italian-speaking congregations actually declined during this period. The primary change appears to be that larger numbers of Canadians of Italian background have begun speaking English or French, rather than Italian, at home.

- Despite commendable reductions in population-to-church ratios among the Chinese, Polish and Vietnamese

Table 13
Fifteen Language Groups Requiring Most New Churches - 1995
(Canada's Largest "Unofficial Language" Groups)

Language	Evangelical Churches 1995	Projected Population 2001	Current Population to Church Ratio	Evangelical Churches Needed
Chinese	187	730,226	3,138	178
Punjabi	3	197,200	51,493	96
Polish	4	151,932	29,911	72
Italian	18	173,033	11,950	69
Arabic	11	121,479	8,325	50
Portuguese	24	133,168	5,139	43
Vietnamese	28	119,221	3,349	32
Persian	2	62,868	22,250	29
Greek	9	66,168	7,633	24
Gujarti	0	30,995	26,685	15
Tamil	16	74,580	3,479	21
Cree	9	53,538	5,538	18
Urdu	1	33,741	27,085	16
Russian	4	39,664	8,440	16
Hindi	3	28,727	7,740	11

communities through successful church planting, many additional churches are needed.[40]

- The church planting needs for churches speaking Persian, Gujarati, Tamil, Cree, Russian and Hindi have replaced, in the order of the top 15 priorities, those churches that speak German, Ukrainian, Inuktitut, Czech and Lithuanian.

- No new Punjabi-speaking congregations are recorded as having been planted despite a projected population growth in this group of over 140,000 persons.

Canada's Least-Reached Language Groups

Tables 12 and 13 focused on needs for church planting among the language groups in Canada requiring the *largest numbers* of new church plants to bring each group to a church for each 2,000 people speaking that language at home.[41]

Tables 14 and 15 draw our attention and prayers to people groups in Canada, regardless of numerical size, that currently have the highest ratios of population to churches. These groups urgently require major inroads in raising up indigenous churches. Many of these groups do not have adequate indigenous leadership to disciple the unchurched among their own people *without cross-cultural assistance*.

It is instructive to compare progress, or lack of it, between 1989 and 1995 (the date for which we have our most recent data).

- First Nation languages Inuktitut and Ojibway show a combined need of 16 new churches.

- Punjabi-speaking people are in greatest need of pioneer church planting. Their population-to-church ratio more than tripled between 1989 and 1995 and is now highest in Canada. Numerically, the need for new churches grew nearly 400% and, given rapid immigration rates, in all probability the need for new cells of Punjabi believers is even higher. Most Punjabi-speaking people are, at least culturally, Sikh.

- There are no known Gujarati, Croatian, Serbo-Croatian, Ojibway or Macedonian congregations. These groups appear entirely unreached in Canada and require adoption for prayer and pioneer church planting efforts. Urdu and Czech-speaking peoples have only one reported church each. Urdu, Persian and Macedonian language groups have shown deterioration in population-to-church ratios between 1989 and 1995.

- It is important to note that many of the European languages included in Table 14 have been replaced by Asian languages in Table 15. Immigration changes, new church plants and changes in home language account for these differences.

- While those speaking Chinese do not appear in Tables 14 and 15, the total number (i.e., 178) of new churches needed is higher than any other "unofficial language" group.

In all this, we must not lose sight of the tremendous need among the two official language groups in Canada. Although there has been an increase in the number of churches (926 for English Canada and 123 for French Canada) between 1989 and 1995, the need for new congregations to disciple the nation is enormous. As has already been stated, French-speaking people remain the largest unreached people group in North America.

Mapping the Land

When Joshua sent out a small advance team, he directed, *"Go, look over the land"* (Joshua 2:1). Accurate information is

Table 14
Fourteen Language Groups Least Reached
in Canada - 1989
(By Current Population-to-Church Ratio)

Language	Evangelical Churches 1989	Projected Population 2000	Current Population to Church Ratio	Evangelical Churches Needed
Greek	0	84,250	84,250	42
Inuktitut	1	20,375	17,455	9
Punjabi	3	55,604	15,878	25
Portuguese	7	122,660	15,011	54
Czech	0	10,179	10,179	5
Urdu	0	9,478	9,478	5
Lithuanian	0	9,362	9,362	5
Hindi	1	10,908	9,345	4
Persian	0	8,877	8,877	4
Macedonian	0	8,171	8,171	4
Thai	0	8,043	8,043	4
Hungarian	3	27,192	7,765	11
Yiddish	0	7,652	7,652	4
Romanian	1	6,858	5,875	2

vital in warfare and in search-and-rescue missions. Both the big picture and its component parts are needed as we seek out God's lost sheep and plant churches to fill the land with the presence of the Lord.

The tables and appendices with this chapter can assist in locating the general area and language group for your next church plant. Computer mapping, while only two-dimensional, can be a valuable tool in finding the specific locations of people groups most in need of new cells of believers. Maps are produced by comparing information on the number of people speaking a given language in any area in Canada with existing congregations ministering in that language. Samples of such mapping can be found in Appendix

Table 15
Fifteen Language Groups Least Reached
in Canada - 1995
(By Current Population-to-Church Ratio)

Language	Evangelical Churches 1995	Projected Population 2001	Current Population to Church Ratio	Evangelical Churches Needed
Punjabi	3	197,200	51,493	96
Polish	4	151,932	29,911	72
Urdu	1	33,741	27,085	16
Gujarati	0	30,995	26,685	15
Croatian	0	25,173	24,200	13
Persian	2	62,868	22,250	29
Serbian	0	23,724	19,935	12
Serbo-Croatian	0	20,440	14,085	10
Italian	18	173,033	11,949	69
Bengali	0	14,072	11,820	7
Inuktitut	2	24,555	11,233	10
Ojibway	0	11,556	11,010	6
Macedonian	0	11,599	10,510	6
Czech	1	8,248	8,385	3

4. Additional field exploration and prayer will always be necessary. Custom maps showing comparative churches-per-capita ratios by census tract are available from *Outreach Canada*.[42]

Our Great Calling and Opportunity

The evangelistic establishment of new cells of believers and congregations within the social fabric of every neighbourhood, apartment block and people group in Canada is the primary task of those committed to the discipling of our nation for the glory of the One who died for all. Church planting is front-line spiritual work and warfare. Front-line spiritual work is never easy, but always worthwhile—for eternity!

Action Points

✓ As Canada becomes less Christian and more pluralistic ("no religious preference" is the opinion growing most rapidly), a new generation is growing up without a clear understanding of the Gospel. Is this kind of culture, which is more like first-century culture than perhaps any previous Canadian generation, a disadvantage or an advantage to the work of the Great Commission? We cannot continue with "maintenance as usual." How should your congregation change its approach to reaching a narcissistic, functionally secular or pagan Canadian community?

✓ One-third of Canadians live in apartments or other high-density housing. How could your church birth new cells of believers in three to five such buildings in your community in the next two to three years?

✓ Ask the Lord to lead your congregation to a language group in Canada, other than your own, to "adopt"— perhaps through your missions budget—to sponsor a new church plant.

✓ How would the understanding of a "church" as, *"Any gathering of Christians meeting regularly for worship celebration, caring, teaching and prayer and actively engaged in evangelism"* affect your approach as you seek to mobilize church planting?

Chapter Notes

[1] Statistics Canada, *Religions in Canada*. Catalogue 93-319. The question of religious affiliation was not asked by Statistics Canada in 1996 and will not be asked again until 2001.

[2] Reginald Bibby. *There Must be More* (Wood Lake Books, 1995) suggests the Church must take immediate action to reach out to an increasingly secular generation still holding memories of a Christian background but with little connection to the Church, before this tenuous connection fades in the upcoming generation.

[3] Worship attendance reported by denominational leadership in another 1996 study was 19%. Lorne Hunter and Dr. Murray Moorman, *An Initial Survey of the "Harvest Field" and "Harvest Force" in Canada* (Richmond, BC: Outreach Canada, 1996).

[4] Worship attendance reported in an Angus Reid poll reported in *Maclean's* magazine, November 4, 1996 included worship in non-Christian traditions.

[5] Statistics Canada, *Religions in Canada*. Catalogue 93-319.

[6] Angus Reid poll reported in *Maclean's* magazine, November 4, 1996.

[7] *Maclean's*, November 4, 1996, p.39.

[8] "Positive tolerance" demands not only the acceptance of *persons* embracing beliefs and lifestyles Christians believe destructive (a Biblical value Christians have always taught), but the embracing of these beliefs and lifestyles *themselves* as of equal "goodness" and "truth" as those which are their logical opposites (a Biblical impossibility).

[9] Brian Stiller. *Was Canada Ever Christian?* Faith Today Publications, 1996.

[10] *The Vancouver Sun,* Monday, August 18, 1997.

[11] Cf. for example two recent works: Brian Seim, editor. *Canada's New Harvest: Helping Churches Touch Newcomers*, Scarborough, ON: SIM Canada, 1997, and Enoch Wan, editor, *Missions Within Reach: Intercultural Ministries in Canada*, Edmonton, AB: China Alliance Press, 1995.

Chapter Notes

[12] Reginald Bibby. *Fragmented Gods*, Irwin Publishing, Toronto, 1987.

[13] These personal definitions of what constitutes a Christian vary greatly in popular culture, often are limited to a general theism (cf. James 2:19) and are too frequently non-Biblical in nature.

[14] Evangelicalism in the following survey is defined as: (1) A focus on Christ's redeeming work as the heart of essential Christianity; (2) A reliance on the Bible as ultimate religious authority; (3) A stress on the new birth; and (4) An energetic individualistic approach to religious duties and social involvement. Such a definition is the minimum (and is perhaps even inadequate lacking reference to the deity of Christ) that might be considered for a person to be a member of the harvest force with the potential of leading others to personal commitment to Christ.

[15] George Rawlyk/Angus Reid Survey, reported by Evangelical Fellowship of Canada in *Canada Watch,* Jan./Feb. 1996, Issue 1.

[16] Dr. George Rawlyk estimated one-seventh, or 14%, of 3,454,574 Roman Catholic worship attendees to be evangelicals.

[17] One seventh, or 14%, of 753,556 worship attendees reported by mainline denominations.

[18] A balance advocated by Dr. Don Posterski in *World Vision's* "Praxis 97" conferences calling for "The Power of the Reconnected Gospel" to be shown by the broader Canadian church.

[19] "Church in Transition" materials for congregational redevelopment are available from Outreach Canada, #16 - 12240 Horseshoe Way, Richmond, BC V7A 4X9, Phone 604-272-0732, Fax 272-2744, or E-mail gkraft@outreach.ca.

"ReFocusing" materials and coaching are available from CRM (Church Resources Ministries), Canada, 1066 - 48th, Delta, BC V4M 2N6, Phone: 604-943-2520. E-mail: canada@crmnet.org.

"Natural Church Development" materials are available from ChurchSmart Resources, 390 E. Saint Charles Road, Carol Stream, IL 60188. Phone 800-253-4276 or E-mail churchsmart@compuserve.com.

Chapter Notes

[20] "Meta-church" materials for assistance in overcoming this common challenge are available from International Centre for Leadership Development and Evangelism, Box 41083 RPO South, Winfield, BC V4V 1Z7, Phone 1-800-804-0777, Fax 250-766-0912, or E-mail leadedge@netshop.net.

[21] For instance, the challenge might begin with each congregation developing community contacts—in a combination of its church directory and "prospect prayer lists"—with 1,000 persons, and continue with focused efforts to deepen relational contact with each person. When a congregation has discovered the 1,000 persons entrusted to it, a new church plant would be undertaken, all the while attempting to bring to be fully devoted followers of Christ each of the 1,000 persons entrusted to the mother congregation.

[22] Roger T. Forster. *Models of Church Planting*. London: Ichthus Media Services. pp.7-13.

[23] Ibid. p.11.

[24] Donald Capps. *The Depleted Self* (Minneapolis: Fortress Press), 1993; and Christopher Lasch, *The Culture of Narcissism* (Northvale, N.J.: Jason Aronson), 1975.

[25] Adapted from *Church Planting Canada* Newsletter, 2nd Quarter, 1997, p. 4.

[26] David Bunch. Harvey Kneisel and Barara Oden, *Multihousing Congregations: How to Start and Grow Christian Congregations in Multihousing Communities*. Atlanta: Southern Baptist Mission Board, 1993.

[27] The Home Mission Board of the Southern Baptist Convention has developed several valuable resources, including a vision overview publication to gain the support of multi-housing managers and owners and two recent paperbacks: (1) David Bunch, Harvey Kneisel, Barbara Oden, *Multihousing Congregations: How to Start and Grow Christian Congregations in Multihousing Communities*. Atlanta: Southern Baptist Mission Board, 1993. (2) Robert L. Perry. *Models of Multi-family Housing Ministry*. Atlanta: Southern Baptist Mission Board, 1989. You may order either from the Canadian Convention of Southern Baptists, Post Bag 300, Cochrane, AB T0L 0W0.

Chapter Notes

[28] 159 Indian Reservations refused enumeration in 1996.

[29] In this and the following cases columns represent known evangelical churches (to the end of 1995) and needed evangelical churches ministering in the language indicated.

[30] Over 100 aboriginal languages are recorded by Statistics Canada.

[31] Those who speak English or French only, or English or French and an aboriginal language.

[32] Cf. Len Cowan. "An Indigenous Church for Indigenous People," in *Faith Today*, July/August 1991, pp.23-26, for a helpful overview of the Christian movement among aboriginal peoples.

[33] Arnell Motz, editor. *Reclaiming a Nation: The Challenge of Re-evangelizing Canada by the Year 2000*. Richmond, BC: Church Leadership Library, 1990. p.110.

[34] A small portion of the improvement in English and French (and some other language groups which follow) population-to-church ratios during these six years may be due in part to improved denominational record keeping and continuing research. Research data is acknowledged never to be entirely complete. Nevertheless we are convinced that the Body of Christ in Canada has reason to be encouraged and affirmed in its task and progress.

[35] "Unreached" people groups are defined by the Joshua Project of the *AD 2000 & Beyond Movement* as over 10,000 people in size with less than 2% evangelical believers.

[36] The conception of God in popular culture throughout Canada varies greatly. Belief in "God" may refer to Jewish or Muslim monotheism, an undefined deism or theism (cf. James 2:19), a new age pantheism or other conception frequently non-Biblical in nature. Yet belief in God, however defined, may provide a bridge to the Creator who came to earth to be our Redeemer.

[37] *Ensemble* magazine, C.P. 602, Succursale B, Montreal, Qc H3B 3K3, Vol. 19, no. 1, p.13.

Chapter Notes

[38] Technically no ratio can be calculated due to no reported evangelical churches in the specified language. In such incidents a ratio will be shown as if one evangelical church were ministering in the language group.

[39] Arnell Motz. p.110.

[40] Due to significant immigration growth in the Chinese, Polish and Vietnamese communities.

[41] We must remember that many more new churches than listed in column 5 are actually needed to disciple these people groups. The numbers suggested reflect only a 1:2000 ratio. We must seek 1:1000 or 1:500 ratios.

[42] Outreach Canada Research Department, #16 – 12240 Horseshoe Way, Richmond, BC V7A 4X9, Phone (604) 272-0732, Fax 272-2744, or E-mail lhunter@outreach.ca.

Chapter Four

Looking to AD 2015:
10,000 New Churches

Dr. Murray Moerman and Lorne Hunter

Jesus issued the challenging call, *"The harvest is plentiful, but the workers are few. Ask the Lord of the harvest, therefore, to send out workers into his harvest field"* (Luke 10:2). It is a call to pray and a call to release more labourers into the harvest.

How many labourers are gathering the Master's harvest? Is the Christian movement in Canada growing? Why are growing sections of the Church doing so and why are other segments in decline? Which denominations are growing and by what means? Perhaps most importantly, what can be done to disciple the nation as all denominations, missions and congregations give priority praying for and releasing labourers for church planting that the Lord may grant a great harvest?

The purpose of this chapter is to overview the effectiveness and great prospects of harvest force commissioned by the Lord of the harvest to be labourers in His vineyard.

The Long View

Figure 8 depicts long-range trends in religious affiliation[2] in Canada, as a percentage of population, during the 20th century to 1991. In general terms, we see long-term trends of:

- Growth in Roman Catholicism affiliation, which overtook a declining Protestantism in the mid-sixties, peaking in 1981 and declining slightly during the last decade.

- A steady decline in Protestantism,[3] increasing in seriousness in the 1960s and showing no sign of slowing.

- Rapid growth, beginning in the 1960s, in the percentage of Canadians claiming, "no religious affiliation."

- An increase in the growth of other religions beginning in the 1970s.

Early in the century few Canadians held publicly to atheism or agnosticism and, at least nominally, identified with Christianity. Eastern religions began to arrive in the

Figure 8
Canadian Religious Affiliation (1901-1991)[1]

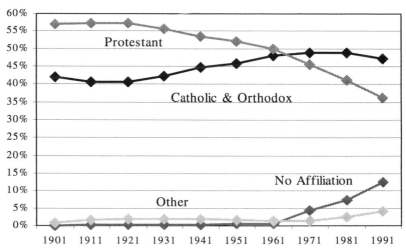

latter third of the century, building slowly. Secularism, encouraged by public policy, has shown strong increases toward the end of the century. Whatever else can be said for the 1960s, the decade heralded an era of change, with effects far beyond the perimeters of that decade.

A breakdown of the Protestant line of Figure 8 is depicted in Figure 9. Difficulties in offering a simple, accurate Protestant picture of the first third of the century arise due to the change of some mainline Protestant denominations from essentially evangelical convictions to more liberal views. The formation of the United Church in Canada in 1925 from streams of Presbyterian, Methodist and Congregationalist sources appears somewhat awkwardly in the 1921-1931 decade.

Despite difficulties depicting the first third of the century, the trend from 1930 onward is clear. Mainline Protestantism continues to slide, the most painful decade coming most recently. Evangelical influence remains stable and low for most of the century, turning upward only in the final decade

Figure 9
Canadian Protestant Affiliation (1901-1991)[4]

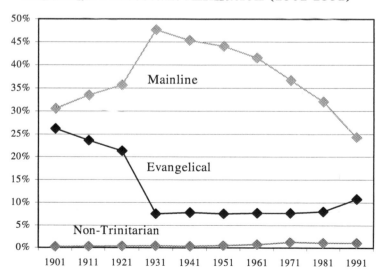

depicted. Figure 10 sheds further light on the fortunes of mainline Protestantism during the century.

The overall picture of long-term decline is a frustrating one for mainline Protestantism. This trend must be stopped if mainline Protestants are to re-engage our culture and figure significantly in the harvest force of the 21st century. The

Figure 10
Canadian Mainline Affiliation (1901-1991)[5]

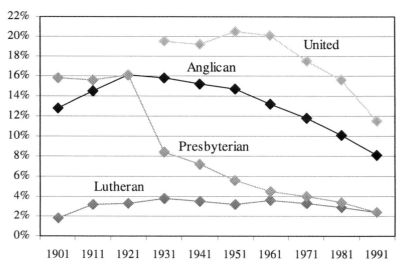

United Church of Canada has declined most rapidly, followed by the Anglican Church and the Presbyterian Church in Canada. Only the Lutheran tradition has maintained stability and some overall growth. It would appear that the larger the denomination, the more difficult and essential it is to reverse decline.[6]

A Closer Look at a Recent Decade

Table 16 shows deep cause for concern as Christians take stock of the harvest force available to disciple the people groups of Canada and beyond.

Table 16
Canadian Change in Religious Affiliation
(1981-1991)[7]

Affiliation	1981		1991		% Change	
	Number	%	Number	%	+	-
Total Population	24,083,495	100.0%	26,994,045	100.0%		
Catholic	11,402,605	47.3%	12,335,255	45.7%		1.6%
Roman Catholic	11,210,390	46.5%	12,203,620	45.2%		1.3%
Ukrainian Catholic	190,590	0.8%	128,390	0.5%		0.3%
Other Catholic	1,630	0.0%	3,235	0.0%		
Eastern Orthodox	361,560	1.5%	387,395	1.4%		0.1%
Protestant	9,914,580	41.2%	9,780,710	36.2%		5.0%
United	3,758,015	15.6%	3,093,120	11.5%		4.1%
Anglican	2,436,375	10.1%	2,188,115	8.1%		2.0%
Presbyterian	812,105	3.4%	636,295	2.4%		1.0%
Lutheran	702,905	2.9%	636,210	2.4%		0.5%
Evangelicals	1,926,115	8.0%	2,907,925	10.8%	2.8%	
Non-Trinitarian Cults	260,930	1.1%	289,360	1.1%		
Jewish	296,425	1.2%	318,070	1.2%		
Eastern Non-Christian	305,890	1.3%	747,455	2.8%	1.5%	
Islam	98,160	0.4%	253,260	0.9%	0.5%	
Buddhist	51,955	0.2%	163,415	0.6%	0.4%	
Hindu	69,500	0.3%	157,015	0.6%	0.3%	
Sikh	67,710	0.3%	147,440	0.5%	0.2%	
Other Eastern Non-Christian	18,565	0.1%	26,320	0.1%		
Parareligious Groups	13,450	0.1%	28,155	0.1%		
No Affiliation	1,783,530	7.4%	3,386,365	12.5%	5.1%	

The percentage of Canadians willing to identify with Christianity declined 6.7% during the decade. While Roman Catholic affiliation declined 1.6% during the decade, mainline Protestant affiliation declined a deeply disturbing 7.6%. At the same time Canadians accepting "no religious affiliation" increased a dramatic 5.1%.

Since eastern religions grew 1.4% during the decade, presumably largely though immigration and birth, it is possible the growth of "no religious affiliation"[8] may be accounted for largely through defections from mainline Protestantism. Defections from mainline Protestantism are more likely than defections from Catholicism for two reasons. First, Catholicism declined far less than "no religious affiliation" grew. Secondly, Dean Kelley has demonstrated how conservative movements grow more effectively over time.[9] Catholicism has tended to remain more conservative than mainline Protestantism, therefore the more liberal movement—mainline Protestantism—is more likely to sustain defections over time.

Table 17 summarizes recent trends in the number of mainline Protestant congregations in Canada.

Table 17
Mainline Protestant Congregations (1980-1995)

	1980	1985	1990	1995
Anglican Church in Canada	3,316	3,210	3,033	2,390
Evangelical Lutheran Church[10]	658	648	659	650
Lutheran Church – Canada	356	360	346	325
Presbyterian Church in Canada	1,015	1,041	1,023	1,004
United Church of Canada	4,265	4,205	4,081	3,909

The primary encouragement for the Canadian harvest force was an "against-the-flow" growth of 2.8%, compared to overall population growth (within evangelical denominations).[11] The proportion of evangelical denominational growth from biological and conversion growth and the proportion of Biblically orthodox members defecting from more liberal mainline Protestant denominations is not currently known. It must be remembered that this 2.8% growth in the evangelical harvest force merely tempers the massive loss to the Body of Christ of 9.3%[12] during the decade to the deeply disturbing overall loss of 6.5%.

Who is Committed to Evangelism?

Canadians were asked in a 1996 Angus Reid poll to respond to the statement, *"I feel it is very important to encourage non-Christians to become Christians."* This question must be recognized as vitally important, in that only those who respond positively can form the core of the labourers available for discipling the nation. The response of Canadians to this question by region, age group and denominational background is reflected in Figures 11, 12 and 13.[13] Greater clarity of purpose in the Canadian harvest force is be found in the Maritimes and Prairie provinces and in conservative Protestant denominations. Particularly disturbing, is the growing weakness in commitment to evangelism shown by age group among Canadians under 55 years of age, reflecting, in all likelihood, the post-modern agenda of pluralism and the denial of absolutes including the very concept of truth.

It is vital that Christian leaders emphasize the role of Christian apologetics in the Body of Christ to address this erosion of belief in the existence of truth in a cultural environment that denies all universal absolutes but tolerance.[14] This, precisely, is our task in discipling the nation to Christ.

Figure 11
By Region

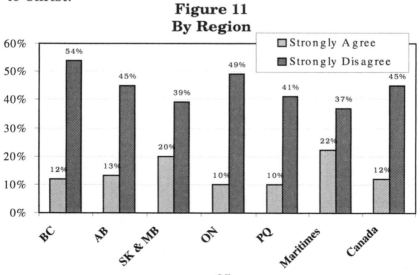

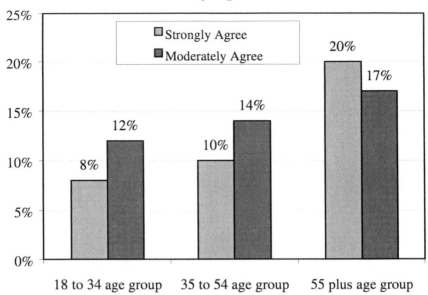

Figure 12
By Age

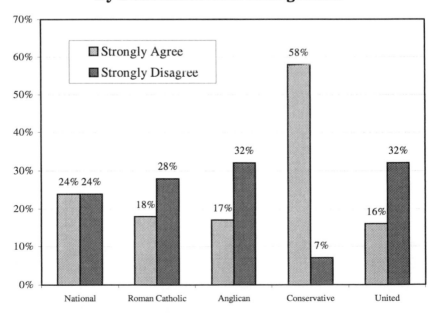

Figure 13
By Denominational Background

Renewal Groups Within Historic Traditions

Most mainline Protestant denominations are benefiting from Biblically orthodox groups working to bring this renewal to their tradition from within. In the United Church of Canada, The National Alliance of Covenanting Congregations (NACC) represents 113 congregations.[15] The Essentials Movement[16] in the Anglican Church in Canada embraces both the Barnabas[17] and Anglican Renewal[18] Movements. In the Presbyterian Church in Canada the Renewal Fellowship[19] encourages pastors sharing its vision, as does the Presbyterian and Reformed Renewal Ministries International.[20] Many Catholic charismatic prayer groups minister within the Roman Catholic Church, but support for these groups varies greatly by diocese and no coordinating body exists to encourage the movement nationally.

The strength of the NACC is its unique focus on renewing congregations per se, who in turn become members of the movement. Renewal groups in other traditions tend to focus on the membership of clergy, who in turn affect congregations. This renewing effect on congregations, however, may be lost when the congregation's pastor leaves, whereas the NACC's efforts to bring Biblical orthodoxy to congregations who become covenanting members is more likely to remain.

While the research team identifying church planting needs for evangelical congregations in Canada wishes to take into account Biblically orthodox congregations within mainline Protestantism in each census tract, only congregations evangelizing their community can be identified as meeting the need for Biblically orthodox congregations in a given community, compaired to more mobile clergy. We invite all mainline renewal groups, in addition to clergy, to consider ways of drawing congregations into membership and ongoing renewal.

Recent Church Planting Trends by Tradition

Changes in religious affiliation depicted in Table 16 are reflected in Table 18 and suggest a linkage between church planting rates and changes in religious affiliation in Canada.

While a decline in denominational membership may be seen to account for decline in the number of congregations in some movements, it also appears the trend toward planting new churches in evangelical denominations accounts significantly for the growth of that movement. While some may argue changes in religious affiliation produce the need for new congregations, it is difficult to account for spontaneous upward changes in evangelical affiliation. It seems more realistic to view the growth in identification with evangelical denominations as a result of the evangelistic church planting efforts of those denominations.[22]

Table 18
Organized Congregations in Canada by Tradition
(1989-1995)

Tradition:	1989	1995	AAGR
Evangelical	7,854	8,848	2.3%
Mainline	9,226	8,358	-2.1%
Roman Catholic	6,173	5,355	-2.6%
Orthodox	300[21]	439	unknown

Several Encouraging Indications

To summarize recent pertinent findings:

- While Canadian identification with Christendom declined dramatically between 1981 and 1991, evangelical affiliation grew 2.8% during that period as reported by Statistics Canada (see Table 16).

- Evangelical church planting rates stood at about 1.1% AAGR (1984-1994).[23]

- Evangelical church planting rates appear to be rising to 2.3% AAGR (1990-1995) (see Table 17).

While the dates of these findings do not coincide so as to draw firm conclusions, indications are positive for the harvest force in Canada—while the culture is in decline, the Evangelical church is growing through church planting, and the rate of its growth appears to be on the rise. What is needed is more and greater effectiveness in evangelistic church planting to counter the drift of Canadian culture, as we disciple our nation.

Who Is Growing and Why?

Table 16 showed the evangelical movement alone, among Christian traditions, growing 2.8% during the 1981-1991 census period. While some denominations decline, others are growing. Why? What lessons can be learned from those movements currently most effective in planting new cells of believers throughout the land?

Let us break out the nine fastest-growing evangelical denominations for this period to see what we can learn. Table 19 shows the church planting rates of these nine denominations for the previous five and ten years.

Initial Observations

As we peruse the following list of growing denominations we observe:

- Both renewal movements and more conservative denominations can be found in the list of most rapidly growing denominations in approximately equal proportion.

Table 19
Nine Canadian Denominations
With the Highest Church Planting Rates

Denomination	Average Annual Church Planting Rate		Current Number of Congregations	
	AAGR[24] 5 years	AAGR 10 years	Larger < 100	Smaller > 100
Apostolic Church of Pentecost	5.4%	1.3%	163	
Association of Vineyard Churches	17.5%	36.2%		44
Canadian Convention of Southern Baptists	4.6%	7.2%	124	
Christian & Missionary Alliance	2.3%	2.8%	378	
Church of God – Cleveland	3.8%	unknown	120	
Church of the Nazarene	1.6%	2.2%	190	
Evangelical Free Church	0.0%	2.9%	133	
Foursquare Gospel Church of Canada	1.4%	4.0%		58
Victory Christian Churches	33.3%	34.2%		38

- Smaller denominations tend to grow more rapidly than larger denominations. All denominations in Table 19 are under 200 congregations in size, with the exception of the Christian and Missionary Alliance.

- Newer denominations tend to grow more rapidly than older denominations. Victory Christian Churches and the Association of Vineyard Churches, with the highest growth rates, are relative newcomers, beginning their development in the 1980s.

- The multiplication of denominations may be as strategic to the discipling of the nation as church planting is strategic to the growth of individual denominations.

Why are These Denominations Growing?

We contacted leaders from each of these denominations for interviews regarding their experiences in church planting. The following reports come from these discussions. There are both practical insights and patterns for the wide variety of ways the Lord of the harvest is raising up new congregations.

The Apostolic Church of Pentecost (ACOP) has its roots in the Azusa Street Mission (Los Angeles) revival of 1906. The ACOP subsequently branched off of the Pentecostal Church of Canada in 1921. Largely a western movement, the denomination has been primarily rural, and subsequently closed a number of its congregations as Canadian rural towns dwindled with population migration to the cities.

The ACOP has been multiplying congregations at a net average rate of 5.4% annually during the last five years and set a goal in 1997 to increase that planting rate to 7.1% annually through 2010. To reach this goal each congregation will be challenged to daughter a new work at least every ten years.

The past 5.4% planting rate has been sustained without a nationally coordinated strategy or specific structure, according to moderator Gil Killam, largely because local churches and pastors have been growing in their awareness of the priority of outreach ministry. The role of district has been one of encouragement and some coordination of financial support, but 90% of church planting has been undertaken by mother churches giving birth to new outreach works— churches planting churches. In Calgary, for example, the Calgary Downtown Full Gospel congregation has planted seven daughter churches, and one of these daughters has entered into second-generation planting. The remaining 10% of church planting is district initiated and sponsored.

Nevertheless, further change in the mindset of pastors and leaders remains a major challenge to realizing the greater harvest potential of the ACOP movement. Many pastors still think they do not have the skills to lead their congregation in birthing a new work. Many leaders are not aware that increasing the size of their existing congregation is, for most leaders, more difficult than birthing a new work. In addition, Rev. Killam is aware of a need to develop more effective strategies and leadership training resources.

Leadership for successful church planting has come largely from experienced staff members of local churches. Recent Bible school graduates are not as successful as church planters, generally speaking, perhaps due to lack of ministry experience.

The ACOP, in addition to church planting, has also seen a small number of previously independent congregations, particularly in the Maritimes and Ontario, turn to them for a denominational home.

In recent years church planting efforts have focused on western urban centres, largely among middleclass Anglo Baby Boomers. The ACOP has not been strong in ethnic planting historically, but change is in the wind as ethnic planting is receiving increasing priority.

The Association of Vineyard Churches began in Canada with a single congregation in 1985, growing to 44 congregations in 1996, an amazing annual average growth rate of 36.2% during the 1986-1996 decade.[25] As a young movement the Vineyard movement is known for its creativity and vigour. "Ninety percent of the Vineyard's congregations have been brought into the movement through church planting," indicates national director Gary Best, who also oversees the development of Vineyard churches in Asia. "There have been very few adoptions," he states.

How is the Vineyard planting so effectively? Key to this growth is the commitment to church planting demonstrated by its leadership. Virtually all major functional leaders of the movement are planting or have recently planted new churches. Gary Best, for example, planted a Vineyard in Langley, B.C., and has seen six new congregations birthed out of this congregation. The Vineyard regional leader for Alberta has planted three congregations in Edmonton and has plans to plant a total of six congregations. Deeper roots go back to John Wimber, Vineyard founder in the U.S., with church growth background at Fuller Seminary, who not only planted the Vineyard in Anaheim but has planted dozens of churches out of it over the last twenty years. "Like begets like," points out Best.

As a result, church planting is in the genetic code of the Vineyard—"Our mission is to plant churches that plant churches," says Best. In the organizational culture where high value is placed on small group experiences, a new believer may lead someone else to the Lord, lead their own small group within a year, be mentoring an apprentice leader and already be dreaming of the day that they can help plant a church. "Many Generation Xers want to be planters," says Best, "many of them overseas."

The movement also develops and draws entrepreneurs by fostering a pioneering culture. "We're still able to take a fair number of risks as an organization," states Best. "We send out people who are learning as they go. Sometimes it looks more like ready, fire, aim or even fire, fire, fire, but we have a corporate environment in which planters can thrive." Despite being a risk-taking culture, the Vineyard's rate of church planting success is high. Best cites only three failed plants out of a total of more than sixty over the past dozen years.

The Vineyard has an orientation toward younger people and the poor—and finds both groups very receptive to the Gospel. "There is a real spiritual hunger in Canada," says Best, "albeit a spirituality often desiring to remain independent of the authority and structure of the established church. Yet it's a starting point." Best sees changes in Canadian culture moving to revisit major components of the culture of the first century and says, "We're not afraid of that. History shows the Gospel competed well in that environment."

The Vineyard places high value on informal servanthood. "You bring down a lot of barriers by serving people," says Best. "We have preconceived images of who is open and who is not, but servants are not easily put aside." Servant-evangelism, as the approach has come to be known, is most effective when it's not organized, maintains Best. "Shovel a driveway. Clean windows. Not as an organization, but as individuals. Serving disarms people who misunderstand the Gospel." Best cites a recent example of a Vineyard youth group buying hookers' time to buy lunch, give flowers and share Christ's love.

The Vineyard has opted for minimal bureaucracy. "We are resisting the desire to create all the structures we think we need but which could strangle us," says Best. "Organization is not opposed to organism, but organization must remain submitted to the purposes of the organism." Best has been influenced by Roland Allan's *The Spontaneous Expansion of the Church*.

Several models of planting have been undertaken. Each approach has benefits and challenges. Pioneer planters are valued and encouraged, but not controlled. "We somewhat try to get out of their way and let them do it," says Best. "But pioneer planters are not often long term. You have to discern when to put in pastoral leaders and release the pioneer to plant again."

Another approach that has been used is one Best calls the "strawberry runner," in which 100 to 200 people are sent out to root a new fruit-bearing plant some distance away—still connected to the mother plant, but functionally autonomous. While this approach seems at first glance to be a fast track to new plants, Best cautioned that they are still evaluating the longer-term benefits of such a strategy. "There is something brought out in a pastor in the process of gathering the first 100 people of a congregation that is missed when the core is readymade."

The Vineyard is flexible regarding formal education for its planters. While seminary is not required, the movement does highly value Biblical knowledge and functional leadership. Several means of moving toward the desired result are used. In some instances young leaders will be urged to take a year or two of formal schooling. All developing leaders are encouraged to read informally and take continuing education classes, as they are able. In addition, a two-year, part-time leadership growth program has been developed with emphasis on reading (leadership and church planting), interacting with experienced planters and being mentored in a local congregation. The primary purpose of the program is to develop self-directed leaders.

Church planting goals tend to be more commonly expressed in terms of mission, vision and qualitatively described desired results rather than numbers. The numerical portion of the goal is to see 200 congregations by the end of the year 2000. "That will be a stretch since the Toronto situation," says Best, "but we'll keep focused on our mission and see what God does."

The Vineyard Task Force for Church Planting remains purposely decentralized. The kinds of new congregations desired are defined and agreed upon. Then nine area directors, each overseeing from five to ten congregations (to keep mentoring relational) cast the vision, gather resources and encourage new plants in their development. Resources given to new plants include little finances—rather one congregation will give the new plant a worship leader, another a youth leader, etc.

Despite the Vineyard's success, Best doesn't consider himself an expert—"We don't really know what we're doing, but we're just doing it and learning as we go. We have a great love and appreciation for the whole Body of Christ in Canada and fully recognize that we are simply a small part of it. We simply want, within our limitations, to play that part as well as we can so the whole may be strengthened."

The Canadian Convention of Southern Baptists (**CCSB**) planted its first Canadian Church in 1953 and has since grown to 124 congregations in six regions across the country. Fifty percent of this growth has taken place in the last ten years. Between 1986 and 1996 the CCSB planted 131 new congregations, with 67 of these (51.1%[26]) taking root, for a net average growth rate of 7.2% annually—the highest rate of an established intermediate-sized denomination in Canada during this period. These figures suggest broad seed sowing in new church starts to be key to the significant growth experienced by the CCSB.

Despite this achievement, the convention restructured in 1997 to further energize church planting efforts. Each district association—currently six across the nation—will now be led by "church planter catalysts," whose role will be to mobilize church planters and to personally do church planting. They will also assemble necessary resources for the growth of the church through church planting. In addition, the services of a national church planting consultant are available to all associations.

Executive director Rev. Allan Schmidt does not perceive Canadians to be resistant to the Gospel. While animosity toward the Gospel is seen in public institutions such as media, government and education, Schmidt sees a real hunger for God in the hearts of average Canadians. "The issue is leadership," says Schmidt, "if we had leadership we could plant a church anywhere in Canada—new communities, ethnic, rural."

While 75% of church planters are seminary trained, the CCSB looks for ability rather than formal education, and actively seeks those with the gift and calling of gathering new believers among lay people.

The CCSB has developed church planter assessment processes to assist in identifying such leaders. Church planters are then linked with mentors for ongoing personal support. Regional groups of planters and mentors are gathered quarterly for prayer, sharing and mutual encouragement. The CCSB assists in the funding of local planters for up to a five-year phase-out period.

A wide range of church planting models have been utilized—ten may be identified—but increasingly the intentional "church planting systems" approaches pioneered by Bob Logan of Church Resource Ministries are being adapted and utilized with encouraging results. In most cases mother churches are sought out to sponsor new works, although supporting parent congregations may be many kilometers from the new planting site.

Rev. Schmidt expresses Southern Baptist attitudes toward goals in terms of trying to recognize what God wants to do next and cooperating with His agenda. Numeric goal setting does draw attention to the primary task. "But we want not only new churches, but Bible believing, soul winning, disciple making churches," says Schmidt.

The main challenge to church planting in Canada is seen as its large geographic size and subsequent very real regionalism. Yet our segmented society also provides opportunities. Much of CCSB growth therefore has been within Canada's visible ethnic communities. Within Québec for instance, the majority of CCSB churches are Haitian, Arabic, Hispanic, etc. Work among francophone Québecers is slow. "Our focus is on finding native Québec sons for leadership," says Schmidt. "We must intentionally plant Anglo and French churches as well as ethnic."

Daughtering by established congregations is strongly encouraged, both for the sake of the Kingdom and the health of the mothering congregation. Observes Schmidt, "The congregation that gets preoccupied with itself will die. If it looks outward it grows. If you give the Gospel away, God's blessing comes back."

The Christian and Missionary Alliance (C&MA) established its first congregation in Canada in 1887 and became autonomous from its U.S. parent body in 1980. A primary core value of the C&MA stresses the connection between a deepening spiritual life in Christ and the resulting heart for evangelism and world mission of the believer. The C&MA had 378 congregations at the end of 1996. An annual average growth rate of 2.7% over the last decade makes it the fastest-growing large denomination[27] in Canada.

The primary reason for this growth record, according to Dr. Stuart Lightbody, vice-president for Canadian ministries, is, "we believe the best way to do evangelism is to do church planting." Personal evangelism is stressed both in established congregations and in new church plants. A second reason for the growth of the C&MA in more recent years is that the global perspective of its historic missionary vision has enabled it to recognize the changing ethnic reality of Canada and respond quickly.

Historically, the C&MA has found its most responsive ground for planting churches in the Prairie provinces, Alberta in particular. More recently it is Toronto and Vancouver where church planting is being done among new Canadians.

The C&MA has been less effective among French speaking Québecers and First Nation peoples. They have responded to these areas of recognized weakness in several ways. By emphasizing the need for indigenous leadership the C&MA has identified an effective francophone district superintendent to develop its work in Québec and a native leader to head its association of First Nations congregations. Further, at the invitation of the Québec district superintendent and consent of other leadership, the C&MA is sending to Québec those who will approach their task as bona fide, cross-culturally trained, language learning, lifetime missionaries to this largest of unreached people groups in North America.

Strong response to the cultural diversity of Canada's people groups is also reflected in the formation of three national multi-cultural associations—Chinese, Vietnamese and Filipino—each with their own leadership structure. For 1998 three additional multi-cultural associations are being considered—Spanish, Korean and a yet unnamed association—that will coordinate ministry among Sikh, Hindu, Buddhist and Islamic people groups.

In the Caucasian community church planting is most commonly done at the initiative of the district office or by the initiation of the local church "mother-daughter process." Leadership for church planting comes from either seasoned pastors with a special interest or gift in church planting or from younger recent Bible college graduates. In the multi-cultural associations new churches are generally initiated by the associations themselves who see the need and approach the district when plans for the new work are already well developed. Due to a lack of seasoned multi-cultural pastors, leadership for these new works is more often recent Bible school graduates.

Finances for church planting are raised largely on a faith promise basis. Every C&MA church is required by its constitution to hold an annual missions conference. During these conferences congregational members are invited to make financial commitments to support global advance and Canadian ministries church planting ventures.

Goal setting has been a strong factor in C&MA church planting growth. In anticipation of the C&MA centennial in

1987, both the Canadian and U.S. bodies publicly covenanted to seek to double in size by that date, and both bodies achieved the challenging goal. The C&MA in Canada then formed its own "Plan 2000" to set the denomination's direction to the year 2000. A key goal was to "plant culturally relevant evangelistic churches." The C&MA is on track to reach 435 congregations by 2000. From 1987 to 1996 a net gain of 114 churches was achieved (127 new plants vs. 13 closures), 59 of these being multi-cultural. By mid- 1997 a net gain of seven congregations had been started, four of these being multi-cultural.

Dr. Lightbody identifies three ongoing challenges: the embracing of the C&MA primary core values by newcomers, additional finances to plant more churches and leadership for new churches, particularly non-Anglo multi-cultural church planters. We, like they, have great confidence the Lord of the harvest, who has given the C&MA movement such great blessings, will continue to provide grace and resources for the task of discipling the nation.

The Church of God (Cleveland) originated in Tennessee in 1887 and began its work in western Canada in 1957, Ontario in 1967 and Québec in 1972. The movement has seen its greatest growth since the mid-eighties, currently growing at 3.8% annually to 120 congregations.

Why is this movement growing so consistently? First, is a focus upon responsive peoples. Bishop Canute Blake believes, "God has a time and season in manifesting His power and grace in a specific ways. Therefore we need to be sensitive to what the Lord is saying and where the Lord is directing the casting of the net. At this time we must be sensitive to the cultural mix and diversity in Canada and not be afraid of it."

Bishop Blake believes the people groups in Canada most responsive to the Gospel are those who have recently immigrated. This is supported by the fact that ethnic and cultural churches have been growing best and are planting the most new churches with great diversity—Romanian, Jamaican, East Indian. Canadians value multi-culturalism, and the Church must realize the potential in this cultural value.

Second, is a practical focus on the power of prayer. The movement is looking for 300 intercessors to pray one hour daily for the harvest. Those committed to this calling are called "faith walkers"—partners in reaping the harvest.

A third key is goal setting by a leader who is a strong promoter of church planting. Bishop Blake, leading in a modified Episcopal polity, establishes church planting goals and appoints leaders for new plants. Between August 1994 and August 1996, a goal of ten new congregations for Ontario was set and achieved. Also, an overall goal of 10% membership increase was targeted—a mark successfully reached in each of the last three years! Currently 12 new plants are planned for the years 1996 to 1998—two Caucasian, a Slavic and an East Indian congregation have already been organized.

Financial support for church planting is not left to chance. Member congregations contribute 5% of local offerings to the support of the regional office, 5% to the national office and 5% to home and world missions. These funds in turn are used to support new and developing congregations. In addition, the Church of God denomination seeks 300 partners to seed $10 a month into the church planting harvest.

Church of God church planting methodology favours the local church birthing, nurturing and supporting the new church with leadership, prayer and finances. Pioneer planting has shown mixed results. Tent-making planters, common in the past, are giving way to younger planters seeking more financial security.

Ensuring that newly planted churches have adequate ongoing support remains a challenge. Yet Bishop Blake would like to see every Church of God plant a new congregation to share in the support and reward of sowing into the great Canadian harvest!

The Church of the Nazarene established its first Canadian congregation in 1908 and grew to 190 congregations by 1995. The Church of the Nazarene has been multiplying congregations at an average annual rate of 2.2% during the 1985/1995 decade, slowing slightly to 1.6% annually during the second half of that period.

A recent study of the contribution of church planting to the overall growth of the movement has been revealing. National leadership reviewed the growth of the movement through congregations established before 1970, then the contribution of congregations planted between 1970 and 1995. The study showed 21% of current Nazarene members resulting directly from recent church plants. Further, 25% of worship attendance, 24% of Sunday School attendance and 23% of finances have resulted from recent church plants.

Mrs. Marjorie Osborne, coordinator of church growth for the Church of the Nazarene, credits the international "General Church" headquarters for keeping church planting continually before its people, particularly as a thrust for the urban and multi-cultural planting. She believes also that Nazarene pastors have become increasingly knowledgeable regarding church growth principles. "In the 1970s six plants were underway at any given point, in the 1980s 12 plants and in the 1990s you can find 24 plants underway at any one time across the country," says Osborne. "We're committed to planting churches."

The Nazarenes have found responsiveness to the Gospel among Anglos in suburbia and among non-Anglos in Canada's urban areas. Before 1985 most church plants were either

Anglo or French. In the 1990s, however, half of new church plants are among non-Anglo ethnic groups.

Haitian and Filipino groups in Québec currently appear most responsive. Lack of qualified French-born indigenous leadership hampers church planting in French Québec.

Nazarenes use many church planting methods, but a single umbrella concept provides the proven context for them all—planting in clusters. The *"Target Toronto"* project began 27 new outreaches in a three-year period. Osborne now believes clusters of about ten new plants in a given region to be optimal and is willing to work with other denominations rather than allow planters to work without the peer support benefits of planting in clusters. Cluster planting benefits church planter morale, provides interaction and practical ideas and offers the larger dream to which the established church will give more generously. Critical also to Nazarenes is that each new work in the cluster is sponsored by a local church in the district for prayer and practical support.

Leadership for new church development within the Nazarene movement may come from the ranks of clergy or lay leaders, with or without a completed seminary education. Appropriate spiritual gifts for planting are the primary criteria. This broadening of the potential selection pool for church planting is a major advantage over other denominations.

To identify lay leaders with church planting potential, the Nazarenes hold annual lay institutes in major centres across Canada. Lay people interested in church growth are invited with the expectation, expressed in advance, that some new work will be initiated as a result of the experience; e.g., an evangelistic Bible study, new church plant or other outreach. Basic theology, pastoral and evangelism skills are reviewed over eight weekends, spaced one month apart. Instructors for the institute are selected, at least in part, for their evangelistic personal lifestyles. Of 30 participants at the first Institute in Toronto, seven went on to be full-time pastors, three of which went on to overseas mission fields in Albania and Kenya. Assessment centres are an alternative method used in conjunction with lay institutes.

Church planting goals set for *Target Toronto* shook up the Nazarene world. One of the values of the goal-setting process was to wake people up to the need for church planting, a desirable result even if the full goal was not achieved. On a national level superintendents currently set goals for their district and these are summed to become the national goal.

A church growth committee (10 elected district superintendents, pastors and lay people) work to stimulate church planting on the national level. Districts also have church extension committees.

Challenges remain. The desire to complete the Great Commission is not yet at the top of the list of denominational priorities at the grass roots level. One additional note of encouragement, however, is that Nazarene colleges, which had focused largely on training academics, are now refocusing to produce mission leaders in a world that has forgotten the eternal value of souls.

The Evangelical Free Church began its work in Canada in 1934, becoming autonomous from its U.S. parent body in 1984 on the 100th anniversary of the ministry of the Evangelical Free Church in America. The movement is now 136 congregations strong in Canada. The Free Church has been adding congregations between 1986 and 1996 at an annual rate of 2.9% per decade, slowing during the last five years.

Existing congregations from other traditions looking for an adoptive home have found the denomination's open and inclusive style appealing. While this growth is welcome, Dr. Charlie Worley, District Superintendent for the Lower Pacific

District, believes a much greater proportion of incoming congregational growth must result from church planting.

The Free Church has been finding Chinese immigrants and first-generation Chinese congregations most responsive to church planting, a fact that has contributed significantly to the denomination's growth rate.

Evangelistic church planting initiatives in Québec, however, have come from the Evangelical Free Church in America which, in 1987, commissioned a mission team cluster of four couples to begin work in the province. Four new congregations have been established since 1987, but birthing daughter congregations has been a challenge due to a lack of indigenous leadership. At present all Québec pastoral leadership remains expatriate.

Most church planting has taken place in the context of the mother-daughter model, usually initiated by a mother church. Leadership for new church plants frequently comes from the mother church, sometimes from the senior pastor personally. Seasoned pastors are preferred to new Bible school graduates as church planters, although mature lay persons may be selected to lead a new plant based upon experience.

President Rick Penner would like to see Free Church congregations multiply at a "double-in-a-decade" rate of 7.14% annually, while recognizing the denomination's need for a unified vision and strategy to move in this direction. There is the possibility that a part- or full-time national director of church planting may be commissioned in the next three to five years.

The denomination is reviewing other means of transforming its structure to serve the local church in fulfilling the Great Commission. One possibility includes moving to regional support, and equipping groups of 10 to 15 congregations coached by national staff portfolios in church planting, pastoral care and revitalization.

The mission of the Evangelical Free Church in Canada is to strengthen and expand in Canada. The challenge created by a denomination stressing local autonomy is that the local church has no formal accountability to the district or the district to national leadership. Leadership, therefore, must motivate by informal relational means rather than formal goal setting.

The Foursquare Gospel Church began its first work in Canada in 1927, growing to 30 congregations in 1981, when it was given autonomy from the International Church of the Foursquare Gospel. Today the movement has 58 congregations.

During the decade of 1986 to 1996, Foursquare congregations increased at an average rate of 4% annually. This rate has slowed to 1.4% annually during the past five years. Just over 50% of this growth has come through the development of new congregations, with the remaining coming through the adoption of existing congregations into the Foursquare movement.

The Foursquare movement is served by a modified Episcopal polity with a local church focus. President Tim Peterson views the role of the denomination simply as "empowering the local church and its laity for their ministry of personifying Christ in the community."

Rev. Peterson prefers the term "birthing" to church planting. Birthing reflects the natural relational process of spiritual reproduction suggested in the Scriptural depiction of the Body of Christ as family. The normal expression of a Biblically healthy church is the birthing of new congregations just as naturally as is the birthing of children to a relationally healthy married couple. Intimacy with Christ motivates further spiritual reproduction.

"New works" (e.g., preaching points or other outreach ministries) are initiated by the local church. Some of these develop to become self-conscious daughter congregations. When a daughter congregation becomes viable and reaches beyond itself in winning people to Christ, the national office recognizes it as a pioneer congregation. At a later stage of maturity the congregation is recognized as a Foursquare church.

Every new church, therefore, is connected to a mother church rather than to the national or regional office. The national office partners with and invests funds in a potential mother church which, in turn, invests in its daughter.

Most leadership for "new works" is raised up relationally in the local church family. Foursquare's Pacific Life Bible College offers ministry training on campus and by video through its "Life Line" extension programs. A seminary degree is welcome but not required for ordination—leaving a wide leadership door open to an empowered laity in their mature "second career" stage of life. The local pastor recommends a mature lay person to lead a daughter church.

Calgary Pastor Arnie ter Mors, coordinator of church planting, is challenging the Foursquare movement to increase its growth rate to an inspiring 12% annually. The church planting representative of each regional unit (of about ten congregations) in turn encourages each local church to participate in giving birth to "new works" regularly and hopefully to begin a daughter church, on average, every seven years.

Even if the lofty goal is not fully subscribed, the focusing effect of the goal is viewed as having great benefits—it is a vision to grow toward, a way to evaluate and improve what is being done and a projection of what could happen as the family pulls together.

The strength of Foursquare growth to date has taken place mostly among young and middle-aged Anglo Caucasian adults through new church development. Also the movement has assimilated some congregations from eastern cultures. No congregations in Québec have yet been developed.

The Foursquare movement desires to continue to grow as a natural outflow of healthy spiritual life. "We just want to let the natural process of life produce more life," says Peterson.

The Presbyterian Church in North America (PCNA) came from a merger with the Reformed Presbyterian Church, Evangelical Synod, some 25 years ago. Five of these congregations formed the nucleus of the PCNA movement in Canada. Further leadership came from the Presbyterian Church in Canada. Approximately ten years ago the PCNA became more proactive about church planting. Its approximately 1,650 congregations endorsed a Vision 2000 church planting strategy to grow to 2000 congregations by the year 2000—and they remain close to the trajectory for accomplishing the goal.

British Columbia coordinator Rev. Steven A. Laug identifies key factors as including, (a) the willingness to take the risk and pay the price (and keep going with successes and failures), (b) the desire to be a part of what God is doing (e.g., moving church planting sites to responsive areas, even midstream), (c) the use of an interdenominational church planting assessment centre in selecting potential church planters and (d) the ability to raise additional funds in the United States.

Population groups most responsive to the Gospel have been Boomers and Asian immigrants, particularly Korean and Japanese. The PCNA has had difficulty in finding appropriate leadership for church plants in Québec.

Laug indicates PCNA experience with church planting methods has led them away from the pioneer model due to stress on the church planter's family. The PCNA would prefer that a planter be available to plant several, even many times and this seems more likely using the "hiving" model. The hiving model cultivates the mother church to become a seedbed for future daughter congregations. Advantages to this model include a starting core group of lay leaders as well as stronger initial finances. However, Laug warns that if the core group does not begin with evangelistic motivation, the new church is not as likely to become evangelistic as when it is begun by a pioneer leader.[28] Laug's perception is that pioneer planting is more successful at gathering the unchurched, while hiving gathers more Christians who want programs. The PCNA has not been using "cell" or "tent-making" models, as these models tend to take too long to gain momentum and face some funding challenges.

The PCNA has found church planter recruitment in seminaries working effectively in recent years for several reasons. First, the average seminary graduate age has been rising, tending to produce more mature leaders. Secondly, because the PCNA produces more seminary graduates than it has vacant pulpits, many students consider planting from the beginning of their seminary experience. Covenant Seminary, the denominational school in St Louis, therefore offers an emphasis in church planting to assist in this preparation. Internship is required. Seminarians, and even undergraduate students, are linked personally with nearby church planters for several years while still in school.

The PCNA has developed a clear process to select and channel potential church planters:

1. Internship with a church planter.

2. A pre-screening interview.

3. A recommendation to an assessment centre, the result of which may be:
   (a) qualified to plant,
   (b) provisional acceptance, or
   (c) disqualified—but free to upgrade and try again.

4. Qualified and provisional candidates may be referred to serve in a mother church or move directly to planting. In either case, candidates and planters are mentored with written learning contracts.

Laug, for instance, serves as mentor to three current church planters and one in-house potential planter. He seeks to make phone contact every two weeks and to arrange for a visit two to three times a year.

In addition, two regional vision casting gatherings are planned annually—the first for planter couples only. The second is a three-day gathering of prayer, praise and worship for clergy and lay leadership teams of all regional mother and daughter churches, up to 150 people, for vision casting, fund raising, training and fellowship.

Goal setting is a major factor in church planting growth—each presbyter meeting (three per year) reviews goal targets and budget implications. A broad five- to ten- year plan develops first, then specific aspects are addressed.

Organizationally, John Smed serves as team leader for the PCNA's Mission to North America vision. Presbytery church planting committees—generally 15 members, including all planters and pastors of potential mother churches, serve on the committee—plan and review new works. Canadian regional coordinators seek to provide day-to-day church planting coaching at a maximum of one-to-five ratio.

Financial support is raised by various means, ranging from an international campaign to local and regional vision casting gatherings. A uniqueness of the PCNA is that all monies invested in a local plant are committed by the local plant to be passed on when the plant is able, without interest, to another church plant in Canada.

The PCNA also uses the Canada Employment "Summer Career Placement Program," which pays nonprofit organizations 100% of minimum wage and basic benefits up to 16 weeks at 37½ hours a week for qualified "job creation" projects. Students must be registered in college for the following fall semester. The mother church supplies the church planting intern housing and an increase over the government-supplied minimum wage.

A problem encountered in PCNA plants is finding committed leaders for elder and deacon roles, in that 30% to 40% of new members are from unchurched backgrounds.

Dr. Stephen Beck, pioneer planter of Toronto Grace Church, leads the PCNA flagship plant in Canada. The benefit of feeling called for life, he says, is that "you can take the particular philosophy of ministry God has placed in you and become a vision-driven church—you can shape it."

Toronto Grace, Beck's second plant, began in September 1994 and now averages 250 persons representing 20 nations. Beck's goal is to plant 20 daughter churches around the metro Toronto area. He began by establishing "life groups" in the city, two of the largest he views as embryonic daughter churches. A Japanese daughter church is beginning to emerge as the church moves toward four weekly services. Worship is translated into several languages—some of these will become the gathering points for new congregations.

Canada ceased being a church culture in the 1960s, Beck believes. Secular Canada is now rather anti-church but open to spiritual matters and spiritually hungry. "They will not go onto our turf, so I go to their turf," says Beck. He gets out of the office purposely every week to meet with people who are unchurched. It's important to get the feel of the culture, to take notes and get referrals.

Early in his ministry Beck received an invitation to lead a Bible study for his non-Christian friends. He repeated the process and began using Alpha principles.[29] Beck calls his adaptation a "School of Discovery"—a weekly dinner to which people bring non-Christian friends, featuring five tracks for group discussion for everyone—wherever you may be on your spiritual journey.

Beck believes that what Christians do in worship services must be understood by non-Christians and touch their hearts. One point of common ground for the Christian and non-Christian is that we are created in the image of God. Beck seeks to raise and answer questions non-Christians are asking so they will learn that the Bible offers answers and so that Christians will simultaneously be trained in apologetics. "Show that people who do not believe actually live as though there is absolute truth," says Beck. "Word and Spirit are inseparably married—just let the Word convince them of the truth."

Finally, the story of a newer denomination. In fact, many may not have heard of the **Victory Christian Churches International** movement until now. George Hill, born in England and now 53, had not knowingly met a Christian until his 30th birthday, while working as an electrician and travelling for adventure. Neither had his Australian-born wife Hazel, until both she and George made the decision to follow Christ in 1975 in Lethbridge, Alberta. Four years later they planted their first church in Lethbridge, which grew rapidly on a 43-acre campus and soon began to birth daughter congregations. Victory Christian Churches organized as a movement with five congregations in 1989.

Victory Christian Churches International was an apostolic movement of 38 congregations in Canada at the end of 1996, 45 by mid-1997 and a total of 150 internationally. It has been planting churches at a remarkable rate of 33% annually during the 1986/1996 decade. Victory Churches recently purchased a 53-room hotel near Canada Olympic Park, Calgary, for its Bible College. It has opened its first church in Jerusalem, hoping to hold an international convention in the year 2000.

Several distinctives mark the rapidly growing renewal movement:

An apostolic leader. The vision, energy and spiritual authority of George and Hazel Hill permeate the movement. Not all 20th century Christians believe in the apostolic ministry in this age, but this characteristic, by whatever name, is consistent with the most rapidly growing denominations around the world.[30]

Closely related is an emphasis on the five-fold ministry of Ephesians 4:11-12. Carefully selected teams composed of an apostle, evangelist, prophet, pastor and teacher open new fields. George Hill calls it "teamwork—getting the right people in the right places."

Big vision backed by challenging five-year goals. The vision of Victory Churches is to change a nation through church planting, media and education. (Victory Churches received Canada's first 24-hour Christian television station license in 1996. CJIL, broadcasting from Lethbridge, hopes to go to satellite for national distribution in the fall of 1997. Victory Churches has also initiated the Canada Family Coalition to influence public policy.)

Adequate finances. To be a part of Victory Christian Churches International, a local congregation agrees to tithe to church planting—5% to national church planting and 5% to international church planting. This enables Victory Churches to offer matching dollars to strategic existing churches with limited resources so they can add and train necessary staff to plant new churches.

Most new Victory congregations are hived from a mother church. Typically a small group leader is released from the mother church to begin a care group in a nearby community. The mother church gives prayer and practical support. As the small group grows its leader's gift grows with the challenge, and the nucleus of a new congregation is born.

To begin a cluster of Victory Churches in a city where none have been planted, an entire apostolic team may move to a given city to found a new mother church. In Calgary for instance, an apostolic team gathered 270 people for a first Sunday service and the congregation has subsequently grown to four weekend services. Then, between 1990 and 1996, this new mother congregation has in turn daughtered nine new congregations in the area.

Until 1996 George Hill continued to pastor a local church, at least on a part-time basis. During this time most new leaders gained experience as part of George's staff and many grew to become new church planters. Leadership is now also being developed in "Finishing Edge" evaluation and training courses for lay leaders or previous pastors in transition who feel called to full-time service, have ministry experience and come recommended. The "Finishing Edge" experience includes advanced reading, exams, interviews, personality inventories, essay writing and times of prayer and vision sharing, as new leaders are matched with new ministry opportunities. Fifty-five people enrolled for the most recent "Finishing Edge."

Two of Hill's key leadership development principles are:

1. Be willing to release your best leaders. Invest for an increase. It takes faith to plant your good seed (Proverbs 11:23).

2. Look for people who are better at what you are asking them to do than you are, and do not be threatened by their abilities. The Lord wants to develop character in leaders, removing insecurity.

George Hill sets five-year goals for the movement, and assists each congregation in turn set five-year goals for evangelism and planting. "Goal setting takes courage, faith and commitment," says Hill, "because each time you do it you take a risk." So Hill sets three levels of goal—victory, hallelujah and miracle—"just to give the Lord a chance to do one."

It Takes the Whole Church to Disciple the Whole Nation

All parts of the Body of Christ are needed. Every denomination, congregation, mission agency and disciple of the Lord Jesus can contribute to the multiplication of new cells of believers in every neighbourhood, city block, high-rise apartment and people group in Canada.

Individuals can lead, form or invite unchurched friends to small prayer and care groups. Congregations can become "seed beds" for new churches, birthing a daughter congregation—alone or in partnership—every three to five years. Mission agencies can partner with denominations in forming new churches and directing new converts to church planters for follow-up. Denominations can pray, develop means of supporting church plants and set goals for the multiplication of many kinds of new congregations.

All can participate—lay and clergy—empowered by the Holy Spirit Jesus promised to pour out for this very purpose. We all can pray diligently for revival of the Church and the transformation of our society, one household at a time, to show the presence of Christ to all.

God can and wants to do great, even miraculous, things as we rely on His supernatural presence and empowerment.

A Faith Goal—How Does the Lord of the Harvest Want to Multiply the Church?

The Lord of the harvest calls the whole Church to unite in discipling the whole nation. We are called to repent of our lukewarmness, seek His face, hear His voice, understand the times and respond with faith, vision and sacrificial obedience.

Annual evangelical church planting rates have tended to be in the 1% to 2% range. An estimate of 1.5% AAGR can be made with reasonable confidence. However the current Canadian population growth rate is at 1.1%.[31] To respond seriously to our call to complete the Great Commission, however, our church planting rate must significantly exceed this rate. The AAGR of the world evangelical church is approximately 5.4%.[32] This should inspire us to think big.

Let us engage in some "for instance" speculation! What would happen "for instance" if all denominations of the Body of Christ in Canada would increase our average annual national church planting rate to 3.5% during the next 25 years (see Figure 14)? At a 3.5% church planting rate the national "population-to-church" ratio[33] would be gradually reduced, as depicted in Table 20.

Let us lay before the Lord another possibility. How might the nation be transformed by the presence of Christ if our faith and planning were stretched to pursue 5% and 7% in national average church planting rates during those 25 years (see Figure 15)? At a 7% church planting rate the national "population-to-church" ratio would be rapidly reduced, as shown in Table 21.

Do you see how we, together, empowered by the Lord's Spirit and presence, could move to within reaching distance of completing the Great Commission? Canada, our homeland, *can* be transformed by the power of the Gospel, and within our lifetime!

Figure 14
Total Cells of Believers at 1.5% & 3.5% AAGR

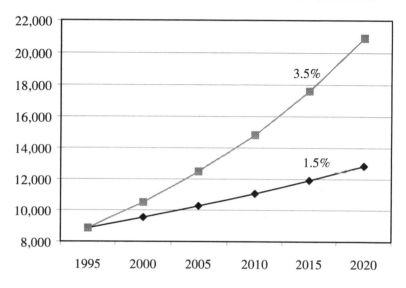

Table 20
Population-Per-Congregation Ratio
Based on a 3.5% Growth Rate

Year	Congregations	Population	Ratio
1995	8,848	29,617,448	3,347
2000	10,509	31,390,050	2,987
2005	12,481	33,319,200	2,670
2010	14,823	35,366,911	2,386
2015	17,606	37,540,469	2,132
2020	20,203	39,847,608	1,906

Figure 15
Total Cells of Believers at 5% and 7% AAGR's

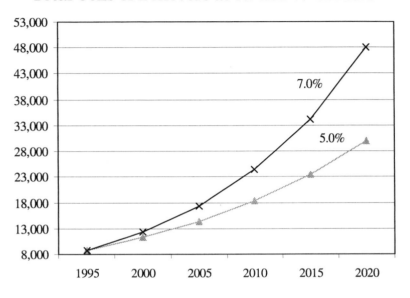

Table 21
Population-Per-Congregation
Based on a 7% Growth Rate

Year	Congregations	Population	Ratio
1995	8,848	29,617,448	3,347
2000	12,410	31,390,050	2,529
2005	17,405	33,319,200	1,914
2010	24,412	35,366,911	1,449
2015	34,239	37,540,469	1,096
2020	48,002	39,847,608	830

What Might This Mean for Each Denomination?

All the above "whole Church" national scenarios are real possibilities. The choice is ours. Church leaders may wonder what such involvement in the harvest will mean for their particular movement.

Table 23, at the end of this chapter, consists of six pages and casts the vision in some detail for individual denominations. This vision does not purport to suggest what will happen or what specific denominations will choose or be able to accomplish in the Canadian harvest field if prayer and human resources are released on a priority basis for church planting.

The table overviews selected denominations:

- Summarizing recent individual church planting rates.

- Suggesting a possible ("for instance") average annual church planting growth rate. Generally a doable 3% increase over current rates is envisioned as realistic, challenging and possible. In a limited number of cases where current AAGR's exceed 10%, future "for instance" rates have been reduced to sustainable possibilities. In all cases it must be clearly stated that projections do not purport to predict future growth rates, and further that individual denominations are autonomous before the Lord and free to set and alter their own church planting goals. Many movements may exceed these "for instance" possibilities.

- Calculating the net number of cells of believers permeating the fabric of our nation with the presence of Christ should a denomination plant new congregations at the "for instance" rate. Every denomination, of course, is free to plant as many new cells as the Lord directs during these years.

15,000 New Cells of Believers by the Year 2020?

Look more closely at the top half of the last page of Table 23. In a summary projection depicted there, we can see and be encouraged by what can be done together as we pray for empowerment, plan boldly and re-commit ourselves to plant new cells of believers in every people group, neighbourhood and apartment complex across the land.

Notice the decreasing church-to-population ratio projection to where the current ratio would be halved before the year 2020. This is one of the best measurable indications of progress in discipling the nation (refer to Chapter one).

Is it really possible that the Body of Christ could birth 15,000 new cells of believers by the year 2020? Yes it is. And perhaps an even greater number.

It is God's will that His lost sheep be found. He enables His people by His grace and by the power of His Spirit to accomplish all that is on His heart. Of this we can be confident!

The Canadian Church Planting Congress '97 Responds in Faith

In October 1997 Canadians gathered in Toronto to consider the challenge before us, consult in denominational and regional groupings and begin corporately to respond to the Lord.

Plenary speakers included international leaders such as Lynn Green, director of England's *"Challenge 2000"* and *DAWN* co-ordinator and missions strategist Dr. Jim Montgomery. Canadian speakers included Dr. Gary Walsh, executive director of the *Evangelical Fellowship of Canada* and Dr. Arnell Motz, chair of the EFC's *Vision Canada*. Jacqueline Dugas, director of the *Centre for Prayer Mobilization (Every Home for Christ)* led the opening Concert of Prayer and daily prayer gatherings.

The Congress theme was "Pray, Plan, Plant." In the closing declaration delegates said:

We, the delegates of the Canadian Church Planting Congress '97—representing 39 denominations, 13 mission organizations and four seminaries—called together to address the urgent spiritual need in Canada, declare concerted prayer and evangelistic church planting to be the key to reaching our nation.

WE ACKNOWLEDGE

That without the raising up of new congregations there are still thousands of Canadians who will not have the opportunity to hear of the saving grace of our Lord Jesus Christ.

That we have a personal and corporate responsibility to reach these people.

That church planting is the key to discipling our nation calling the people to worship and serve our Lord Jesus Christ.

WE COMMIT

To earnestly pray for the harvest field and the harvest force.

To the goal of planting 10,000 new churches by the year 2015.

To plant churches that are geographically accessible and culturally relevant to every Canadian.

To develop networks for support and accountability.

To work together as the whole Body of Christ to accomplish the task of the Gospel for every person and a church for every people.

The Congress[34] affirmed a corporate 18-year goal of planting 10,000 new churches which are geographically accessible and culturally relevant to every Canadian. What a clear, specific focus for our combined intercession, resources and energies for the harvest!

This corporate goal involves an increase of 3% in our average annual church planting rate—from approximately 1.5% AAGR to 4.5% AAGR—a *tripling* of effort!

The following table will show, in the years to come, how near to our corporate goal we are coming. Note especially the encouraging reduction in the "Churches-per-Capita" ratio. A declining "Churches-per-Capita" ratio is the key indicator of our progress in discipling our nation. Please review, if you have not done so recently, the relevant section of Chapter 1 outlining this critical "Capita-per-Churches" measurement.

Since the Congress many denominations have set goals, revised budgets and adjusted infrastructure to re-focus on the task. In addition several schools have begun to respond to the need for training thousands of new church planters, many of them cross-cultural. District superintendents and other leaders have also met in each of Canada's six regions to establish means of resourcing needed church planting support systems.[35]

Table 22
Measuring Our Corporate Progress in Discipling Our Nation

Year End	2000	2005	2010	2015
Number of Churches	9,968	12,192	15,101	19,001
Projected Canadian Population	31.4 M	33.3 M	35.7 M	37.5 M
Capita-per-Churches	3,149	2,733	2,342	1,976

Moving Forward!

We must pray, not out of duty but out of an urgent desire to see God's glory revealed to millions who do not know Him.

Planning must take place because we are created in the image of God, and God Himself plans. Church planting goals can be proposed or set, leadership teams appointed or reviewed, financial plans developed. Planning not completed during Congress breakout sessions scheduled for that purpose must be scheduled for priority attention and continual monitoring.

Planting must take our best attention, leadership, prayer and financial support. All mature existing congregations must be encouraged to parent regularly, individually as often as possible or in teams.

May we give the Lord—and the lost—our best so that Christ will be incarnate in every segment of society and glorified throughout the earth—that *"the earth will be filled with the knowledge of the glory of the LORD, as the waters cover the sea"* (Habakkuk 2:14).

Table 23
A Vision for Discipling a Whole Nation
Multiplying Cells of the Body of Christ: 1997 - 2025

Updated: 10/16/97

Selected Denominations:	1985 [1] Cong.	1995 [2] Cong.	Last Known Decadal AAGR [3]	Last Known Five-Year AAGR	A Future "For Instance" AAGR	At 3%[4] Increase in Rate of Church Planting					
						2000 Cong.	2005 Cong.	2010 Cong.	2015 Cong.	2020 Cong.	2025 Cong.
Apostolic Christian Churches (Nazarean)	14	12	-1.3%	unknown	1.7%	13	14	15	16	18	19
Apostolic Church in Canada		14	7.8%	unknown	10.8%	19	32	53	89	148	247
Apostolic Church of Pentecost		163	1.3%	5.4%	7.1%[5]	200	283	400	564	796	1,124
Associated Gospel Churches	110	134	2.0%	1.9%	5.0%	155	198	253	322	412	525
Association of Free Lutheran Churches		7	unknown	unknown	11.0%	10	16	27	46	77	130
Atlantic Canada Association of Free Will Baptists	17	17	unknown	unknown	3.0%	19	22	25	29	34	39
Baptist General Conference		84	1.6%	2.3%	5.3%	98	127	164	213	276	357
Bible Holiness Movement		16	unknown	unknown	3.0%	17	20	23	27	32	37
Brethren in Christ, Canadian Conference	33	38	2.0%	0.4%	3.4%	42	50	59	69	82	97
Canadian Baptist Federation (composed of):											
- Atlantic United Baptist Convention	554	556	0.0%	0.2%	3.2%	611	715	837	980	1,147	1,343
- Union of French Baptist Churches of Canada	24	25	1.4%	-1.5%	1.5%	26	28	30	33	35	38
- Baptist Convention of Ontario & Quebec	389	388	0.0%	0.2%	3.2%	426	499	584	684	801	937
- Baptist Union of Western Canada	162	165	0.2%	-1.0%	2.0%	175	193	213	236	260	287

Table 23, Cont'd

Updated: 10/16/97

Selected Denominations:	1985[1] Cong.	1995[2] Cong.	Last Known Decadal AAGR[3]	Last Known Five-Year AAGR	A Future "For Instance" AAGR	At 3¾ Increase in Rate of Church Planting					
						2000 Cong.	2005 Cong.	2010 Cong.	2015 Cong.	2020 Cong.	2025 Cong.
Canadian Conference of M.B. Churches	169	208	2.1%	1.8%	4.8%	239	303	383	484	611	773
Canadian Convention of Southern Baptists	57	124	7.2%	4.6%	7.6%	154	223	321	463	669	961
Christian & Missionary Alliance in Canada	287	378	2.7%	2.3%	4.9%	436	554	704	894	1,136	1,443
Christian Reformed Church	209	219	0.4%	0.4%	3.4%	242	286	338	400	473	553
Churches of Christ, World Convention (composed of):											
- Churches of Christ in Canada (Accapella)	149	122	unknown	unknown	3.0%	133	155	179	208	241	279
- Christian Churches (Independent)	66	84	unknown	unknown	3.0%	92	106	123	143	166	192
- Disciples of Christ in Canada	37	36	unknown	unknown	3.0%	39	46	53	61	71	82
Church of God, Anderson	54	51	-0.5%	0.4%	3.4%	56	67	79	93	110	130
Church of God, Cleveland (composed of)[6]											
- Quebec/Maritime District	30	unknown	unknown	unknown	3.0%	33	38	44	51	59	68
- Eastern Canada District	61	unknown	unknown	3.7%	6.7%	74	102	142	196	271	375
- Western Canada District	29	unknown	unknown	0.8%	3.8%	32	39	47	57	68	82
Church of God in Christ (Mennonite)	39	unknown	unknown	unknown	3.0%	43	49	57	66	77	89
Church of God of Prophecy in Canada	38	26	unknown	unknown	3.0%	23	33	38	44	51	59
Church of the Nazarene	153	190	2.2%	1.6%	4.6%	217	272	341	427	535	669

135

Table 23, Cont'd

Updated: 10/16/97

Selected Denominations:	1985 [1] Cong.	1995 [2] Cong.	Last Known Decadal AAGR [3]	Last Known Five-Year AAGR	A Future "For Instance" AAGR	At 3% [4] Increase in Rate of Church Planting					
						2000 Cong.	2005 Cong.	2010 Cong.	2015 Cong.	2020 Cong.	2025 Cong.
Conference of Mennonites in Canada (composed of):											
- Mennonite Conference of Eastern Canada	85	94	1.0%	1.0%	4.0%	106	129	157	190	232	282
- Conference of Mennonites in Manitoba		52	0.4%	0.0%	3.0%	57	66	76	89	103	119
- Conference of Mennonites of Saskatchewan		41	unknown	unknown	3.0%	45	52	60	70	81	94
- Conference of Mennonites in Alberta		21	unknown	unknown	3.0%	23	27	31	36	41	48
- Conference of Mennonites in British Columbia	26	36	3.3%	6.6%	9.6%	47	75	119	187	296	469
Congregational Christian Church	5	91	33.5%	5.8%	8.8%	117	179	272	415	633	965
Estonian Evangelical Lutheran Church	13	12	-0.8%	unknown	2.2%	13	14	16	18	20	22
Evangelical Covenant Church	23	20	-1.6%	-3.2%	-0.2%	20	20	19	19	19	19
Evangelical Free Church	102	133	2.9%	0.0%	3.0%	145	168	195	226	262	304
Evangelical Mennonite Conf.	50	53	0.6%	1.2%	4.2%	60	74	90	111	137	168
Evangelical Mennonite Missions Conference	30	27	-1.0%	-1.0%	2.0%	29	32	35	39	43	47
Evangelical Missionary Church of Canada (composed of):											
- Eastern District	72	77	0.7%	1.4%	4.4%	88	109	135	167	207	257
- Western District	69	62	-1.0%	-2.1%	0.9%	64	67	70	73	76	80
Fellowship of Christian Assemblies	54	85	4.1%	5.4%	8.4%	108	162	243	363	543	813

Table 23, Cont'd

Updated: 10/16/97

Selected Denominations:	1985 [1] Cong.	1995 [2] Cong.	Last Known Decadal AAGR [3]	Last Known Five-Year AAGR	A Future "For Instance" AAGR	At 3% Increase in Rate of Church Planting					
						2000 Cong.	2005 Cong.	2010 Cong.	2015 Cong.	2020 Cong.	2025 Cong.
Fellowship of Evangelical Baptist Churches	464	506	0.9%	0.6%	3.6%	563	671	801	956	1,141	1,362
Fellowship of Evangelical Bible Churches	20	21	0.5%	1.0%	4.0%	24	29	35	43	52	63
Foursquare Gospel Church of Canada	39	58	4.0%	1.4%	**12.0%**	81	144	253	446	786	1,385
Free Methodist Church in Canada	137	130	-0.5%	-1.4%	1.6%	136	148	160	173	187	203
Independent Assemblies of God[7]		110	unknown	19.1%	7.1%	135	190	268	378	533	751
Italian Pentecostal Church		24	4.3%	4.5%	7.5%	30	43	61	88	127	182
Latvian Evangelical Lutheran Church in America	9	17	8.4%	16.0%	7.1%	21	29	41	58	82	116
Native Evangelical Fellowship	20	25	1.8%	0.8%	3.8%	28	34	41	49	59	71
North American Baptist Church	114	122	0.7%	0.0%	3.0%	133	155	179	208	241	279
Northwest Mennonite Conf.	18	19	0.5%	unknown	3.5%	21	25	30	35	42	50
Old Order Amish Church	14	14	0.0%	0.0%	3.0%	15	18	21	24	28	32
Open Bible Faith Fellowship[8]		48	unknown	unknown	10.0%	64	103	166	267	430	692
Partners in Harvest		22	unknown	unknown	3.0%	24	28	32	37	43	50
Pentecostal Assemblies of Canada		1,120	5.4%	1.9%	3.0%	1,224	1,419	1,645	1,907	2,210	2,562
Pentecostal Assemblies of Newfoundland		146	unknown	-2.1%	0.9%	150	157	164	172	179	188

Table 23, Cont'd

Updated: 10/16/97

Selected Denominations:	1985[1] Cong.	1995[2] Cong.	Last Known Decadal AAGR[3]	Last Known Five-Year AAGR	A Future "For Instance" AAGR	At 3%[4] Increase in Rate of Church Planting 2000 Cong.	2005 Cong.	2010 Cong.	2015 Cong.	2020 Cong.	2025 Cong.
Pentecostal Holiness Church of Canada	27	28	0.3%	-1.7%	1.3%	29	31	33	35	38	40
Plymouth Brethren (Christian Brethren)	405	442	1.1%	unknown	4.1%	499	610	745	911	1,114	1,362
Presbyterian Church in North America (Canada)	14	15	1.3%	-1.1%	1.9%	16	17	19	21	23	25
Reformed Church in Canada	28	41	3.9%	2.6%	5.6%	48	63	83	109	144	189
Salvation Army in Canada		385	unknown	unknown	3.0%	421	488	565	655	760	881
Seventh-Day Adventist Church		331	1.3%	0.8%	3.8%	370	446	538	648	780	940
United Brethren in Christ (Ontario)		11	unknown	unknown	3.0%	12	14	16	19	22	25
United Pentecostal Church		198	unknown	0.0%	3.0%	216	251	291	337	391	453
Victory Churches International[7]	1	38	34.2%	33.3%	15.0%	58	116	234	470	946	1,902
Vineyard Christian Fellowship[7]	1	44	36.2%	17.5%	12.0%	62	109	192	338	596	1,051
Wesleyan Church (composed of:											
- Atlantic District		46	unknown	0.4%	3.4%	51	60	71	84	99	117
- Central District		22	unknown	-5.6%	2.0%	23	26	28	31	35	38
Wisconsin Evangelical Lutheran Synod - Canada	16	16	5.9%	9.9%	12.9%	23	42	77	142	261	478
Independent Congregations		379	unknown	unknown	3.0%	414	480	557	645	748	867
Others not listed elsewhere[9]		478	unknown	unknown	3.0%	522	606	702	814	943	1,094
TOTAL[10]		8,876				9,968	12,192	15,101	19,001	24,388	32,083
Total Canadian Estimated Population					1.2%	31,390,050	33,319,200	35,366,911	37,540,469	39,847,608	42,296,537
Population per Evangelizing Congregation		3,149				3,149	2,733	2,342	1,976	1,634	1,318

Table 23, Cont'd

		Summary Projection: at 3% Church Planting AAGR			
Year	Canadian Pop. in M	Total Cong's	Net New Ch. Plants	Running Total	Population Ratio
1997	30,286,596	8,876			3,412
2000	31,390,050	9,968	1,092	1,140	3,149
2005	33,319,200	12,192	2,225	3,365	2,733
2010	35,366,911	15,101	2,909	6,274	2,342
2015	37,540,469	19,001	3,900	10,174	1,976
2020	39,847,608	24,388	5,387	15,560	1,634
2025	42,296,537	32,083	7,696	23,256	1,318

Notes:

[1] If known.

[2] Last known number. Please forward corrections/updates to Lorne Hunter, Outreach Canada, #16, 12240 Horseshoe Way, Richmond, BC V7A 4X9 or phone: (604) 272-0732 or fax: (604) 272-2744 or email: lhunter@outreach.ca.

[3] AAGR = "Average Annual Growth Rate" of net new congregations.

[4] Projections are generally made at a 3% AAGR increase over previous growth rate, and do not purport to predict future growth rates. Each denomination can, of course, make its own decision regarding future growth rate, and some movements may exceed these "for instances."

[5] Bold text under 'A Future For Instance AAGR' indicates growth rate goals proposed or targeted decided upon by that denomination.

[6] Our goal is to have every denomination broken down into regions or districts. The difficulty lies in the availability of regional statistics for some denominations.

[7] Three smaller denominations currently growing in excess of 15% are projected conservatively.

[8] Newly formed in 1997. Includes Open Bible Standard, Word of Life and independent congregations.

[9] "Others not listed elsewhere" include smaller denominations of less than ten congregations.

[10] This total does not yet include Biblically orthodox congregations in mainline denominations. Research continues.

139

Action Points

✓ Have you carefully reviewed your denomination's church planting history and devised your own process leading to specific goal setting?

✓ What new insights for church planting can you implement from the experiences of other denominations shared earlier in this chapter?

✓ Identify the next three priorities you must attend to in order to proceed effectively and strategically.

Chapter Notes

[1] Statistics Canada Census reports on religious affiliation.

[2] Religious affiliation necessarily indicates neither membership, regular attendance, firm commitment or doctrinal orthodoxy. Rather, affiliation suggests a general association with the religious tradition, an affiliation which may range from high commitment to nominalism.

[3] Mainline and evangelical trends are to some degree difficult to track in that some mainline denominations were essentially evangelical through the first portion of the century.

[4] Statistics Canada Census reports on religious affiliation.

[5] Ibid.

[6] This may be an argument for the formation of new denominations, almost all of which grow best in their youth.

[7] Statistics Canada, Catalogue no. 93-319.

[8] The segment, "No religious affiliation," is now the most rapidly growing "harvest field" in Canada.

[9] Dean M. Kelley, *Why Conservative Churches Are Growing,* Harper & Row, 1977.

[10] The Evangelical Lutheran Church merged with the Lutheran Church in America (and Canada) in 1986. These numbers are combined to reflect that merger.

[11] The best use of language is under discussion. Dr. Reginald Bibby tends to call this group "conservative Protestants," since most within it relate to the Evangelical Fellowship of Canada and are comfortable with the term "evangelicals;" others prefer "Biblically orthodox."

[12] When evangelical gains are removed.

[13] Don Posterski, editor. *Context* (MARC Canada/World Vision) Fall 1996, vol. 6, issue 2. p.7.

Chapter Notes

[14]Teaching the Body of Christ to hold to and share absolute truths with confidence against the stream of politically correct relativism requires careful and continual education and courage. Christians also require training in sensitivity as we learn to "speak the truth in love."

[15] The NACC represents approximately 2.9% of total UCC congregations and 4.1% of UCC worship attendance respectively. Sec'ty-Treas: Bob Blackburn, 5300 Hrenkelly Court, Mississauga, ON L5M 2H4.

[16] Essentials Coordinator is Canon Jerry Smith, 1225 Cassells Street, North Bay, ON P1B 4B8.

[17] Less "charismatic" in orientation, the Barnabas movement is led by General Secretary Rev. Tom Robinson, R.R.2, Hatfield, NB E0G 2A0.

[18] More "charismatic" in orientation, the Anglican Renewal Movement is led by National Chairman Rev. Ed Hird, 1384 Deep Cove Road, North Vancouver, BC V7G 1S5.

[19] Rev. Calvin Brown serves as Director, 3819 Bloor Street West, Etobicoke, ON M9B 1K7.

[20] Zeb Bradford Long serves as Executive Director, 115 Richardson Blvd., P.O. Box 429, Black Mountain, NC, 28711-0429.

[21] Research on orthodox congregations was incomplete in 1990; only an estimate was provided.

[22] An example of the effect of church planting on the growth of a denomination (Nazarene) may be found in the chapter titled, "Can Canada be Discipled?"

[23] Murray Moerman and Lorne Hunter, *An Initial Survey of the "Harvest Field" and "Harvest Force" in Canada.* Richmond, BC: Outreach Canada, 1996. p.14.

Chapter Notes

[24] AAGR calculated over five years. Both five and 10 years, AAGR's are depicted when data is available to show whether a movement is planting at a higher or lower growth rate in the most recent five years as compared to the previous five.

[25] Not including seven congregations leaving the Vineyard movement with the Toronto Airport Christian Fellowship in 1995.

[26] This percentage of new starts taking root does not factor in previously established churches closed for other reasons during this period, a factor that would increase the "success" rate of new church starts.

[27] Large denominations are defined for the purpose of this study as those composed of more than 250 congregations.

[28] Dr. Beck, pioneer planter of Grace Toronto Church, believes "hiving" is easier because it is not perceived by the public as arising from something new. Canadians, he says, are suspicious both of "something new" and of that which is not "already successful"—a "double-whammy" for the pioneer planter. The pioneer is charged with elitism— "Who does he think he is?" People want to know there is accountability and connection to a larger whole. Canadians, Beck believes, are more suspicious of the new and of the entrepreneurial than are their American counterparts.

[29] David C. Cook can provide further information on the Alpha model and curriculum.

[30] For more on this trend cf. C. Peter Wagner. *Church Planting for a Greater Harvest*. Regal Books: Ventura, CA, 1990. pp.73-74.

[31] Between July 1996 and July 1997, the AAGR for the previous decade was approximately 1.7%.

Chapter Notes

[32] Patrick Johnstone, *Operation World: The Day-by-Day Guide to Praying for the World*. Grand Rapids, MI: Zondervan Publishing House, 1993. p.23.

[33] "Population-to-church ratio" is the key indicator of progress toward discipling the nation. Please see Chapter 2: "Can Canada be Discipled" for further details of the importance of this measurement.

[34] The term "Congress" rather than "consultation" or "conference" was used to underscore our need, not only to consult or confer, but in addition to make historic corporate decisions affecting the discipling our nation.

[35] Dates and events planned in each region may be accessed on Church Planting Canada's website: www.outreach.ca/cpc.htm or quarterly newsletter.

Section Three

Our Focus: Unreached People

"It has always been my ambition to preach the gospel where Christ was not known, so that I would not be building on someone else's foundation. Rather, as it is written: 'Those who were not told about him will see, and those who have not heard will understand'" (Romans 15:20,21).

Chapter Five

Unreached People Groups In Canada

Brian Seim

In the mid-1980s, when I first heard the phrase "unreached people," I thought of the "countless millions," *out there*. Over the next two summers I led Jesus Film teams, first to the central Amazon basin, and then to Northern Thailand. People who had neatly fit into the category of unreached people became friends, and some also became "reached." Back in Canada, my evangelism now focused on new immigrants. I did not say it out loud, but I began to realize that many of these people had never heard the Gospel in a way that made sense to them. It hit home—Canada was a country made up of reached and unreached people groups.[1]

This chapter identifies 82 unreached people groups in Canada, both from among the 2.5 million who have immigrated in the past 12 years—as well as others who have been part of Canada since its conception as a nation. The goal is to identify unreached groups, explain some of the barriers that retain them, identify needs within our evangelistic strategies and encourage the "adoption" of unreached people groups by churches so that spiritual, financial and manpower resources begin to reach these unreached people.

Unreached people are: *"A people for whom there is no viable indigenous church movement with sufficient strength to sustain and ensure the continuous multiplication of churches."* The group of researchers processing the raw data for this book further defined "Unreached People Groups" as: *"any group of more than 5,000 people around the world, whose makeup reflect less than 2% evangelical."* Canadian populations, even among First Nations figures, may be far less. We have defined "evangelical" by a New Testament theology of the Church in which Christians participate in redemptive worshipping communities and are involved in evangelizing the world.

What makes unreached people difficult to reach for Christ? Ethnicity, culture and language are certainly three non-spiritual elements that separate us. Prejudice and religion are issues that the empowerment of God's Spirit can help us overcome. Another issue here in Canada, and around the world, is urbanization. How do Christians reach people they refuse to live among?

To cluster the information on these people groups who are without the Good News, there are five tables in this chapter, indicating unreached peoples in Canada. Each is accompanied by an issues sheet. These tables show population statistics from Statistics Canada 1996 publications, which are then compared with *Joshua Project 2000* data, as well as the listing given from the Southern Baptist Convention (with 1991 data) in the table at the end of this chapter.[2]

The issue sheet that accompanies each chart asks questions which may: a) define plans to minister to people within the area, b) understand prayer and mobilization needs and, c) help your church see the value of adopting one or more of these people groups as a focus of your outreach, giving and prayer.

Table 24
Unreached People Groups In Canada of
African Origin

	Canadian Population		Canadian Population
Algerian Arab	6,830	Ghanaian	14,925
Berber	2,425	Moroccan Arab	14,605
Burundi	680	Nigerian	6,215
Egyptian Arab	35,560	Other Arab	48,925
Ethiopian	14,960	Somali	30,180
Eritrean	6,220	Sudanese	2,640
		Tunisian	3,825

Issues on Reaching Africans In Canada

• *The African Christian diaspora has not found its way into Canadian churches and lack church leadership. Only about 1,200 are attending African churches.*

• *The majority of Africans who are moving to Canada—those listed above—come from north of the equator and are firmly Muslim.*

• *Ethiopian, Ghanaian and Nigerian have many people groups within their respective countries—some reached and others unreached in Canada.*

Ethnicity

Ethnicity makes clear delineations, even in small geographical areas. It is unwise to confuse a Norwegian with a Swede, an Armenian with an Iraqi or a Korean with a Japanese. Ethnicity determines how we respond to someone from another ethnic background, based on historic treatment, either positive or negative.

On a vacation to Cape Cod I met a Catholic student from Northern Ireland working on the ferry to Nantucket. I mentioned my Protestant faith and he eagerly began to try to understand the differences. As an experiment, I mentioned a student from England, curious how these different students had received work visas. He shared how he received his own visa but wouldn't mention the other student. He couldn't tell me the difference between the Protestant and Catholic faith, yet he had set his mind against a student from England whom he'd never met. This student was not responding to a religious difference, but an ethnic one.

Culture

Culture is the everyday unwritten and written rules that a group of people use in order to live in harmony with each other, show respect, develop moral codes, build leadership, eat, sleep and dress. All are a part of culture. Leo Driedger, in his book, *Multi-ethnic Canada: Identities and Inequalities,* says that these rules exist so that we "feel at home in a culture... because humans want to live by habit rather than decide constantly what to do next. It is comfortable to sense a "consciousness of kind" where you are accepted as you are."[3]

Cultures can be similar without being synonymous. Canada and the United States have, by virtue of ethnic background, religion, economy and geography, chosen *some* of the same rules. In other distinctions, they have chosen not to be the same. Guns as personal property have not been a major issue in Canada, whereas U.S. citizens have demanded the right to bear arms since the establishment of their country. Lack of refuse on our streets and orderliness of crowds in major Canadian cities waiting for mass transit are far different from most of our U.S. cousins. Response to crowds, humour and world view all force us to say that Canadians do not act the *same* as Americans.

Culture should not only play a part in evangelism but also in discipleship. People from a Catholic background may leave the Catholic Church to explore a more personal relationship with Christ, but what will they look for in a church—probably high structure and a clear order of worship. It must also meet social needs, such as family, friendship, humour and moral code.

Some practices within any culture are sinful. People harden their hearts within a culture and no longer have the same guidelines for moral values that God placed there at creation, and in that sense no culture is "Christian" (Romans 2). Therefore people must be redeemed out of a culture and into His kingdom. But we must recognize that they, as well as we ourselves, will struggle far deeper with the systemic sin within the culture of our birth than others from another culture do. The unreached peoples to whom we are instructed to bring the Good News all live within cultures, many quite diverse from our own. As we disciple them, we must distinguish between a Biblical and a cultural message. Otherwise they may reject the message of the Gospel in response to our rejection of their culture.

Language

We do not speak the language of most first-generation immigrants today. If culture is a barrier based on "the way things are," then language is an audible barrier of that culture which forms a measurable, technical difference. These differences are based on the sounds and meanings of words, sentence structure, thought development and interpretation. There are different "mom and apple pie" words in each culture that have little to do with the technical structure of words. So language is a measurable, technical difference, but it also punctuates or influences a culture.

Table 25
Unreached People Groups In Canada of
Asian Origin

	Canadian Population		Canadian Population
Afghan	13,230	Japanese	77,120
Pashto	1,885	Laotian	17,305
Burmese	2,100	Malay	8,165
Cambodian	21,440	Mongolian	1,200
Chinese (Hokkien)	23,455	Nepal	540
East Indian	548,080	Pakistani	38,635
Bengali	10,645	Urdu	27,085
Gujurati	2,755	Palestinian	11,440
Hindi	28,945	Sri Lankan	46,565
Marathi	1,125	Sinhalese	3,085
Punjabi	154,480	Syrian	19,385
Telugu	965	Thai	5,015
Iranian	64,390	Tibetan	780
Kurdish	3,115	Turk	18,135
Iraqi	10,785		

Issues Relating to Asian Unreached Peoples in Canada

• *Our new Asian neighbours are urban people. What urban methodologies are in place to reach them?*

• *All people of India, though divided by primary language and ethnicity, have a national language of Hindi.*

• *Beyond ethnicity and language, the Asian people are often divided by religion—even within a major religious group.*

• *The Southeast Asians (Burmese, Khmer, Lao, Malay, Thai) are animists as well as being either Hindu, Buddhist or Muslim.*

Linguistic differences can be overcome. I have a snapshot of two young women walking down a muddy road in the jungle of Brazil. Their arms are over each other's shoulders and they are laughing heartily. They have become friends, *but they don't speak each other's language.* One is from Washington D.C., a professional nurse of some capability—the other from a tribal background in Western Brazil—new even to an urban centre. They spent time together, listened to the tone of the other's voice, watched the other's body language and listened as they prayed or read the Bible. In essence they became friends. Later, they learned each other's language. In the same way, language may be a temporary barrier as you reach out to new people groups and the language of love overcomes it.

It is far easier to reach a self-contained group. That certainly describes most first-generation immigrant groups. We must either pay the cost of learning their language or we must disciple people who do speak both languages. We must disciple to full Christian maturity and capability of church planting. But to complete the picture, we must send enough resources for them to finish the job.

Religion

David Lyon speaks of the different religions existing in Canada as groups. The "other" (than Christian) main groups may be numbered in thousands.

Table 26
The "Other" Main Groups

Jews	318,000
Muslims	253,000
Buddhists	163,000
Hindus	157,000
Sikhs	147,000
(Statistics Can. 1991	

Religion is another way of subdividing the unreached people groups, yet in surveys many people do not want to indicate their religion because in their own country people were persecuted for religion other than the predominant faith. So these figures from Statistics Canada about religion are incomplete.

Table 27
Unreached Newcomer People Groups In Canada of European Origin

	Canadian Population		Canadian Population
Albanian	4,140	Italian	1,207,475
Basque	2,645	Jewish	351,700
Bosnian	9,010	Maltese	29,815
Bulgarian	12,370	Romani, Sinte (Gypsi)	1,320
Croatian	84,485	Serbian	40,170
Cypriot	2,540	Slovenian	25,860
French	5,597,830		

Issues of European Unreached Peoples

• *If a people have ignored the Gospel for two thousand years, some may say God has hardened their heart. But this is a new opportunity.*

• *Ignoring these people would be just as dangerous for Christians as ignoring other unreached peoples.*

• *Messianic Jews across North America are making headway toward the Gospel. But it is not only prayer that they need from us, it is the Good News in "lives lived out" form.*

• *Many "secondary" cultures like Basque and Serbian are war shocked. What helps and ministries are available for them?*

• *The Italian evangelical population desperately needs a focused boost to reach second- and third-generation populations.*

Religion exists in every culture. When the truth is unknown or rejected, people, out of desperate need to see beyond themselves, create a religion—a connection with God. These are a complex sets of moral structures created to explain why people are the way they are, why they are not happy, how they are supposed to deal with the world around them and what makes a person admirable or despicable. Because the majority of people in a given culture see things in the same way, it is obviously difficult to begin to penetrate the culture with a new idea, unless God steps in, in a way that makes sense to a few of the gifted communicators from that culture.

Prejudice—the Silent Sin

Prejudice is made up of generalizations that bring about a negative response toward a group of people. Although we clump our cultural values together because we do not understand the other person's culture, we do not know whether he is violating a cultural value. Therefore we must get to know more than just a few people from that background before we can understand their culture. To be prejudiced is not a neutral act. *Judging is an action of the mind.* Pre-judging is judging without all the data available. Spiritually, prejudice is our sinful response toward God's initial division of the nations at Babel.

When somebody from our own culture has a lesser "garbage or yard ethic" than our own, we may think, "that person disgraces our neighbourhood." But in prejudice, if someone from another culture, skin colour or ethnicity in our neighbourhood has that same "garbage or yard ethic," we place a label on *them* along with *all the other people in that group.*

Of course that is a very simplistic example, but it illustrates the problem we face—pre-judging many individuals in a "group" based on one person's behaviour.

In one ethnic church, a missionary named John met a leader who was obstinate, mistreated people and twisted truth for his own good, rather than God's. John fought constantly not to pre-judge this ethnic group based on his opinion of that one person. Since he worked for some time at this church and met other leaders who were upright, devoted men and women of God who gained his respect, he was able to overcome his prejudice of that people group. There is one overriding rule in breaking the power of prejudice—prejudice is overcome through *relationship*.

Jesus makes it clear in His teaching in the Sermon on the Mount that if we as Christians judge others by the colour of skin, the language that is spoken or the dress that is worn, then we stand in judgement before God. We stand in judgement because the Bible's teaching clearly defines our responsibility to love all humanity as He, for God's sake, loved us. And we have the ability to overcome this sin, just as we have the ability to overcome any other sin, because the Spirit of God resides within us (Romans 8:13).

Urbanization

Recently, CBC radio reported that the 1996 census indicates that over 75% of our population live in urban areas with populations of over 100,000 people. Now that does not include places like Cornerbrook, Cape Breton or Charlottetown...nor places like Shawinigan, Stratford, Grand Prairie or Gander. No! Contained within nine small urban corridors across Canada are 75% of our approximately 32 million people! Virtually all of Canada, despite its huge geographical area, is an urban country.

According to 1981 figures, 43% of the population of Metro Toronto were born outside Canada. That is just within the metro limits. By 1996, 47% of the new *"Greater Toronto Area"* was made up of people born outside Canada.

In 1990, less than 2% of the core of our cities were made up of evangelicals attending church on a regular basis. Less than 2% had even the possibility of being able to share their faith with these urban, immigrant newcomers.

Although many parts of the suburban and rural church are growing, much of this is simply a regrouping, a fortress mentality revisited. Very few groups in Canada—some would argue none—are doing well in true urban ministry or church planting. We are largely running from the opportunity of bringing Christ to the city and the newcomer.

Denominations, churches and seminaries all need to rededicate themselves to work in the city, develop new methodologies for the city and stimulate vision for the city among their youth. In short, we need to love, work and pray for our cities, for Christ's sake.

Aboriginal Peoples of Canada

My first job after university was in an inner city school in Edmonton. Fifty-six mother tongues were represented in that single middle school. Several students came from six or seven Cree tribes, each speaking a different dialect. They arrived in class in the city in mid- to late October and returned to their reservations in late May.

As I got to know two students with Biblical names, I realized one student represented his Biblical namesake. He was wise, hardworking and would become a prophet for his people. His godly grandmother taught him to love Jesus

Christ, and pray and learn from other godly people. The other student was late, got into trouble and wore dirty clothes. One very cold day in January, when he did not show up, the vice principal visited his tiny, shabby house. He noticed a spot under the porch where someone had spent the night. The boy's mother arrived at the door wearing a dirty, torn T-shirt that was too short to cover her. The student, finally awakened, said he had spent until 6:00 a.m. under the porch because the man who had been with his mother the night before beat him, causing him to grab his coat and run out. That is where he drifted off to sleep most nights.

These two young men became a spur to my prayer life. As I prayed, God forced me to examine my prejudice toward aboriginal people. One godly grandmother, who had been discipled by a believing nun—one poor mother caught in prostitution, old at 25. Both were from the same reserve. How did these lost people find hope? How can they have hope without Christ? Who will reach them?

Yet, the job of evangelizing Canada's aboriginal peoples is really in its birth stages. Prayer will be an important component of reaching these first nations. Personal friendship is what will break down the barrier of prejudice that keeps us from reaching the North American native.

Table 28
Canadian First Nations

First Nation members by Tribe/Nation	Population	On Reserve	Off Reserve
Total First Nations	486,790	227,955	258,840
Algonquin*	9,375	3,640	5,735
Blackfoot*	13,395	8,480	4,910
Carrier*	8,815	4,310	4,500
Chipewyan*	11,830	5,900	5,930
Coast Tsimshian*	5,575	2,235	3,340
Cree**	168,670	90,225	78,445
Dakota*	12,330	7,580	4,755
Dogrib*	3,505	10	3,495
Gitksan*	5,595	2,860	2,735
Gwitch'in (Kutchin)*	2,540	10	2,535
Haida*	3,200	1,265	1,935
Halkomelem*	12,385	7,405	4,980
Iroquois	15,320	80	15,245
Kwakiutl*	4,875	2,180	2,700
Lillooet*	3,260	1,430	1,835
Malecite	4,215	2,325	1,890
Micmac*	20,830	12,140	8,690
Montagnais-Naskapi*	14,215	8,430	5,785
Nishga*	4,985	1,865	3,120
Nootka*	4,975	1,880	3,095
Ntlakapamux*	4,915	2,345	2,565
Ojibway*	102,910	41,240	61,670
Shuswap*	6,395	3,255	3,140
Slave*	6,665	1,925	4,740
Squamish*	2,615	1,210	1,410
Other Nations	24,285	9,880	19,030
Population By Aboriginal Groups			
Aboriginal Origins	799,005		
Metis*	204,115		
N.A. Indian	529,040		
Inuit	40,220		

* Indicates unevangelized people

** The Cree stretch from Quebec to Alberta. There are several subgroups—some reached, while others are totally unreached. For more information see the table at the end of this chapter.

Issues Raised from the Aboriginal Peoples List

- *100,000 of Canada's 799,000 aboriginal peoples are among unreached people groups.*

- *The majority of the language groups among Inuit population are "reached."*

- *North Eastern peoples, the majority of the language groups are "reached."*

- *Therefore, those who are furthest from the majority of Christian population are the most reached.*

- *Effect on strategies to reach unreached people groups:*

  ⇨ *It is easier to target someone who is isolated, yet urban non-isolated groups have larger populations.*

  ⇨ *What is close seems more "common," and therefore without need of the Gospel.*

- *Less than a third of those indicating home language, indicated their own historical language or French. English is their language.*

- *Giftings in leadership, education and business lead people to greater contact with more people in urban settings. This creates new developments in culture, sets them apart from others of their people and creates new hope for youth. It also sets a false hope for those who come to cities without those giftings.*

- *There are few Christian outreaches to aboriginal peoples in urban settings.*

- *As believers, how can we help these people retain their ethnicity, while discovering a true spirituality in Christ (and this without restricting them to reservation life)?*

Québec

In the province of Québec, according to *Christian Direction's* figures, there are approximately 5.5 million francophones. Only 0.54% of these people have an affiliation with a Protestant church, certainly not enough to be self-sufficient in reaching this vast unreached people group. This is the largest unreached people group in Canada, and in all probability in North America.

Table 29
Is Québec Reached?

Is Québec Reached?	French	English
Total Religious Responses	5,556,215	599,345
Protestant Affiliates	101,835	224,585
Protestant Churches	369	408
Churches per total Population	1:15,060	1:1469
Sources: Statistics Canada 1991, Religious Affiliation		

Issues In Reaching Québec

• *Anglo Christians ignore Québec as much as the secular Anglo population.*

• *The Catholic Church has been denigrated by evangelicals. Why have we been unwilling to bring the Gospel to people who affiliate with this religion? Do we need an object to hate? Is that why we will not share with a fracophone from Québec or an Italian from Toronto?*

• *Are Christians unconvinced that there is any* real *need to bring the Gospel to those who have the same or greater economic standing than ourselves?*

We must bring whatever resources we have to bear on reaching Québec with the Gospel. These people need to be reached, not for the sake of evangelical positioning in the unity of Canada, but for the sake of the Kingdom of God. As people of that Kingdom, we have a great responsibility in the spiritual future of Québec. Surely there is an immediacy needed in our response, but what is it?

One Québécois pastor interviewed about French Canada as an unreached people group noted, "There's a need for new models of ministry that are fitting for Québec and that originate in Québec, not western Canada. These existing methods haven't worked in Anglo-Canada, and they don't work in Québec." We must look realistically at our efforts in urban centres in English Canada and develop new methodologies that work here, before, as a Church movement, we try to import ministries that "should work in Québec." About 80% of Québec's population live in urban areas. To reach Québec we need effective urban methodologies.

I asked those same pastors what the Anglo-Canadian church can do to help reach the Québec people. At first they said there is not much they can do. However, when asked whether an "adopt-a-people" strategy would be feasible, where Anglo-Christians began to pray, not in big rallies, but one by one, or in one church at a time, on an ongoing basis, one pastor's eyes lit up, and he said, "If even one person prayed for me, and got in touch with me by phone or e-mail and really prayed on a regular basis, God would change my church." The other pastor's eyes lit up with hope as well. "Now that would change things," said another pastor. "In fact that might even change the outcome of Québec, especially if teams from churches began to come out to work with us to evangelize and pray for our province." We as Anglo-Canadians need to adopt a people—our own people in Québec—and pray and communicate with individual leaders and pastors and go as churches to Québec.

One issue we cannot ignore is leadership. The future of Québec's Church depends on its leadership and the training of future leaders. Glenn Smith and Wesley Peach both develop this theme well in their chapters. We must invest in the training of young Québécois leaders. Returning to the conversation with Québécois pastors, one said, "Discipleship of young leadership is key to the future of the Church in Québec." When asked, "Is God raising up an evangelist for the people of Québec?" one pastor talked about a young man in Montreal (from another denomination) pastoring a church of 700. He started it as a youth ministry that grew to 200 in a very short time.

Finally, we need to prepare quality people with the right abilities to go to Québec. Those needed for this task are not our average missionary candidates. Specific skills are essential. Pre-proven cross-cultural abilities are necessary and speaking the language is imperative. Given the character of the ministry to Québec, we need to pray that God will raise up some from within and some from without. It is He who raises up the "right stuff."

Conclusion

Canadian churches need to adopt one of these people groups and begin to pray for them, get to know them and understand the things that keep them from accepting the Gospel. As a church, we need to begin to consciously focus on that people group in terms of financial, personal and prayer investment.[5]

God has chosen to use Christians to accomplish His task of helping the world respond to His love for them. One hundred and eighty-six nations are recorded as sources for people groups living in Canada. It is both a tremendous opportunity and a terrible burden of responsibility. Only with commitment to obedience and God's help can we fulfil it.

We can no longer ignore the unreached people groups of Canada. We need to review the problems, seek solutions that work and mobilize our churches for action. Crossing these boundaries is difficult; comfort zones will be stretched by ethnic identities, cultural differences, language hurdles and religious understandings. We need to teach how to overcome prejudice in our churches, through authentic relationships over time. Ministering in an urban context is certainly something few evangelical leaders understand and must be addressed, or else our whole country will be unreached. Love, understanding and adoption of other cultures are ingredients that must be taught in seminaries and pulpits and demonstrated throughout the Church.

Looking at a country that had become urban, multi-cultural, divided and distracted spiritually, the prophet Isaiah did not lose hope. He urged the country to bring true justice and hope through God's love, message and standard to the disparate parts of the society. That caused their own spirituality to blossom. He issued a prophetic challenge applicable to us:

"Your people will rebuild the ancient ruins and will raise up the age-old foundations; you will be called Repairer of Broken Walls, Restorer of Streets with Dwellings" (Isaiah 58:12).

Table 30
Ethnolinguistic Peoples[6]

Language	People Group Name	Canadian Pop.	World Pop.	Scripture	Audio	Jesus Film	Status
ABNAKI-PENOBSCOT	Abnaki-Penobscot	1,900	1,920				Unevangelized
ABNAKI-PENOBSCOT	Western Nbnaki						Unknown
ALGONQUIN	Algonquin	3,000	3,000				Unevangelized
AMERICAN ENGLISH	English	900,000	1,100,000				Unreached
ARABIC, JUDEO-MOROCCAN	Moroccan Jew		1,646,100				Unknown
ARABIC, LEVANTINE	Palestinian Arab	28,000	11,844,100				Evangelized
ARABIC, LEVANTINE	Lebanese Arab	28,000	3,058,600				Evangelized
ARABIC, MODERN STANDARD	Egyptian Arab	28,000	5,661,770			Yes	Evangelized
ARMENIAN	Armenian	19,000	5,496,900			Yes	Evangelized
ASSINIBOINE	Assiniboin	2,800	3,000		Yes		Unevangelized
ATIKAMEKW	Atikamek	3,200	3,200	Portion			Unreached
BABINE	Babine	1,600	1,600		Yes		Unevangelized
BEAVER	Beaver (Tsattine, Castor)	300	300	Portion	Yes		Unevangelized
BELLA COOLA	Bella Coola	200	200				Unevangelized
BELORUSSIAN	Byelorussian	700	10,479,590	Bible		Yes	Evangelized
BENGALI	Bengali	3,200	179,025,800	Bible	Yes	Yes	Unevangelized
BLACKFOOT	Blackfoot (Piegon, Blood)	12,000	21,000	Portion			Evangelized
BLACKFOOT	Piegan						Unknown
BULGARIAN	Bulgar	2,200	8,322,200	Bible	Yes	Yes	Evangelized
CARRIER	Carrier	1,500	1,500				Unevangelized
CARRIER, SOUTHERN	Southern Carrier	500	500				Unreached
CAYUGA	Cayuga	400	410		Yes		Unevangelized
CHEHALIS, UPPER	Halkomelem	8,000	8,010				Unevangelized
CHILCOTIN	Chilcotin	1,200	1,200		Yes	Yes	Unevangelized
CHINESE, MANDARIN	Han Chinese	254,000	861,305,630		Yes	Yes	Evangelized
CHINOOK WAWA	Chinook Wawa	100	110				Unevangelized
CHIPEWYAN	Chipewyan	4,000	4,000	NT	Yes	Yes	Unevangelized
CHIPEWYAN	Yellow Knife						Unknown

165

Table 30, Cont'd

Language	People Group Name	Canadian Pop.	World Pop.	Scripture	Audio	Jesus Film	Status
COMOX	Comox	400	400				Unevangelized
CREE, CENTRAL	Central Cree	4,500	4,500				Evangelized
CREE, CENTRAL	Eastern Swampy Cree						Unknown
CREE, CENTRAL	Moose Cree						Unknown
CREE, COASTAL EASTERN	Eastern Coastal Cree	5,000	5,000				Evangelized
CREE, INLAND EASTERN	Inland Eastern Cree	2,200	2,200				Evangelized
CREE, WESTERN	Western Cree	45,000	80,000			Yes	Evangelized
CREE, WESTERN	Plains Cree						Unknown
CZECH	Czech	26,000	10,463,800	Bible		Yes	Evangelized
DAKOTA	Dakota (Sioux, Santee)	5,000	25,000	Bible	Yes		Evangelized
DANISH	Danish	29,000	5,162,000	Bible		Yes	Evangelized
DOGRIB	Dogrib	2,300	2,300		Yes	Yes	Unevangelized
DUTCH	Dutch	164,000	20,408,500	Bible		Yes	Evangelized
ENGLISH	Anglo-Canadian	16,615,000	314,346,940	Bible	Yes	Yes	Evangelized
ESTONIAN	Estonian	15,000	1,149,900		Yes	Yes	Evangelized
FARSI, EASTERN	Persian	5,100	4,665,000			Yes	Unevangelized
FARSI, WESTERN	Persian		23,607,300	Bible	Yes	Yes	Unknown
FINNISH	Finn	38,000	5,367,700	Bible	Yes	Yes	Evangelized
FRENCH	French	6,000,000	45,813,480	Bible	Yes	Yes	Unevangelized
FRENCH	Walloon	28,000	3,301,000			Yes	Evangelized
FRENCH, CAJUN	Acadian (Cajun French)	11,000	1,011,000			Yes	Evangelized
FRISIAN, WESTERN	Frisian	2,000	741,000	Bible			Evangelized
GERMAN, HUTTERITE	Tyrolese (Hutterite)	15,000	20,000				Unreached
GERMAN, PENNSYLVANIA	Pennsylvania Dutch	10,000	70,000				Evangelized
GROS VENTRE	Gros Ventre		10				Unknown
GWICHIN	Kutchin	1,400	2,900				Unevangelized
GWICHIN	Western Canada Gwich'in						Unknown

Table 30, Cont'd

Language	People Group Name	Canadian Pop.	World Pop.	Scripture	Audio	Jesus Film	Status
HAIDA	Haida	1,100	1,300	Portion	Yes		Unevangelized
HAISLA	Haisla	30	30				Unevangelized
HAISLA	Kitimat					Yes	Unknown
HAITIAN CREOLE FRENCH	Haitian	5,500	7,422,940	Bible		Yes	Evangelized
HALKOMELEM	Halkomelem	500	500				Unreached
HALKOMELEM	Cowichan						Unknown
HAN	Han (Moosehide)	300	320				Unevangelized
HEILTSUK	Heiltsuk	300	300				Unevangelized
HUNGARIAN	Hungarian	95,000	14,472,150	Bible		Yes	Evangelized
ICELANDIC	Icelander	6,200	264,500	Bible	Yes	Yes	Evangelized
INUKTITUT, EASTERN CANADIAN	Copper Eskimo	14,000	14,000				Evangelized
INUKTITUT, NORTH ALASKAN	North Alaskan Eskimo	2,800	12,100				Evangelized
INUKTITUT, NORTH ALASKAN	Point Barrow Eskimo						Unknown
INUKTITUT, WESTERN CANADA	Northwest Alaskan Eskimo	4,000	4,000				Unreached
KASKA	Kaska	200	200				Unevangelized
KHMER, CENTRAL	Khmer (Cambodian)	4,600	8,991,000	Bible		Yes	Unevangelized
KOREAN	Korean	19,000	65,533,500	Bible	Yes	Yes	Evangelized
KUTENAI	Kutenai	100	300				Unevangelized
KWAKIUTL	Kwakiutl	300	300	Portion			Unevangelized
LAKOTA	Lakota	11,000	17,000		Yes		Unevangelized
LAO	Lao (Laotian Thai)		3,123,900	Bible		Yes	Unknown
LATVIAN	Latvian (Lett)	14,000	1,233,800	Bible	Yes	Yes	Evangelized
LAURENTIAN	Laurentian						Unknown
LESSER ANTILLEAN CREOLE EN	West Indian Black	36,000	1,181,200				Evangelized
LILLOOET	Lillooet	300	300		Yes		Unevangelized
LITHUANIAN	Lithuanian	15,000	3,560,000	Bible	Yes	Yes	Evangelized
MACEDONIAN	Macedonian	12,000	1,651,500	NT		Yes	Evangelized

167

Table 30, Cont'd

Language	People Group Name	Canadian Pop.	World Pop.	Scripture	Audio	Jesus Film	Status
MALAY	Malay	2,300	8,243,370	Bible		Yes	Unevangelized
MALAYALAM	Malayali	2,300	33,398,900	Bible	Yes	Yes	Evangelized
MALECITE-PASSAMAQUODDY	Malecite	1,500	3,000				Unevangelized
MALECITE-PASSAMAQUODDY	Malecite						Unknown
MALECITE-PASSAMAQUODDY	Passamaquoddy						Unknown
MICMAC	Micmac	6,000	8,000	NT	Yes		Unevangelized
MITCHIF	French Cree	11,000	16,200				Unevangelized
MOHAWK	Mohawk	3,900	6,900	Portion	Yes		Evangelized
MONTAGNAIS	Montagnais	7,000	7,000		Yes		Unevangelized
MUNSEE	Delaware (Lenni-Lenape)	1,900	1,900				Unevangelized
NASKAPI	Naskapi	400	400				Unreached
NASS-GITKSIAN	Nass-Gitksian	2,500	2,500				Unevangelized
NASS-GITKSIAN	Nishka						Unknown
NASS-GITKSIAN	Gitksian						Unknown
NOOTKA	Nootka	600	600				Unevangelized
NORWEGIAN, NYNORSK	Norwegian	22,000	888,010	Bible			Evangelized
OJIBWA, EASTERN	Eastern Ojibwa (Chippewa)	19,000	27,000				Evangelized
OJIBWA, EASTERN	Ottawa						Unknown
OJIBWA, NORTHERN	Cree	8,000	8,000				Unreached
OJIBWA, NORTHERN	Northern Ojibwa	9,500	9,500				Evangelized
OJIBWA, WESTERN	Western Ojibwa (Chippewa)	23,000	58,000				Evangelized
OKANAGAN	Okanagon	3,200	3,700				Unevangelized
ONEIDA	Oneida	200	250		Yes		Unevangelized
ONONDAGA	Onondaga	50	100				Unevangelized
PANJABI, EASTERN	Sikh	200,000	21,527,160		Yes	Yes	Evangelized
PAPAGO-PIMA	Papago-Pima	600	17,100				Unevangelized
PENTLATCH	Pentlatch						Unknown

Table 30, Cont'd

Language	People Group Name	Canadian Pop.	World Pop.	Scripture	Audio	Jesus Film	Status
PLAUTDIETSCH	Low German	80,000	332,900	NT		Yes	Evangelized
POLISH	Polish (Pole)	145,000	41,071,200	Bible		Yes	Evangelized
PORTUGUESE	Portuguese	187,000	167,379,250	Bible		Yes	Evangelized
POTAWATOMI	Potawatomi	100	600		Yes		Unevangelized
ROMANI, SINTE	Sinti Gypsy	2,800	143,400		Yes		Unevangelized
ROMANI, VLACH	Romanian	15,000	2,225,400	Bible	Yes		Evangelized
ROMANI, VLACH	Kalderash Gypsy (Rom)	39,000	571,200				Evangelized
RUSSIAN	Russian	31,700	150,621,400	Bible	Yes	Yes	Evangelized
SALISH, STRAITS	Straits Salish	1,700	1,730				Unevangelized
SARSI	Sarsi	50	50				Unevangelized
SECHELT	Sechelt	40	40				Unevangelized
SEKANI	Sekani	100	100		Yes		Unevangelized
SENECA	Seneca	30	230	Portion	Yes		Unevangelized
SERBO-CROATIAN	Croat	93,900	11,534,900			Yes	Evangelized
SHUSWAP	Shuswap	500	500		Yes		Unevangelized
SINHALA	Sinhalese (Cingalese)	1,000	13,408,500	Bible		Yes	Unevangelized
SLAVEY	Slave (Tinne, Mountain)	4,000	4,000	NT			Unevangelized
SLAVEY	Hare						Unknown
SLOVAK	Slovak	22,000	5,109,000	Bible		Yes	Evangelized
SLOVENIAN	Slovene	6,400	2,256,400	Bible		Yes	Evangelized
SPANISH	Spaniard	79,000	311,364,060	Bible	Yes	Yes	Evangelized
SQUAMISH	Squamish	20	20				Unevangelized
STONEY	Stoney	1,000	1,000				Unevangelized
SWAHILI	Swahili	700	871,170		Yes	Yes	Unevangelized
SWEDISH	Swedish	19,000	8,971,200	Bible		Yes	Evangelized
TAGALOG	Filipino (Tagalog)	51,000	16,777,950	Bible	Yes	Yes	Evangelized
TAGISH	Tagish	10	10				Unevangelized

169

Table 30, Cont'd

Language	People Group Name	Canadian Pop.	World Pop.	Scripture	Audio	Jesus Film	Status
TAHLTAN	Tahltan	40	40				Unevangelized
TAMIL	Tamil	2,300	59,841,300	Bible	Yes	Yes	Evangelized
TANANA, UPPER	Upper Tanana		300				Unknown
TELUGU	Telugu	800	67,311,900	Bible	Yes	Yes	Unevangelized
THAI	Thai	8,400	18,620,200	Bible	Yes	Yes	Unevangelized
THOMPSON	Thompson (Ntlakyapamuk)	500	500	Portion	Yes		Unevangelized
TLINGIT	Tlingit	100	2,100		Yes		Unevangelized
TSIMSHIAN	Tsimshian	2,200	4,300				Unevangelized
TURKISH	Turk	4,600	50,257,600	Bible		Yes	Unevangelized
TUSCARORA	Tuscarora	10	40		Yes		Unevangelized
TUTCHONE	Tutchone	500	500				Unevangelized
TUTCHONE	Athabascan: Northern Tutcho						Unknown
TUTCHONE	Southern Athabascan						Unknown
UKRAINIAN	Ukrainian	331,000	45,050,100	Bible	Yes	Yes	Evangelized
URDU	Urdu	14,000	51,612,700	Bible	Yes	Yes	Unevangelized
WELSH	Welsh	3,000	645,900	Bible		Yes	Evangelized
WYANDOT	Huron		1,300				Unknown
YIDDISH	Jewish	341,000	4,759,200	Bible		Yes	Unevangelized

Action Points

✓Unreached peoples are defined as, "any group of more than 5,000 people whose makeup reflects less than 2% evangelical." Were you surprised to find so much of the "mission field" (so defined) in Canada?

✓Would you consider Canadian groups of 5% evangelical as "reached?" What about 10% or 25%? How does this affect the way you see Canada and your calling to disciple our nation?

✓How could your congregation "adopt" a Canadian unreached people group for church planting?

✓Who are your neighbours? Do you have the opportunity to get to know, on a personal basis, a family or household from an unreached people group?

Chapter Notes

[1] Brian Seim, *Canada's New Harvest—Helping Churches Touch Newcomers*, SIM Canada, Vision Canada, 1997.

[2] Charting the work of small ethnic churches is sometimes difficult, and if you have data in this area, please contact me.

[3] Leo Dreidiger, *Multi-Ethnic Canada—Identities and Inequalities*, Oxford University Press Canada, 1996.

[4] Edward Opuku-Dapaah, *Somali Refugees in Toronto—A Profile*, York Lanes Press, Toronto, 1995.

[5] Churches wishing to participate in such a French-English church prayer partnership may contact Suzanne Morin-Mackenzie who has agreed to serve as communication coordinator: 1773 Dansey Avenue, Coquitlam, B.C. V3K 3J4, or by email: smackenzie@bc.sympatico.ca. Suzanne is a nineth generation Québecois "beauceron" married to an English husband, Stephen, both of whom share in a ministry of intercession. Their children are fluently bilingual.

[6] Integrated Strategic Planning Database - Global Research, Foreign Mission Board of the Southern Baptist Convention

Chapter Six

Rethinking Revival in Québec

Rev. Wesley Peach

Introduction

"Those were the days, my friend..."

F rancophone evangelical churches grew very rapidly in Québec between 1970 and 1985 (see Figures 16-19). It is not without some pain, however, that we look back nostalgically at that wonderful time of excitement and blessing.

Nowadays we often hear evangelicals in Québec asking hard questions, their disappointment occasionally bordering on frustration. They wonder what happened to make the Québécois population so cool to the Gospel now after such a great time of warmth and openness in the past. Some church members feel guilty for not witnessing like they used to. Pastors who remember the "boom" days are well aware they aren't seeing as many or the same type of conversions and baptisms. Denominational leaders ponder why they have to spend so much of their efforts on maintaining harmony in their existing churches. They see that new church plants are very rare.

Leaders of parachurch ministries—Christian day schools, theological schools, Christian camps, literature ministries, campus ministries, etc.—have virtually all reduced their expectations for their ministries aimed at French Canadians. With few exceptions, their organizations are surviving in Québec primarily by diversifying their ministries to work with the growing numbers of ethnic evangelicals. The Québécois Baby Boomers converted during the revival wonder why their young adult children of the '90s see so little "good news" in the evangelical message and way of life.

Hard questions indeed. Where did we come from? Where are we going? The purpose of this chapter is to propose an interpretative analysis of the evangelical revival in Québec in a way that will shed some light on our strategies for the future. To do so, we will use a time-tested anthropological theory of how revivals work. Our goal is to show what the revival accomplished and what evangelicals are doing to maximize its accomplishments in the province. The lessons of the recent revival will also point us to new challenges Québec evangelicals must face to prepare for a new wave of Church growth. For a more detailed analysis of the Québec revival, look for a forthcoming book by Richard Lougheed, Wesley Peach and Glenn Smith, published in French by *Les Editions la Clarière*.

Before we go any further, however, we must pause to reaffirm our conviction that only God brings revival. Our theology is clear that the sovereign God of history worked in Québec in ways we will never completely understand. By using an anthropological theory we will attempt to identify some of the human factors by which God is building His church. The following graphs give us an important overview of the tumultuous church growth of the Québec revival.

Figure 16
Total Number of Organized Churches of the Three Major French Evangelical Denominations in Québec 1960 - 1995

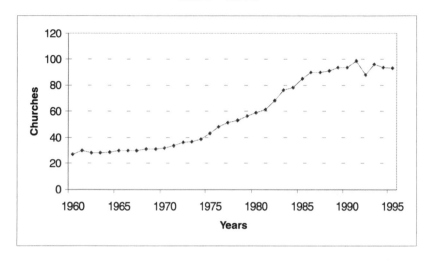

Figure 17
Total Membership of the Three Major French Evangelical Denominations in Québec 1960 - 1995

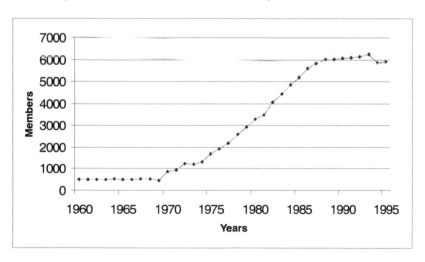

Figure 18
Total Baptisms of the Three Major French
Evangelical Denominations in Québec 1960 - 1995

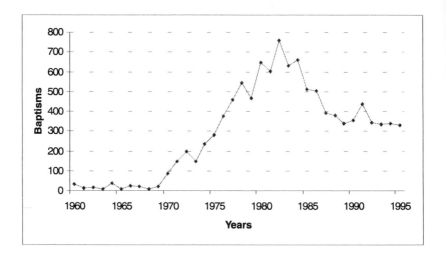

Figure 19
Percentage of Baptisms per Members 1960 - 1995

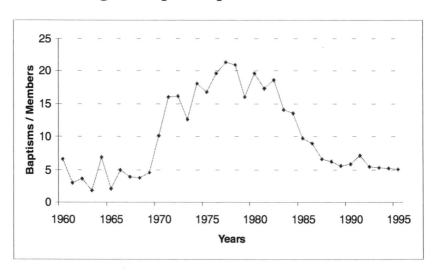

Whose Idea Was This?

Anthony F.C. Wallace, an American anthropologist now retired after a teaching career at the University of Pennsylvania, has shed much light on the individual and corporate human processes that are at work during religious revivals. He published articles and books that articulated and refined elements of his theory over a period of 28 years (from 1951 to 1978). In his first definitive presentation of the theory, Wallace defined a Revitalization Movement as a special kind of culture change phenomenon that is a "deliberate, organized, conscious effort by members of a society to reduce the stress level prevalent in the system by constructing a more satisfying culture."[1] He observed that a new religious fervor is almost always at the centre of a cultural Revitalization Movement. In addition to emphasizing the importance of religion in cultural change, Wallace's theory spells out the logical stages of what he calls a revitalization cycle.

As we review the following steps, or phases, we must keep in mind that Wallace intended his theory to delineate the functions that a religious Revitalization Movement accomplishes. Although we will follow somewhat chronologically through each phase of the Québec revival, we must understand that each phase can vary in order and intensity. Sometimes phases are addressed simultaneously, and sometimes they can be repeated or reworked at a later point in the movement.

The more we understand these functions, the more we will be able to make pertinent observations and predictions concerning the challenges of church planting in Québec.

Phases of Revitalization

1. Steady State
2. Increased Individual Stress
3. Cultural Distortion
4. Revitalization movement
   a. Paradigm Resynthesis
   b. Communication
   c. Organization
   d. Adaptation
   e. Cultural Transformation
   f. Routinization
5. New Steady State

Before we begin our detailed analysis of the Québec revival, we would do well to become a little more "at ease" with the revitalization cycle. To do that, let us recall the period of the judges in the Old Testament.

The children of Israel were prone to forget Yahweh, and the result was moral, economic and military decline. When things became unbearable, Israel cried out to God for a deliverer. Each time God sent a judge to call them back to God, revitalizing their worship and culture. Each divinely appointed leader would bring them victory over their enemies and clearer devotion to God for a generation or two. In the generations that followed, however, the Israelites would again forget Yahweh, initiating a slow deterioration in worship and culture that would result in judgement followed by repentance. God would appoint a new judge to set Israel free from her enemies. The history of Israel is a clear example of a culture that experienced the revitalization cycle.

The Québec Revival Seen as a Revitalization Movement

As we examine the recent evangelical revival in Québec, we will appreciate all the more the clarity and valuable contributions of the revitalization theory. Our format will be to present a somewhat theoretical description of each phase of the revitalization cycle. We will attempt to illustrate each phase with an analysis of some of the dominant characteristics of the Québec revival.

The Steady State Phase

Before a Revitalization Movement begins, the society is in what Wallace calls a "Steady State." His term can be misunderstood to mean that there are no changes in the culture. Wallace insists that his term is intended to mean that the culture makes small, or controlled changes. The Steady State can continue as long as the individuals in the society are able to make minor or gradual adjustments in their cultural and religious "status quo" in ways that continue to respect and defend the validity of their basic culture.

Québec in the Steady State

The Steady State that the Québec culture knew before the evangelical revival of the 1970s and 1980s was in fact the century-old legacy of an earlier revitalization cycle. According to historian Louis Rousseau, French Québec went through the stages of a Revitalization Movement from 1830 through the 1860s. Although a small evangelical movement grew in that time of rapid cultural change, there was a much larger revival of interest in and dominance by the Roman Catholic Church. After 1900, the evangelical movement was unable to maintain its momentum within the then much stronger Catholic cultural infrastructure. The modernist theological debates among Protestants, new pressures toward urban migration away from the rural evangelical churches, and the inescapable reality that life was easier for Québécois evangelicals when they migrated to English circles, all took a toll on the French evangelical movement. After peaking at perhaps 30,000 members in Québec at the turn of the century, the French evangelical movement had virtually disappeared by the 1950s.

Rousseau claims that the Steady State legacy of the last Catholic Revitalization Movement began to deteriorate in Québec after World War II. Thus began a new revitalization cycle that is only now drawing near completion. We believe that the recent evangelical revival in Québec is part of this broader revitalization process whose first stages are apparent in what is often called the "Quiet Revolution."[2]

Increased Individual Stress and Cultural Distortion Phases

When it is not adequately maintained, the cultural stability of the Steady State deteriorates slowly and almost imperceptibly. The individuals within the culture gradually discover that their traditional beliefs and ways of life are less and less adequate for solving their daily problems. It is an increasingly confusing time for the individuals who must come to the conclusion that fewer of their culture "cues" work any more. Traditional goals of their culture can no longer be reached by traditional means. Wallace sees a direct correlation between the disorder in a culture, and the level of stress symptoms experienced by individual members of the community. The more the culture is confused the more individuals become unstable. In a broad analysis of all the evangelical awakenings in North American Church history, William McLoughlin uses Wallace's theory to point to the disintegration of the nuclear family as the first sign of deterioration in this phase of increased individual stress.[3]

One of the symptoms of this phase is the increasing ineffectiveness of the culture's religious rituals to answer the questions or even soothe the pain of the conflicts caused by cultural confusion. Participation in the "national religion" is viewed by many with contempt or apathy. Personal salvation is no longer considered possible within the confines of the existing religious paradigm.

As individuals become less and less able to satisfy personal wishes in the existing cultural confusion, there comes a point where they conclude that the changes and the stress are not the root cause of their dissatisfaction. They begin to see the culture itself as the major source of their frustration because it is not able to provide reliable satisfaction to their expectations. Thus begins the phase of cultural distortion, when the majority of the population has lost confidence in the way things work. They are openly seeking a new cultural order. Many are openly defying the existing "establishment" as inadequate. This sense of desperation is the ultimate stress pushing individuals toward cultural revitalization.

Québec in Increased Individual Stress and Cultural Distortion

The Quiet Revolution can be interpreted as a multi-dimensional cultural crisis. Québécois were openly rethinking their culture as a whole. No aspect was left unquestioned, be it the economy, morality, family roles, religion, education, politics or Québec's place in the world and in Canada, *everything* was declared to be in need of profound and rapid restructuring. The rapid reforms of Jean Lesage's Liberal Party, followed by the rise of the Parti Québécois, were the political manifestations of the sweeping revitalization processes at work in Québec.

Consistent with Wallace's description, the "national religion" came on hard times. In the decade of the 1960s, weekly Mass attendance dropped from 60% to 30% of the population. The percentage of practicing Catholics dropped by half again in the following decade. Catholic sociologist Jacques Grand' Maison describes the result: "The Québécois threw the Catholic Church in the St. Lawrence River and went on with their lives without her." Ironically, when the cultural disillusionment with traditional Catholicism was at its highest, the radical changes of Vatican II hit the remaining faithful worshippers. If the old ways had clearly become irrelevant, the new ways were equally unpopular with many traditionalists. The national religion was at an impasse.

At this point in the revitalization cycle we must keep in mind that Québec culture was not primarily "secularizing" in the sense of an outright rejection of Christianity. Québécois were trying to evaluate, rethink and restructure the unsatisfactory elements of their religious heritage, rather than totally abandon them. This was the open door for the revival that brought many individuals to an evangelical conversion experience resulting in rapid evangelical Church growth in Québec.

Resynthesis of the Religious Paradigm

Wallace states that when individuals in a revitalizing culture have come to the point of questioning their whole way of life, they do so by rethinking four fundamental psychological needs. Their first need is for a satisfying divine parental figure to provide authority and protection. Such a need is all the more evident for those whose world has become unpredictable and confusing.

Their second basic human need is the assurance that one is part of a coherent cultural system. This confidence gives the peace of mind of predictability and order, and a basis for stable personal identity as a part of that order. Wallace refers to the individual's new reference point for self-identity as a "goal culture." When everything crumbles and becomes unpredictable in the old way of life, the individual finds a new focus of transcendent absolutes, which in turn yields a new set of directions for daily living. This reorganization provides individuals with an idea of who they are in the universe and what they are to do in their world.

Turning the page to a brighter future with a new sense of divine approval is not entirely possible until individuals can make some kind of sense of their own actions in their chaotic past. The third need that individuals must find a solution to is their crushing sense of guilt, failure and anxiety. Along with a new definition of sin comes the redefinition of a way for atonement for past failures, and new rules for avoiding further transgressions. The new "code" is the vital link between the chaotic present and the peace of the envisioned goal culture. This "code" becomes people's daily assurance that order, self-esteem and an intimate relationship with the divine are possible and in fact is being realized by their faithfulness to it.

Having lived in chronic personal and social confusion, individuals have to put to rest a fourth basic question: "What is to become of the old order and those who cling to it?" In the process of rejecting the old way, revitalized individuals relate their new vision to apocalyptic terms of the destruction of the "old" order and of all those who refuse to accept the new code. Hence Wallace also observes a "preoccupation with the concepts of sin and hell," in the early phases of Paradigm Resynthesis of Revitalization Movements. The condemnation of certain vices by a new code can be seen as a "divinely sanctioned" statement of lessons learned by personal failure. The new list of sins and judgements with the threat of eternal destruction becomes a kind of "death certificate" confirming the old order as passé and useless.

Québec in the Paradigm Resynthesis Phase

True to Wallace's observations, the personal and cultural revitalization process for individuals in Québec was indeed a search for intimate contact with God, for a new form of social order and community, for a new way of forgiveness and for a clearer eschatology concerning the righteous and the wicked. These four needs were exactly what the evangelical believers and churches had to offer. Perfectly positioned in their responses to the culture's pressing needs, the evangelical message and lifestyle were distinct from but clearly relevant to those who wanted to rethink the doctrines of Catholicism. The message proclaimed by evangelicals referred to as the "plan of salvation" corresponded directly to the needs of the revitalizing Québécois.

Table 31
Parallels Between the "Four Crises" and the
"Plan of Salvation"

The Four Personal Crises of Revitalization	Important Elements of the Evangelical Plan of Salvation
1. Intimate contact with a divine authority figure and protector.	1. God loves you personally. You can invite Jesus Christ into your life.
2. A new goal culture which gives a new personal identity.	2. God has a wonderful plan for your life. You can be part of our new Church.
3. New ways for atonement and for avoiding sin.	3. Salvation is by faith alone, not by works. The Holy Spirit gives victory over sin.
4. Apocalyptic destruction of the old system.	4. Jesus is coming back soon. God will judge those who reject Christ.

The Communication Phase of a Revitalization Movement

According to Wallace's theory, the people who have experienced a radically revitalizing religious conversion set out immediately to communicate their vision to those around them. Preaching "the good news" is a primary activity of the new movement even during later stages of its organizational life. Wallace proposes that when new believers have dared to reformulate their entire lives in a way that initially sets them out as marginal or non-conformist, they will experience the inescapable urge to find "safety in numbers." The doctrinal and behavioural injunctions they preach carry two fundamental motifs—that those who adhere to the new movement come under God's care and protection, and that they and society in general will benefit from an identification with the new cultural model.

The methods of communication chosen by those who proclaim the message can vary widely according to the unique situation of each Revitalization Movement. The preaching can take place in mass rallies or through quiet individual persuasion and may be directed at various sorts of audiences. In more complex societies, usually only a small target audience is responsive. Wallace notes that Revitalization Movements tend to be more successful if their initial message is directed to a limited few, rather than a diluted message to a general audience.

The Communication Phase of the Québec Revival

Before the Quiet Revolution, a tiny evangelical community of less than 2,000 believers had been faithfully witnessing in Québec in a context of very strong opposition. As the culture was "cracking open" to new ideas, the Sermons from Science pavilion at the Expo '67 in Montreal was a strategic beginning to the Communication Phase of the evangelical revival in Québec. Over the course of the pavilion's existence, one-quarter of the entire population of Québec passed through its doors to see and hear a clear, credible plan of salvation. The pavilion organizers received over 160,000 response cards! The Sermons from Science pavilion at Expo '67 did not, however, result in instant church growth. Its primary accomplishment was to announce on a grand scale the existence and credibility of the evangelical message. Other mass evangelism efforts followed. Leighton Ford preached at crusades in 1983 and 1990. Alain Choquier from France, Gaston Racine, Walter de Sousa, Fernand St-Louis and the Janz team, "Québec pour Jésus" all organized local crusades from the early 1970s through the 1980s.

As important and visible as these macro-communication efforts were, most evangelism and disciple making was done at the individual and small group network level. This movement of lay witnessing was spontaneous and unorganized. New converts had their greatest effectiveness witnessing to members of their own family and their closest friends. Many young people brought in their parents. To this day it is possible to trace relational "genealogical trees" from the series of conversions that created entire new churches.

Young adult Baby Boomers, especially college students, were the primary group of new converts. They were the driving force and prime beneficiaries of the Quiet Revolution. They had the intellectual and logistical freedom to change their religious affiliation overnight—many did.

Wallace states that the Communication Phase never completely ends. Evangelicals continue to witness and see some conversions. But we can identify Mission Québec in 1990 as an important turning point. Jacques Marcoux and Richard Toupin from, "Québec pour Jésus" expended enormous amounts of time and money to "ride the wake" of Mission Québec through a series of high-quality evangelistic television shows and a whirlwind tour of mini-crusades. The momentum never translated into increased church attendance. If anything, Mission Québec confirmed to the participating churches that the cost of mass evangelism was too high to justify the mediocre results. Although there was a slight increase in baptisms in 1991, the ratings for the TV series were very low and the tour of crusades fizzled in local church fatigue. It was a great disappointment for "Québec pour Jésus."

The Organization Phase of a Revitalization Movement

Revitalization movements often start as spontaneous, informal gatherings to share a new common vision. As the preaching of the new vision continues, the movement gains adherents who eventually form a clearly recognizable group with its own well-defined doctrinal beliefs and organizational structure.

Wallace observes that the Organization Phase of a Revitalization Movement is an inevitable consequence of its new vision dealing with the realities of human group dynamics. Hence the original visionaries or spokesmen come to be esteemed by the group with "prophetic" reverence. These prophet figures may assume a superior role in the organization as mediators or even divine representatives. A relatively small group of fervent, highly committed disciples gathers close to the prophets. These "revitalized" believers become the workers (professional or volunteer) of the new organization. Outside this inner circle is a larger group of followers who sincerely agree with the new vision but who for one reason or another do not have the same profound persevering commitment as the core group of disciples. These people follow along when the music, the messages and the momentum of the group catch their attention. They attend the meetings and occasionally give money. The followers' allegiance is often directed more to the prophetic leader than to God. Because they lack a first-hand lasting personal commitment, followers are equally likely to be swayed "out of sync" by other personal interests that create conflicts with those of the organization.

The Organization Phase of the Québec Revival

Expo '67 was followed by the work of missionaries, pastors and dramatically converted lay people to bring their network of family and friends into the fold of local evangelical churches.

The number of evangelical churches doubled in the 1970s and increased by 50% in the 1980s. The number of active members quadrupled in the 1970s and doubled again in the 1980s (see Figure 17). Québec church historian Richard Lougheed pinpoints the strategic role of new church planting at this point in the revival. He observes that some denominations dared to organize the impromptu gatherings of enthusiastic but immature converts into daughter churches. Other evangelical groups were slower to organize new churches and thereby missed much of the influx of new converts who were looking for places to meet together for fellowship. The Association of Evangelical Baptists was particularly effective in strategically locating their experienced leaders throughout the province with a view to supervising a network of new "pastors-in-formation." These interns were therefore assured more success in their efforts to organize new churches.

The rapid church planting that characterized the Québec revival plateaued in the mid-1980s. As the revival wound down in momentum, many of the later church plants were forced to rejoin their larger "mother churches" for lack of new converts and finances necessary to continue growth. The strategy of subsidizing many small churches became counter productive. There have been some new church plants in the 1990s, however there seem to be more conversions and church growth in the larger "full service" churches. We believe this is true partly because the larger churches have retained a sense of momentum by the quantity and quality of their ministries. Obviously there are still urgent needs for church planting in Québec. Given however that the rapid church-planting phase of the Québec revival is now history, we must be exceedingly wise as to the type, place and duration of our church planting efforts if we hope to maximize the chances for long-term fruitfulness.

The Adaptation Phase of a Revitalization Movement

In the same way that a Revitalization Movement attracts varying degrees of loyalty, it also creates various types of opposition. The success of a new movement depends on its ability to adapt to and overcome the realities of the opposition that arises from the complex (sometimes subconscious) expectations of individuals in the society. Wallace calls this function "adaptation," which he says can take a variety of courses to improve the "fit" of the movement in the society. Any Revitalization Movement that does not adequately respond to its sources of opposition will eventually be ignored or suppressed, regardless of its initial success.

Those outside the movement, in the name of protecting their over-zealous acquaintances from error, organize varying degrees of opposition to the new movement. Their motivation to oppose the movement can stem from genuine ignorance, their mental association of the movement with another "foreign" culture or from fear that the new movement will threaten the existing power structure from which they benefit. The degree of opposition can vary from physical repression to more subtle forms of social disapproval.

A second source of opposition can be found, surprisingly, from within the movement itself. Although new believers have radically reshaped their lives and their beliefs, not everything "fits" together ideally between their lives, the other members of the new organization and all the nuances of the new doctrines. If these "irritants" cannot be worked out over time, the movement will lose adherents.

The Adaptation Phase of the Québec Revival

The momentum of the revival in Québec grew as new converts witnessed to their network of family and friends and saw successive waves of conversions. We dare say that traces of the evangelical message filtered down virtually every relational tributary in the society. In contrast with the concerted physical opposition that was common before the Quiet Revolution, Québécois evangelicals faced relatively diluted though persistent social disapproval. Some young adults were "cut off" by their angered parents for a while after their conversion. Some students received lower grades on papers in which they mentioned their new faith. In most cases, however, peace has been re-established either by "never talking about religion," or by the credibility gained as the young people became successful adults. "Religious fanatics" of all types have been specifically shunned in the workplace and as a result evangelicals have learned to be more discreet in their profile. At the relational level, the Adaptation Phase has usually ended in a truce.

For all the talk of religious pluralism, there is still considerable opposition to the evangelical movement relative to their needs for legal and civic recognition of their institutions. We know of villages in Québec that have recently refused to zone land for a non-Catholic church, stating openly that the basis of their refusal was that they did not want a "cult" in their town. Fortunately, even the Roman Catholic bishops have not allowed such discrimination to continue when they are made aware of the problem.

The Québec revival saw its share of "internal opposition" as many adherents lost enthusiasm for their church involvement. The combined factors of the rapid influx of so many new believers with their unusually high expectations, under the supervision of so few mature leaders, led to many defections from the movement. Most of these departures were not caused by doctrinal disagreements but rather by interpersonal conflicts. Adherents were disappointed that the "goal culture" that they were looking for was not materializing as they had envisioned it should. Some leaders wonder how many of the "converts" of those boom days were in reality only followers rather than true disciples.

The Adaptation Phase is still an active function of the Québec revival. Perhaps it was most evident in the early 1990s when in some churches the number of departures equaled the number of new converts. Further evidence of this phase is seen as "backslidden" Baby Boomer believers are quietly returning for worship and healing, often after the break-up of their families. Québécois evangelicals also have yet to find an identity that is free from the connotation that their movement is "English" in origin. This association could create a major need for further adaptation in the future. Perhaps the recent creation of the French Canadian equivalent of the Evangelical Fellowship of Canada (EFC), called the Alliance Francophone des Protestants Evangéliques du Québec (AFPEQ), will be a step toward this goal.

Cultural Transformation by a Revitalization Movement

As individuals take up the cause of personal and societal salvation preached by the Revitalization Movement, individual symptoms of stress reduce rapidly. As a result of multiple "conversions" to a successful Revitalization Movement, the symptoms of cultural distortion are reduced, being replaced by an enthusiastic embracing of an organized program of group action. Wallace says that the transformation of the culture happens most effectively when a movement has the support of a controlling portion of the population. This control can be measured by the sheer numbers of converts, or by the strategic roles that certain converts play in the leadership structures of their society. By exerting its influence, the movement is able to bring into public policy elements of the "goal culture." Thus the religious teachings of the Revitalization Movement are not relegated only to private life. The movement may not necessarily control the beliefs or the votes of a majority of citizens. It is, however, a credible, publicly recognized voice that is part of the cultural landscape. In the exchange of ideas in public debate, many members of the society will choose to follow the teachings of the new vision because they are convinced of its advantages for them and their society as a whole.

Another indication of the transformation of the society is when the Revitalization Movement has demonstrated that it includes a successful economic system. Some Revitalization Movements must perform major changes in the economic system to set their society on the road to prosperity after cataclysmic failures. Some movements limit their reforms to certain aspects of the whole (such as establishing a new work ethic, banning slavery or returning to a market economy). Wallace's key concept is that the organizations that embody the Revitalization Movement must themselves be economically viable and they must propose economic guidelines that are realistic and beneficial for the society in general.

Cultural Transformation as a Result of the Québec Revival

The Québec media have yet to finish "settling accounts" with past abuses by the Catholic Church. "Church" in general and obedience to a "divine" code in particular are concepts that carry negative connotations in the public arena and are viewed with suspicion on the personal level. Québécois are no longer rethinking the answers proposed to them by Christianity. They have generally come to believe that no answers are possible.

Québécois evangelicals have a huge challenge engaging their culture in the public arena. The efforts of the major denominations and parachurch ministries are still woefully marginal in a society whose older generations (Builders and Boomers) saw the Gospel pass by, and decided that the Church (Catholic or evangelical) was not for them. With a few exceptions, the Baby Busters who are not in acute crises are generally untouched by evangelical ministries.

Even with all the boom conversions and church planting, Québécois evangelicals account for about one-half of one percent of the French Canadian population in most areas of the province. The one happy exception is the town of Granby which has an evangelical penetration of about 3% of the population. The evangelical churches in the Granby area have a united, positive public image. Granby area pastors are "on a roll," talking optimistically of moving ahead with more aggressive church growth and participation in the public life of their region. One Granby pastor said recently, "We want Granby to start taking evangelicals seriously." Unfortunately, few pastors in other parts of Québec feel any momentum for entertaining such thoughts.

Sensing the need to develop a higher level of public visibility and credibility, the "Québec pour Jésus" evangelists turned deliberately from "conversion crusades" to credibility campaigns. Singer-evangelist Richard Toupin tried (with mixed success) to penetrate the public media with his high-quality concerts and recordings. Jacques Marcoux shifted his focus to teach young Québécois men how to make real transformations in their relationships at home and at work. Christian Direction's heavy involvement in public education, YWAM's (Youth With A Mission) street ministry to Montreal's gay community and other specific public ministries to Québec's needy all show that the evangelical movement is taking up the challenge not to stay shut out of the public arena.

Whether by choice or by force, Québécois evangelical churches are facing the challenge of demonstrating the economic viability of their new vision. It is not so much for lack of leaders nor for lack of outreach ministries that evangelical churches are regrouping for survival. Their struggle is mainly economic. As we have seen, the end of the Organization Phase left many daughter churches in the beginning stages of growth without the influx of new, employed believers to complete their planned expansion. Montreal's profound political and economic difficulties have only compounded the lack of internal resources. Since the early 1990s the evangelical movement has been "downsizing" the number of Québécois churches and at the same time upgrading the size and quality of those churches which have survived. Given the realities and challenges of this phase of the revival cycle, we must not be too concerned at the loss. But we must keep asking when, where and how to begin planting new churches that will be better equipped to overcome the now less favourable growing conditions.

Routinization of the Revitalization Movement

As the Revitalization Movement progresses through its phases, the organizations that carry the new vision must sooner or later take on an additional focus, that of routinization. The innovations that initially caused some to convert to the new movement soon become "normal" because of their proven ability to reduce stress in individuals and in the society. As these innovations become routine, the movement's organization no longer has the role of bringing about change, but rather that of maintaining the gains of the accepted innovations. The only responsibilities that the organization retains are those of: 1) preserving and interpreting the doctrine and practices of the movement, 2) reminding the society of the history of the movement and 3) maintaining a system of transfer of leadership. The transmission of the beliefs of the movement to the next generation, and more specifically handing the reins of power of the organization over to a new generation of leaders, is a crucial step in the Routinization Phase.

Ironically, the elements that brought revitalization; i.e., rapid restructuring of a new way of life and dynamic preaching by revitalized leaders, are now of little use and may even be censured because the focus of the organization has changed from innovation to maintenance. The drive of the movement's leaders changes from engaging and influencing the whole society to maintaining the purity and practice of their specific organizations. Wallace says that religious Revitalization Movements reduce their expectations from being forces for cultural change to maintaining themselves as denominations.

The children born in the movement face a very different set of motivations from those of their revitalized parents. Whereas joining the movement in the first generation was a question of tearing down the old way and rebuilding a new order, the challenge for the second generation is to appreciate and preserve the heritage handed down to them. If the first generation leaders and members are not able to meet this challenge their movement will basically die out with them. If the young people of the movement are able to successfully embrace the vision of their parents and if they are given permission to continue to adapt it to their world, then the movement will have completed the Routinization Phase and is heading into a new Steady State. Hence McLoughlin observes that each Revitalization cycle, from increased individual stress through the completion of the Routinization Phase, takes from 30 to 40 years, the time required for a new generation to embrace and live out freely the full consequences of the new vision.

Routinization of the Québec Revival

The dynamics of the Routinization Phase are presently very apparent in the Québécois evangelical movement. In the late 1970s almost every denomination attempted to start a school to meet the pressing needs for leadership training. Since that first wave of excitement, a handful of training centres has been able to focus their programs for a particular niche of the evangelical student clientele. Another indication of the change from organization to routinization is the shift away from evangelism and church planting. The young Québécois leaders want formal, high-quality education so they can become recognized teachers. One school's recent motto reflects the agenda of the Routinization Phase that now characterizes the evangelical movement: "20 years already, let's transmit our heritage!"

Some of the first Québécois pastors of the revival have continued innovatively formulating their doctrine and practice in ways that have caused friction and division within their denominations. Some of the strongest leaders have left and divided the very denominations they helped found. Innovation is no longer appreciated by the organizations that would rather solidify their gains than take on a new vision.

Evangelical parents are struggling to raise their children to appreciate the value of their church's message and lifestyle. Organizing and maintaining Christian day schools are now primary activities of the evangelical movement. Evangelical youth ministries are just beginning to take shape. Our observations lead us to believe that over half of the Baby Boomers' children do not pursue their faith into their twenties. We have yet to see how the evangelical movement will meet these pressing challenges as it carries into the next generation.

More than 30 years have gone by since the Sermons from Science pavilion launched the Communication Phase of the Québec revival. The Revitalization cycle is rapidly drawing to an end. If we heed the lessons from the revival's phases, wise strategies for ministry in Québec can make a difference for the Church as we "complete the race" at the end of the present revival and as we prepare for future revival.

Lessons to Learn from the Québec Revival

1. Richard Lougheed's research has shown that few people saw the revival coming when it was already well under-way. Even those pioneers who were praying for one and preaching for one were often late in seeing how open the door was for a time. Hence we dare not stop preparing infrastructures for expansion just because the potential for growth seems limited at the moment. The denominations that lacked trained Québécois leaders were the least able to respond at the time of unexpected openness for church planting.

2. The Québec revival started with young adults. Yet young adults are now on the outer fringes of our Baby Boomer dominated churches. If we want to be in a position to "ride the next wave" of disciple making in Québec, we will have to focus on young adults.

3. We need not be too discouraged that the rate of conversions and baptisms dropped after the revival. We haven't necessarily "done something terribly wrong to deserve this." Revivals are a time of exceptional interest and growth. Over time, however, they are not the norm. European francophone evangelicals have maintained steady church growth even with slower conversion rates. Increased religious fervour cannot be maintained by programs alone. We must be creative, prayerful and patient in our present circumstances.

4. Church planters in Québec will see their churches grow if they are able to attract and retain "rebounding" evangelical boomers. There is a significant population of revival "drop-outs" who are working through their own "adaptation phase" after being "burned" by difficulties in their evangelical church experience. Many of these folks are now divorced. A loving stable church can help them

heal. Healthy churches can also attract new believers of the Baby Buster generation. Those who are willing to pay the price for creative, long-haul disciple making will see an increase in worship attendance.

5. James Engel introduced English-speaking evangelicals to the idea that there are many steps in the journey toward repentance and faith.[4] Jim Petersen called these steps "mini-decisions."[5] Our post-revival tendency is to measure our evangelism efforts by the number of decisions and baptisms, *particularly compared to revival time*, and therefore conclude that we are now relatively ineffective. Perhaps we should give ourselves the conceptual "space" to see that any concerted effort to move people up the Engel scale is evangelism, whether we see conversion imminently or not. Evangelicals saw very little fruit from 1900 to 1967. But they were faithful in their sowing. By the events of the Quiet Revolution, God brought Québécois to conversion in massive numbers. Let's celebrate the sowing as well as the reaping.

6. It has been our thesis that the Québec revival came mostly because the evangelical message and lifestyle fit very closely with what the culture was searching for, for a specific time. We are now faced with the choice of either staying the same and waiting for Québec to come around to us again, or of restructuring the logic of our message and methods to respond to what Québécois are searching for now.[6] We have come to a point where we need to rethink, once again, the way we do church, daring to experiment and open to taking risks to explore current modes of receptivity. Neither Jesus Himself nor the apostles presented the "good news" in the same way to each audience. They adapted their message to human and social situations, the dominant religious conceptions, and the capacity for change within each individual. The greatest miracle of the book of Acts was that the Church

as a social organization was able to radically restructure itself to include non-Jews. It was this profound reorganization of doctrine and practice that moved the Great Commission forward.

7. If we decide to rethink our approach, we must be willing to pay a price. Our restructuring may well have to be more profound than adding "contemporary seeker services." We must forthrightly consider two new problems that were not issues in the last revival.

First, the vast majority of Québécois are not presently "seeking" in traditional theistic avenues. The farther Québécois progress as a post-modern society (and research shows that they are farther down that road than the rest of North America), the more unlikely they are to relate to the Biblical concepts of an infinite, personal Creator from whom they are alienated by their sin. A "creed crisis" results—how will we relate the Gospel more effectively given this culture's post-modern worldview? We are in a fresh evangelistic setting.

The second problem is more logistical. Research of the Québécois culture shows their growing tendency to shun all structured religious organizations. In other words, we have a profound "confidence crisis" as it relates to the institutional church in the province. Our present efforts to improve church ministries are helping us to attract and retain believers. This is an important step. But we must not be content with these efforts inasmuch as they do so little to engage the majority of distant and distrustful unbelievers.

8. The Organization Phase that could result from the next mass movement of personal conversions could differ radically from all existing church paradigms. Let's dream a little. If, for example, the Buster generation is really as "colour blind" as some researchers say it is, then perhaps

the rapid growth of ethnic churches in Québec could embrace young French-Canadians in a way that the established all-white Baby Boomer churches could not. There may come a day when evangelicals participate in the restructuring of the culture's concept of what is "Québécois."

9. As we contemplate the history of Québec evangelicalism, we cannot avoid the conclusion that revivals are not the result of our schemes. As we look to the future it is time to begin a concerted effort of prayer for God to work in Québec, first in His church, and then in the population as a whole. Perhaps we should invite all of the Canadian churches to join us in prayer for God's powerful, gracious moving in Québec. Prior to the Québec revival, evangelicals prayed fervently because they were painfully aware that their efforts in evangelism accomplished very little. Our greatest need again is a deeper sense of our need for God to work. What we do in prayer, faithfully and fervently in the "slow times," will contribute to a greater harvest in God's time.

Action Points

✓ Does the rise of New Age thinking in Québec "freeze out" the Gospel at every point? What possible new doors do New Age religions open for us to pass through with the Gospel?

✓ What evangelical ministries should be prioritized in a culture that distrusts organized religion of any kind?

✓ What can be done realistically to revitalize campus ministries in Québec?

✓ Are we wise to maintain racial distinctions in our church planting (English, French, First Nations, specific immigrant groups)? American church growth theories say we should. Under what conditions should we change our approach?

✓ What can evangelicals do to maximize French-English partnership in church planting in spite of the Canadian unity dilemma?

✓ What are appropriate strategies for recruiting new church planters in Québec?

Chapter Notes

[1] A.C. Wallace, "Revitalization Movements", *American Anthropologist*, Vol LVIII, pp. 264-281, April 1956.

[2] Louis Rousseau, "Crise et éveil religieux dans le Québec du XIXe siècle", *Interface*, Jan-Fév, pp.24-31, 1990.

[3] William McLoughlin, *Revivals, Awakenings, and Reform*, Chicago, University of Chicago Press, pp.13 and 205, 1978.

[4] James F. Engel and Wilbert Norton, *What's Gone Wrong with the Harvest?*, Grand Rapids, Zondervan, p.45, 1975.

[5] Jim Petersen, *Living Proof*, Colorado Springs, Navpress, pp.150-152, 1989.

[6] This is one of the important points of Dr. Reginald Bibby's *Unknown Gods: the Ongoing Story of Religion in Canada*, Toronto, Stoddart, 1993 and Jacques Grand'Maison's *Le défi des générations*, Montreal, Fidès, 1995.

Chapter Seven

The Québec Protestant Church

Dr. Glenn Smith

Tucked away in the annals of Québec history is a fascinating yet little known story of the growth, death and now sudden surging rebirth of Protestant congregations among anglophones, francophones and allophones. After briefly reviewing the history of the movement through its stages, we will look at its present state and the primary reasons for this growth, particularly in the French-speaking population.

Preamble

A distinguishing trait of French Protestantism in Québec is its evangelicalism. Any liberal or high-church tendencies have been isolated and ephemeral. The movement, although it lacks a precise, universally accepted definition, includes congregations that can be described by four main characteristics:[1]

1. An emphasis of the new birth as a life-changing experience, referred to as conversion or being "born again."

2. A concern for mission, primarily referred to as "sharing one's faith."

3. A reliance on the Scriptures as the source of knowledge of the Creator and the guide to Christian living.

4. A focus on the life, death and resurrection of Jesus Christ as Saviour and Lord.

To this list, we would also need to mention the role of the Holy Spirit and the importance of the Christian community. As numerous others have underscored, although evangelical believers are often identified with certain Protestant movements, such as the Christian Missionary and Alliance, the Pentecostals or the Fellowship Baptists, they can be found in mainline Protestant denominations and even in Roman Catholic parishes. This is certainly true in French Québec and among allophone congregations in the province.[2]

This chapter has five sections. The first section will provide an overview of the historical roots of Québec and the growth of her urban centres. The second section briefly traces the religious evolution of the province and helps the reader understand the place the Protestant church has played in Québec. In the third section, we will examine the rapid social changes that have affected life during the present period, often referred to as *La Révolution tranquille* (The Quiet Revolution). Although Québec society as a whole has undergone massive cultural shifts, we will examine four trends of significance for the future mission of the church. In the fourth section, we will examine how the Protestant church grew in this period by looking at the initiatives of the largest collective effort of the period, The Sermons from Science pavilion. In the final section, we will examine the state of the Protestant church in Québec.[3]

1. The Historical Context

Paul Chomedey de Maisonneuve arrived in 1642 at the confluence of the St. Laurent and the Ottawa, with some 50 people, 40 years after Samuel de Champlain joined with the native peoples of Stadacona (Québec City) to develop a community, a fur trading centre and a base for future explorations. Upon arriving, de Maisonneuve saw the hill that overlooks the plain from the river. Naming it Mont Royal, he climbed it with the help of the Indians he met that day and planted a cross that was to dominate the city ever since. Local folklore says that he prayed over the area and dedicated the new community to the glory of God. The origins of the city are found in the desire to establish a religious utopia on the new continent.[4]

Contrary to the popular myth about the province of Québec, it has historically been a rather urban state. Urban areas were growing four times faster than the rural regions. This, in part, was due to a massive economic plan initiated by Louis XIV at the beginning of his reign. Over one-third of the colonists to come to Québec during the French era came between 1665 and 1672.[5] Both Mirowsky and Fortin,[6] Lachance[7] and Dechêne[8] conclude that in the period up to the British Conquest (1767), better than 40% of the 65,000 people in the colony lived in the three main cities of Québec, Trois Rivières and Montréal. By 1765, Québec (with a population of 8,900) and Montréal (with a population of 7,736)[9] would have been only slightly smaller than the three principal American cities of the period—Boston, New York and Philadelphia.

From the conquest (1760) until Confederation (1867), Montréal was to continue to be an important commercial centre but stayed relatively small. In fact, it is during this time period that the province was to develop its rural reputation. In 1825, better than 83% of the people of Québec lived in a rural setting—defined in this country as communities that have less than 1,000 people. Considering that the majority of anglophones of the period were in Montréal, the number of French Québecois in rural areas would easily surpass the percentage just cited.

This urban exodus took place for three reasons. First, and most important, was the ultramontanist theology of the church. Because of the increasing anti-clericalism that touched France after the French Revolution, the Québécois held that France was apostate. As Latourette commented, "In few countries did the Roman Catholic church have so firm a hold on all phases of the lives of its members as it did on the French in Canada."[10] The clergy had absolute control of education and worship (part of the settlement after the conquest signed in the Québec Act of 1774) and encouraged people in the outlying regions to preserve the culture and language of Canadiens. Second, an agricultural survival culture was born that was to keep the province alive economically for generations. Farms produced better than 50% of the gross national product of the province well into the 20th century. And third, there was an immigration of significant proportions from the second half of the 19th century. This was controlled by the clergy to protect the culture. Many of these people went to New England to establish the French communities there or to Manitoba to create the community of St. Boniface which is now part of Winnipeg. Between 1870 and 1880, the francophone population of New England would grow from 103,000 people to 208,000.[11]

Since confederation, the city of Montréal has grown steadily, becoming not just the regional centre of Québec, but also the manufacturing capital of Canada. Up until 1980 it was the largest city in the country, and is now the second-largest city in the French-speaking world and a leader in its cultural/political/economic affairs. The comparative Table 32 from Census Canada plots the growth of Montréal since 1871, Canada's first census.[12]

Before embarking on a study of the role of the French-Protestant, it is important to underscore that French Québécois society up until 1960 was amazingly homogeneous.

Table 32

The Growth of the Canadian Population in the Major Metropolitan Areas from 1871-1996

Metropolitan Areas	1871	1901	1931	1961	1986	1996
Toronto	59,000	208,040	631,207	1,824,481	3,427,168	4,263,757
Montréal	115,000	267,730	818,577	2,109,509	2,921,357	3,326,510
Vancouver	---	26,183	246,593	790,165	1,380,729	1,831,665
Ottawa - Hull	24,141	59,928	126,876	429,750	819,263	1,010,498
Edmonton		4,176	79,197	337,568	785,465	862,597
Calgary	---	4,392	83,761	249,641	676,321	821,628
Québec	59,699	68,840	130,594	357,568	603,267	671,889
Winnipeg	241	42,340	218,785	265,429	625,304	667,209
Hamilton	26,850	52,634	155,547	395,189	557,029	624,360
London	18,000	37,981	71,148	181,283	342,302	398,616
Kitchener	2,743	9,747	30,793	154,864	311,195	382,940
St. Catharines - Niagara	7,864	9,946	24,753	84,472	343,258	372,406

Table 32, Cont'd

Metropolitan Areas	1871	1901	1931	1961	1986	1996
Halifax	29,582	40,832	59,275	92,511	295,900	332,518
Victoria	3,270	20,919	39,082	154,152	255,547	304,287
Windsor	4,253	12,153	63,108	193,365	253,988	278,685
Oshawa	3,185	4,394	23,439	62,419	203,543	268,773
Saskatoon	---	113	43,291	95,526	177,641	219,056
Regina	---	2,249	53,209	112,141	186,521	193,652
St. John's	---	---	---	90,838	161,901	174,051
Sudbury	---	2,027	18,518	110,694	148,877	160,488
Chicoutimi - Jonquiere	1,393	3,826	11,877	31,657	158,468	160,454
Sherbrooke	---	11,765	28,933	66,554	129,960	147,384
Trois-Rivières	7,570	9,981	35,450	53,477	128,888	139,956
Saint John	41,325	40,711	47,514	63,633	121,265	125,705

Numerous studies have been undertaken by Québécois scholars that address this issue. Dale Thomson,[13] Denis Monière[14] and Marcel Rioux[15] are only a few that have undertaken this study. But it is Fernand Dumont, sociologist and former director of *l'Institut québécois de recherche sur la culture*, who described this cultural ethos of years gone by where faith dominated the society.[16] This urban past, anchored in a religious world view is a particularity of Québec that is crucially important if one is to understand the mission of the church today. Until well into this century, being francophone was synonymous with being Roman Catholic.

Being Protestant meant one was an anglophone. Although the third section of this chapter will nuance this cultural trait, the ethos of society had been established.

Christian Dufour analyzed the same question and summarized the cultural context as an escape on the part of the *Canadien-Français* into a sort of religious imperialism because they had effectively been excluded from political and economical power as the result of both the conquest in 1767 and the defeat in the popular rebellion in 1837.[17]

2. Who Were the First Protestants in Québec?

Those annals of the history of Québec include the story of a people known as the Huguenots; they formed the first Protestant community in Canada.

The initial immigration of colonists to New France prior to the Conquest included at least 800 French-Protestants who were merchants, sailors and soldiers. They were an urban people who came principally from La Rochelle in France. They were entrepreneurs and contributed extensively to the good economic climate that existed during the first 60 years of the colony. Their spirit of initiative and enterprise, coupled with their ardent desire to found a colony loyal to the crown, greatly contributed to the establishment of Québec and francophone

Canada. New France certainly began with a Protestant collaboration.

Two significant histories of Québec written in the past decade make no mention of them at all. But, as one author has pointed out, "This is another example, however, of 'majoritarian history,' concentrating attention on larger elements or forces in history whose records are more readily available, and so overlooking smaller elements such as minority groups or movements."[18]

Interestingly, their arrival and integration into New France were part of both the Protestant and Roman Catholic reformation that swept France after 1550. An ardent spiritual renewal swept the country, resulting in bold initiatives to worship freely, to pursue mission in the New World and to found colonies loyal to the French crown. From 1540 until 1630 seven of the governors of the Québec colony were Huguenots.

But this Protestant presence was most evident in the founding documents of the city of Montréal. In 1627, in the Charter of the "One Hundred Associates Company," the colony was officially dedicated to the promotion of the Christian faith. Up to that time, the reformation spirit had prompted men and women to explore the New World in order to instruct the native people (called savages) "in the love and fear of God and the holy faith and Christian doctrine." No qualifying adjectives (the Reformed faith or the Roman faith) had been added. That spirit encouraged a strong Huguenot presence.

In 1640, La Société de Notre-Dame de Montréal was created. When those 50 people arrived in 1642 with Paul de Chomedey de Maisonneuve to launch the new city of Montréal, near the site of the Indian village Hochelaga, they carried a document called *Les Véritables Motifs de Messieurs et Dames de la Société de Notre-Dame de Montréal* (known in English as *True Motives*). Its opening lines underscore tenets of the

Protestant Reformation, in which a lay movement committed to the Scriptures would proclaim God's grace by faith. Their philosophy of ecclesiology was remarkably different from the hierarchical structures which marked Québec from the 18th to the 20th centuries.[19]

This cooperative spirit changed over time, however. The Huguenots' influence waned for four reasons. First, they were terribly disorganized in the new colony. In comparison with the strength of the Roman Catholic church, they were far too spread out to benefit from their numbers. Second, they suffered under a spirit of intolerance within the community, even if their presence was permitted. Gradually, the forbiddance against Huguenot child baptism and education, civil marriage ceremonies and attendance at non-recognized worship services was enforced, depriving the French-Protestants of their basic institutions. Third, in 1659, François de Montmorency-Laval arrived in the colony as its first bishop. Sent as part of the Jesuit world mission of the period, he dedicated himself to the return of the church to her Roman roots. His first mass included the abjuration of a Huguenot and he repeatedly called on the French government to stop sending Protestants to New France out of respect for the agreement signed with the trading company, the One Hundred Associates. Fourth, in 1685, when the Edict of Nantes was revoked in France, the French-Protestant presence declined quickly. By the advent of the British period (1763), there is little trace of them.

As these Huguenots were more interested in successful trade than settlement, we get a first glimpse into their theological practices. They rarely reacted to political measures taken against them as a group. Rather, many complied and became Roman Catholic in practice or simply in name. As well, discreet groups were formed and many Huguenots fled to New England for religious liberty.

It would be an exaggeration to call this first presence either the emergence of a sustained Church presence or a true Protestant mission. The lack of continuity and transformative action shows that this first wave of Huguenots in Québec was mostly an economic enterprise. They suffered immeasurably at the hands of restrictions that went into effect after 1627, and especially after Protestants were exiled from France in 1685. One must wait until the 1840s to see the birth of a permanent Protestant ecclesiological presence in Québec.

The next waves of the French-Protestant church in Québec are closely linked to the political upheavals that have marked this province over the past 150 years. After the virtual disappearance of the French Huguenots since the mid-17th century, it is not until 1835 that the growth of a Protestant presence in Québec reappears and begins to grow.

The Conquest, instead of facilitating the establishment of the French-Protestant church, strengthened the Roman Catholic church. The British government could not impose religion on the francophones while maintaining good relations with them which were necessary to prevent their forming an alliance with the Americans. How were they to convince the French people to abandon their faith and language? Opting for a French-Protestant faith was too difficult even for the government to conceive. More and more, the governors (even Lord Durham) respected the Catholic faith and tried to avoid unnerving the bishops.

When revival broke out in Lausanne, Switzerland, in the 1830s, a mission society was born and began sending missionaries to the Montréal area. Henri Olivier, Henriette Feller and Louis Roussy began these noble efforts. Little information exists as to the number or size of the French Protestant churches at this time. The Anglican church had moved away from the French work after the death of three rectors near the turn of that century. Perhaps the report of the British and Foreign Bible Society best reveals the state of French Protestantism leading up to this period. They wrote, "It has been found impracticable to find suitable men for the office among the native Canadians who speak the French language; as this class is a very low condition...in regard to education and to religion."[20]

Therefore, God raised up a woman!

Much of the initial efforts of Madame Henriette Feller were geared to educating youth. The clergy of the period were so opposed to "heretical" education that they publicly ridiculed her efforts and those of the mission society. Yet both Feller and Roussy dedicated the majority of their time to this dimension of mission work. Feller stated that the evangelization of the French Canadian people should start with school. Hardy summarized these efforts in stating:

In its fight against ignorance, French Protestantism in Canada understood...that the education of the young should go hand in hand with moral and spiritual uplifting of the parents...The object of the French missionaries was not so much to teach knowledge as to enable the child to be in a better position than their elders to understand the Truth.[21]

But perhaps their most outstanding success came after the failure of the Lower Canadian Rebellion of the French Canadians against the British in 1837. Feller and Roussy were forced to flee their homes in November of that year and to spend the winter in Champlain, New York. Upon returning to their desecrated homes, they refused to prosecute the French patriots and, instead, used the money sent from Switzerland to feed and care for the poor who were left destitute after the uprising. Previously perceived to be a part of the British administration that was out to deprive the people of their morals and their religion, this new approach changed all that. On May 4, 1838, Feller wrote, "In general, I believe that the spirit of the people is so changed toward us that there is no house that I cannot go into. They show as much respect and confidence now as they showed disrespect in the past."[22]

The response was overwhelming. Within 40 years a new mission society, the French Canadian Mission Society, had eight churches, 400 members and over 1,000 adherents. Soon after, the Methodists and Presbyterians began their missionary activities. In 1847, the Anglicans initiated their efforts. By 1900, there were over 100 French-Protestant churches. This period of French Protestantism illustrates a remarkable shift from the Huguenot period.

The French-Protestant convert was isolated from his family, his work, his school and, therefore, from his language and culture. Not many were ready to pay that price. However, the Swiss and French missionaries were almost entirely replaced by French-Canadians by 1880. The conversion of the well-known French Catholic priest Charles Chiniquy[23] in 1858 gave some confidence and a limited number of converts. As champion of a small band of persecuted Protestants, Chiniquy became indispensable. The English-speaking evangelicals used him worldwide either in person or through his writings to promote missions among the Catholics. In Québec, his efforts, however, helped increase the resistance of the ultramontanist view.[24] After the death of Chiniquy, the French-Protestant community had no social recognition at all.

Some of the English-Protestant leaders and inactive members wanted to avoid a conflict with the Catholics. Therefore, a shift occurred in the mission to the French-Canadians. This resulted in an emphasis on overseas mission to the detriment of local French-Canadian missions. A shift toward teaching a more liberal theology in the Protestant faculties was favoured (opposing the proselytization of

Catholics). Evangelical influence greatly decreased by the time of the First World War. The French mission lacked a *raison d'être* and the necessary structures to build on. In Québec, the absence of schools for French-Protestants was the last straw for the then small community. They were rapidly assimilated in english-Protestant schools (even the few French schools became bilingual) and in bilingual churches. Persecution, Catholic domination in education of all French professions, combined with mixed marriages, also helped reduce their numbers. The most talented French-Protestants left the province or remained to be assimilated by anglophones.

All the Protestant churches suffered. Even the founding of the United Church in 1925, which brought together two-thirds of the French-Protestant churches, didn't help matters. In fact, this closed the only French language seminary. Churches were stagnant and heavily dependent on outside financial help. Without local training, they had to rely more and more on European or English pastors. Apart from a few exceptional pastors from the United States, the Anglicans, the Presbyterians and *Grande Ligne* Baptists, a vision for evangelism was replaced by the simple goal of preserving what was left.

In the 1920s, new groups came to evangelize French-Canadians. The Brethren (since 1927) and the Fellowship Baptists (around 1950) chose Québec as a mission field, while the Pentecostals (since 1920) developed their ministries more from their English assemblies.[25] With an evangelical and even fundamentalist vision (as opposed to the mixed messages of older denominations), these three groups made slow progress in rural areas. They established the *Institut biblique Bérée* (Pentecostal 1941) and the *Institut biblique Béthel* (Brethren and Christian and Missionary Alliance 1948) to provide training for church leaders. Persecution followed. However, the incidents in Lac-St-Jean[26] in 1933, in Shawinigan in 1950[27] and in Abitibi during the summers 1950-1953[28] inspired many anglophones. Such a denial of religious freedom required a stronger Evangelical response. Evangelicals contributed time, money and even entire ministries to French missions. The Mennonites, the Christian and Missionary Alliance and other groups sent missionaries in the 1950s, even before the Quiet Revolution.

During the fall of 1935, J. Edwin Orr, a great Church historian had just started a trip that would take him from one end to the other of Canada. Having come from England, he wanted to encourage people to prayer and renewal. He was anticipating with great eagerness what he would discover in the churches, but he left Canada deeply embarrassed by the materialism and the lack of prayer of Canadian Christians. His words about Montréal were stinging. He said of Montréal,

> *The spiritual position of Montréal is tragic...and little is done by the Protestant minority to witness for Christ to the majority...One of the tragedies of the Protestant churches of Montréal is the dearth of prayer meetings. The ensuing spiritual poverty is a part of a vicious circle—lack of prayer, lack of power, indifference, worldliness.*[29]

3. The (Not So) Quiet Revolution

The year 1960 is certainly an important date in the history of Québec, but it doesn't stand out as its turning point.[30] It was the year that the provincial Liberal Party was elected to power, with Jean Lesage as Premier. The Liberal slogan: *C'est le temps que ça change*, Lesage set in motion the process of secularization of the province (until then, the Roman Catholic church was the major decisive force in the province). With this major shift, Québec was entering into the era of modernity.

The Quiet Revolution—an expression coined by a journalist working at the Globe and Mail in Toronto—refers to the period characterized by the social development that Québec has been going through since 1960. From 1960 until 1968, Québec was rapidly changing in a remarkably peaceful atmosphere. In studying cultural revolutions elsewhere, especially in African and Asian countries where there were transitions from a colonized past to a more modern structure, rarely will one find a cultural revolution that was as quiet as the one in Québec. In 1961, Pierre Elliot Trudeau (then law professor at the *Université de Montréal* and soon to become Prime Minister of Canada) described the necessary changes that Québec needed. He stated that, "Québec needs to free its superstructures, to desacralize its civil society, to democratize politics, to make a mark in the world of economy, to relearn French, to rid its universities of narrow minds, to open wide the doors of culture and the minds of progress."[31]

The change, properly understood as modernity, brought about three new tensions to the Christian faith which had dominated Québec for 300 years: the marginalization of religion, the process of retreating into oneself and ideological pluralism. The Church failed to respond. Not having much sensitivity to social description and no skill in cultural analysis, it was undermined by the worldview that it had cleverly created at the time of the Reformation. Having abandoned, or excluded from, the public sphere of society, the Christian movement no longer had a voice.

Moreover, it is interesting to note that the discussion on "postmodernity" started in the French world through the works of French philosopher Jean-François Lyotard, after the universities in Québec had ordered its study.[32] In medieval Europe, a stable social order rooted in divine revelation gave way in the Enlightenment era to a rational, scientific and never-ending bureaucratic approach to reality.[33] The consequences of modernity included unprecedented economic activities, the exponential growth of technical skill and knowledge, education, the exploding urbanization, rootlessness, mass-media communication and the separation of work from home, including mechanization of work. But this "metanarrative" came apart. In fact, Lyotard wrote,

> *What I am arguing is that the modern project (the carrying out of universality) was not abandoned, forgotten, but destroyed, liquidated. There are many modes of destruction, many names which figure as its symbols. Auschwitz can be considered as a paradigmatic name for the tragic incompletion of modernity.*[34]

The consequences are more than evident. Multiple worldviews and manners of expression, tensions between order and disorder, symbols, the flux of life—all these define the new order. Life is being deconstructed. Ernest Gellner clearly states the reason, "Postmodernity would seem to be rather clearly in favour of relativism, insofar as it is capable of clarity, and hostile to the idea of unique, exclusive, objective, external or transcendent truth. Truth is elusive, polymorphous, inward, subjective..."[35]

Québec society, in general, and Montréal, in particular, began to evolve as postmodern cultures, and neither the Protestant nor the Roman Catholic churches were able to help the people face the changes that were occurring, four of which we will soon describe.

Yet what were the conditions—inherited from the past—which have been transformed in these last 30 years that help us understand its present state?[36] This is the fundamental question we need to explore if we are to understand the cultural soil in which the Protestant church has grown. Numbers of studies have been published on the subject. But our concern points in a further direction with a second question: "How will the church reflect Biblically and pursue relevant mission in the Québec context in the years ahead?"

To answer these two questions, an attentive ministry practitioner can employ an ethnographic analysis of the culture so as to understand how social structures and human behaviour interact and influence the evolution of culture. The Christian practitioner who desires to study "the knowledge and practices of people on earth, the manner they use their liberty to dominate, to transform, to organize, to arrange and to submit space to their personal pursuit so as to live, to protect themselves, to survive, to produce and to reproduce"[37] will find in ethno-methodology an excellent tool. To do this one must master four "heavy" tendencies so as to grasp where we have come from and where we are going as a society and what mission in culture will look like.[38]

But what do they discover?[39]

A. The Decline of the Ecclesial System

The cultural shift in the urban milieu is most dramatically seen in the decline in the influence, power and presence of the Roman Catholic Church in the city. In the years leading up to the Quiet Revolution, the number of priests rose from 4,000 in 1930 to 5,000 in 1945 to 8,400 in 1960. Today, there are less than 3,000 and the average age is 63 years. Although Québecers still maintain the highest level of commitment to religious affiliation in North America (79% still consider themselves Christian and 50% identify themselves as profoundly committed to their faith), religious practice is the lowest on the continent. Only 15% go to a religious service once a week and 5% in the urban context.[40]

Compare this with France, for example. Joseph Moody has shown that from 1861 to 1905, the population of Paris grew by 100% but the number of parishes only grew by 33% and the number of priests by 30%.[41] Os Guinness describes the result:

The churches were neither ready nor able to cope with the explosion...There is no striking sight in the environs of Paris and other cities than the little church, intended for a village but now feebly serving a sprawling urban area. Inadequate by itself, it is marooned from the main currents of modern life and left to its own irrelevance.[42]

Gabriel LeBras, the founder of religious sociology in France studied rural immigration from outlying regions to Paris in the 19th century. Normandy, one of the most conservative Roman Catholic regions of the hexagon was a particular concern of his research. He often wondered if there was not a magical place in the Gare du Nord on which one would step, after getting off a train from the northwest of France, and be transformed from a practising Catholic into one who would have lost all interest in religious issues. His conclusions resonate with similar studies done among working classes in Victorian England. As one British clergyman wrote, "It is not as if the Church of God has lost the great towns; it has never had them."

Québec, on the other hand, had a rather dominant church in the cities well into this century. This has evolved, however.

Local parish studies illustrate the shift.[43] In the parish of Plateau-Mont-Royal, it was found that on any given weekend, some 7-10,000 people attended mass in 1960. Today, that number is 700, or 3%, of the total population of that parish. In a study undertaken in the parishes of St-Laurent, the figures are similar.[44] Even the Québec Assembly of Bishops in describing the church today have stated:

In the course of the past thirty years, the Church in Québec has undergone a rapid and considerable erosion of its membership. There has been a very widespread slackening of any sense of belonging. Driven by some sort of centrifugal force, the majority of the baptized have moved toward the outer circles. The central nucleus has dwindled to such an extent that parishes can no longer count on anything but a reduced number of active members to assume pastoral responsibilities...Can we estimate the number of these active Christians? Perhaps only one percent of the total number of the baptized. [45]

This shift in a major institution of the culture also has implications for the world view and the ensuing contextualization of the Gospel. When initial attacks came upon the Church in the late 1950s, the intent was to restore the spiritual vacuum that existed because the Church was sterile. This included the "desacralization of civil society" to which Trudeau referred. But the end result has been otherwise. Because of the rejection of the religious past, Dumont refers French Québécois as "orphans."[46]

Québec, and more specifically Montréal, represents one of the clearest examples of the process of secularization.[47] Guinness, Gilbert,[48] Gilkey and Quek,[49] all emphasize the evolving nature of this trend on western societies. Far from a philosophy or conscious ideology (i.e., secularism), this process is conceived as "(1) the decline of religion; (2) conformity with this world; (3) the disengagement of society from religion; (4) the transposition of beliefs and patterns from the 'religious' to the 'secular' sphere; and (5) the desacralization of the world."[50] At a time when there is a great need to think theologically and missiologically, it is crucially important to understand the intricacies of this process, particularly in North-Atlantic French cultures. Montréal, Paris, Brussels, Lyon and Marseilles are world class metropolitan areas where religious beliefs and values for a large number of peoples and sub-cultures are no longer a means for integrating and legitimating all dimensions of life. The social significance of faith has been marginalized.[51]

Numerous authors attempt to define and to elaborate theories on the process of secularization—this intersection within modernity of an increasing industrialized and scientific society, religious faith and the decline of religious practices. Some link this process entirely to industrialization and urbanization. Others associate it more directly to the conflict between science and religion.

But a clear discussion of secularization must consider the relationship of religion to the "modern project." From a medieval framework where the social order was fixed and based on revelation, the Enlightenment was born with the hope of a rational, scientific and increasingly bureaucratic approach to reality (remember, we described the consequences of this "modern project" as unprecedented economic urbanization, rootlessness, mass media and communication, and the separation of work from the home, including the mechanization of work). Too often, religious faith is reduced to "human contact with the divine" or a denominational affiliation. This reductionism is another example of how our culture has divided the secular from the spiritual. The discussion of secularization is greatly enhanced when we link religious belief and worldview issues. Religion includes that which one holds to be of ultimate importance. As Paul Tillich said, "Religion is the substance of culture and culture the form of religion."[52]

From a Biblical point of view, no one can escape the religious aspects of life; God is ever present in the affairs of all people and cultures. One can do with the Creator what one wants—worship, love, hate or run, but God cannot be ignored. The sense of God is still what Calvin referred to as *semen religionis*, the seed of religion. Secularization implies a decline in the ability of traditional beliefs to bring meaning to life for large numbers of individuals and cultures as a whole. It includes the reshaping of the "religious components" of a worldview and initiates the transfer of beliefs and values from the religious sphere to the secular sphere. It leads to the desacralization of the world.

The past prestige of faith has lost out to technology and the modern economy. Certainly there are exceptions to this process and the extent of its influence. But it is real. Church structures have been increasingly marginalized.

In Québec, this phenomenon is in many ways relatively new. The message that Pierre Elliot Trudeau conveyed in 1961 was hardly a brave agenda; yet, contextually, it was a radical cry.

B. The Rise of the Educational System

In the election of 1960, Jean Lesage advanced the reform of the antiquated educational system as a major plank in his series of election promises. Stealing an image from the days of the conquest, when high birth rates were viewed as the way to protect the culture, he stated, "The revenge of the cradle is no longer enough, we need the reconquest of the brains."[53] This stands in stark contrast to the intervention of the Québec Solicitor General, Antoine Rivard, in the election of 1942, when he declared, "Education? Not too much! Our ancestors have passed on to us a heritage of poverty and ignorance and it would be treasonous to educate our children."[54]

It is little wonder that Lesage felt compelled to radically alter the state of affairs. By the mid-1950s, only 15.4% of boys completed grade 11. There were very distinct discrepancies along sexual and confessional lines. Male Protestants, by and large, were receiving 25% more funding than their counterparts on the Catholic side and 67% more than female Catholics. Female Protestants were funded 44% more than their Catholic counterparts. Montréal school libraries were in a terrible state and university enrolment was horrific on the Catholic side. In fact, one of the great reversals of this reform is seen in this simple comparison: in 1961, only 23,000 students were in Québec universities. By 1988, that number had risen to 235,000.[55]

The process of reform within the existing educational act included free primary and secondary education for all, free school books and compulsory education up to the age of 16. The process was accelerated when the Parent Report was made public in April 1963. Within a year, the Ministry of Education was formed and the process of secularizing education began. As a former member of *le Conseil supérieur de l'éducation*, I can only salute the enormous and wonderful changes that have taken place in the past 25 years in spite of many of the shortcomings of the public school system.

- In 1965 only 57% of 14 year olds attended school— today 100%.
- In 1965 only 40% completed high school—today 72%.
- In 1966 only 45% started college—today 63%.[56]

This massive reform has had incredible implications on the French Québécois worldview. Today, education has become the avenue to advancement in the society. Although that might not be viewed as radical in the rest of the western world, it is again important to underscore the rapidity with which that principle has become axiomatic in this society. In article after article, the call to a better system of education is now viewed as the way to improve the culture.

C. The Impact of Urbanization

All theories of modernization chronicle the growth of cities. We have already seen the relevant historical data for Montréal. Yet there are three important issues to highlight in this important shift in city life.

First, it is crucial to understand the recent growth even of the city of Montréal. The rural mentality still manifests itself in the culture. This is most evident in the art forms that are uniquely French Québécois. The songs of the *chansonniers* evoke images of the St. Laurent plain, of islands in the great river and of life in rural Québec. Wood sculpturing, photography and tapestry often evoke these same images. Most sociologists today continue to chronicle this rural past. Bertin says that, "the attachment to the land"[57] is the principle pole of attachment for the Québécois. The political scientist, Léon Dion claims that the image of the Québécois as "habitant" dominates our history. Ever since the advent of industrialization, French Québécois writers who do write about life in the city rarely see it in positive terms. Dion pleads for new roots in this era for the French urban Québécois.

This is seen demographically when we realize the transitions that have come upon Montréal and the society at large in the past generation. Table 33 illustrates the urbanization of the province of Québec during this period.

The sudden growth in 1941 by 3% of rural inhabitants can be explained by the vigorous efforts on the part of the clergy for a "back to the land" movement. But with the increasing industrialization required by war efforts in the early 1940s, the trend is reversed forever.

It is important to grasp the recent nature of urbanization in the three distinct francophone societies of France, Belgium and Québec (Figure 20 serves as a point of reference). In each case, the urban population did not surpass its rural counterpart until the 1930s (as compared to 1850 in England, 1920 in the U.S. and English Canada). This has led to interesting national perspectives on urban issues.

In France, the predominance of Paris (now representing 20% of the total population[58]), the system of "departments" and the centralist policies of the national government (to the point where many mayors are also nationally elected officials) have all contributed to a cleavage between the city and the country, or more specifically between "Paris et Provence." In Québec, the recent nature of urbanization is even more marked. Today, the Census Metropolitan Area of Montréal represents 48% of Québec's 7.2 million people.

Secondly, this urban shift was to open old wounds that have always existed in Québec society. As industrialization had drawn huge numbers of French Québécois to the city, it soon became obvious they did not have the same access to economic power that was held in the hands of the English Québécois.

Table 33
Urbanization of the
Province of Québec

Year	Rural	Urban
1931	42%	58%
1941	45%	55%
1951	33%	67%
1961	21%	74%
1971	20%	80%
1981	22%	78%
1986	21%	79%
1990	19%	81%
1996	19%	81%

> *To begin with, anglophones played a dominant role in politics, commerce, professional services and the development of natural resources. They trained francophones who would eventually succeed them. The progress of francophones allowed them to compete with and displace anglophones from certain areas of activity, such as municipal and provincial politics and administration, while creating a dual linguistic and religious structure such as exists in Montréal in education, hospital and municipal services. Other fields, such as finance, were preserved as ancient fiefs while new areas of activity were continually emerging.*[59]

And finally, this very observable shift in both the structure of the city (its role in the lives of all peoples) and the underlying values it purports, has brought about a significant alteration in the worldview. In response to the essential tenets of a world and life perspective, the city has become the focus for the functions of that perspective. It is the Priorities Committee of the Québec Assembly of Bishops that has

Figure 20
Urban Population in European Countries 1800-1950

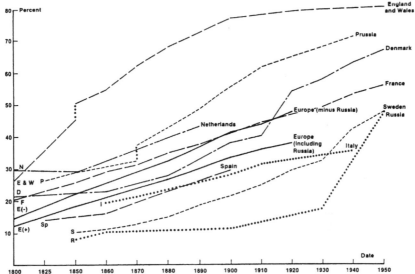

Percentages of urban population in European countries, 1800-1950. (Data from Bairoch 1977:7 for Europe; Berry and Horton 1970:75 for England and Wales, France, Sweden and Russia; W. Lee 1979:120, 231 for Denmark and Italy; Schmal 1981:173-174 for Prussia; and A. Weber 1899:115,119 for the Netherlands and Spain.)

understood this best. Although there is an implicit anti-urban flavour to their reflections, they understand the implications of the shift.

During the last fifty years, Québec society has changed considerably. Urbanization has entailed a dislocation of natural communities and traditional groupings. This society is looking for new forms of communal life; some new avenues are visibly opening up, but it is still impossible to foresee with any certitude which ones will prevail.

Ecclesial life is now suffering from the backlash of these social and cultural changes. It is a whole way of life— which used to be called la civilisation paroissiale (parochial civilization)—that is now inexorably disappearing.

The most visible indicator is the considerable decrease in membership. Other signs exist—the absence of our young people, the difficulty of initiating the children, the very intermittent participation which has replaced for many people their former diligence, etc.[60]

Any effort to contextualize the Gospel in this culture must take into consideration the impact of urbanization on the culture.

D. Ideological Pluralism

That Christians in Québec face diversity on multiple levels is a fact that few individuals would contest. During the past 35 years, the percentage of peoples from different ethnic origins and with different religious beliefs and with varying styles of life or points of view, have come to live in our communities and share our public culture. The growth of this diversity in the years ahead, especially in cities in Québec, will continue.

Cultural diversity refers to the presence of an increasing nucleus of peoples from other countries or ethnic backgrounds. Although Canada has tended to define herself historically as two founding nations, today the image of a true mosaic reigns supreme. For example, among the some 200,000 students in the eight boards of the Montréal Island School Council, there are 168 countries represented. A former European immigration has shifted to a truly global movement.

Religious diversity is also the order of the day. The old paradigm of English being Protestant and French being Roman Catholic has fundamentally changed. Although 92% of Québecers still identify themselves as Christians, Table 34 illustrates the diversity in religious affiliation in Québec according to Statistics Canada.

Table 34
Québec's Religious Affiliations
(According to Mother Tongue)

Affiliations	French	English	Total	QC %	Canada %
Roman Catholic	5,259,145	249,005	5,861,205	86	46
Protestant	101,835	224,585	398,730	6	36
Eastern Orthodox	5,435	8,260	89,285	2	1
No religious affiliation	163,875	51,605	262,800	4	13
Other World Religions	11,705	10,910	100,500	1	3
Jewish	14,100	54,780	97,730	1	1

Source: Statistics Canada 1991 (Languages other than French/English and multiple choice of mother tongue not shown but included in totals.)

Much confusion exists in Québec between cultural and religious plurality. For example, the move to "get religion out of the school" is in large part driven by people who think that the increasing ethnic plurality necessarily implies religious diversity. Because of this pluralism, "religion should not be taught in school."

However, the demographics of Québec schools are a mirror of society. Of the province's 1,037,826 students 97% register as Roman Catholic or Protestant. Even in Montréal, with the ethnic diversity we have just described, 71% of the students register as Roman Catholic or Protestant.

Plurality also has a third dimension—often referred to as ideological pluralism. At the level of one's basic assumptions about the way the world operates, a former consensus of basic beliefs has given way to what we often refer to as relativism. Today, society encourages us to be "tolerant" and in all our thinking to see that there are several ways to believe and to behave and all are equally true. Recently a survey raised the question, "Is what is right and wrong a matter of personal opinion?" Table 35 illustrates the extent to which ideological pluralism dominates the society on this fundamental issue.

Table 35
"What's Right and Wrong is a Matter of Personal Opinion"

Percent Who "Moderately Agree" or "Agree Strongly"

By Region						
National	BC	AB	MB / SK	ON	QC	Atlantic
57	54	53	59	54	65	54

By Age			By Gender	
18-34 yrs.	35-54 yrs.	55+yrs.	Female	Male
65	52	54	61	54

By Church Attendance			
Weekly	Monthly	Occasionally	Never
49	52	63	59

By Denomination			
Roman Catholic	60	Conservative	46
Anglican	51	World Religion	59
United / Presbyterian	49	No Religion	64
Lutheran	60		

Angus Reid Group: July'94; N=1,502

Throughout much of history, most human beings have found themselves in a lifelong, very uniform cultural context. Today, we constantly encounter people of different cultures, religious beliefs and various lifestyles. The suggestion now is that this plurality of beliefs is justified in intellectual, cultural and religious life. To claim that one group has an exclusive claim to the truth is at best viewed as, *"That's a unique perspective!"* and at worst as "arrogant" and "imperialistic."

It is important for Christians to grasp the historical, philosophical move to this advocacy for diversity that we now call pluralism.

The roots of this approach to life came in the 18th century when European philosophy placed its confidence in the power of reason to provide a foundation for knowledge. This confidence is often referred to as *Rationalism*. The idea that divine revelation is essential was gradually discarded. For over two centuries the debate has raged on about how to rationally find "true-truth" and morality based on reason alone. This move created an implicit trust in science as the answer to all humanity's problems.

But in the last century cracks began to appear in the trust people were willing to put in Rationalism. A new movement appeared called *Romanticism* that tried to capture the God-consciousness in each of us. One philosopher wrote in reaction to the scientific-rationalism of his age, "Man is weak if he looks outside himself for help. It is only when he throws himself unhesitatingly on the God within that he learns his own power."[61] Even the painters and the poets of the movement called *Symbolism* depicted the despair of a world gone wrong in thinking and science. There was no hope within or without for them.

The "post-modern condition" of philosophers like Lyotard said that nothing can be known with certainty, history is devoid of purpose, universal stories or quests for truth had to be abandoned, everything is relative. As we saw, truth is elusive, inward, subjective, even polymorphous.

Therefore, it is not hard to see that pluralism, in this sense, is an ideology or philosophy of life. In this sense, it does not just describe a state of affairs (plurality) but prescribes a bias for a state of life where relativism reigns. This describes the net effect of the evolution of Québec in this period.

Yet to fully grasp how pluralism is advocated in Québec society, we need to see how issues get discussed. Increasingly, we make a distinction between the public world of facts and the private world of values. In the former, we discuss "truth" and issues that are viewed as objective and verifiable. This is what we know. In the latter, we find beliefs and issues that are subjective.

Religion, therefore, is excluded from the "public world of facts" in the primary institutions of community building. But as human beings, we live out of a basic set of beliefs, core values or ideas which inform and guide our actions. We act in the world around us in terms of a "worldview" with which we make sense of life and which directs how we live. One's religious beliefs are an integral dimension of a worldview.

We would, therefore, disagree with those who view public reflection as religiously or ideologically neutral or private. Religion or ideology is the ultimate commitment, which provides personal and communal direction to life. It is what is of ultimate importance to a person, community, group or institution. It informs the worldviews, which are foundational to any political plan or, for that matter, any human enterprise in the public arena.

The Christian who wants to engage pluralism in the diversity of Québec's society has a huge task but a noble ambition. The process of engagement must begin with a commitment to contribute to the development of a common public culture. This means we will want to articulate that nucleus of values, those "rules of the game" and those crucial institutions that must be for all a source of profound inspiration for life in society and the glue for unity and social coherence in our culture. This common public culture obviously includes a commitment to the Québec Bill of Rights and the United Nations Universal Declaration of Human Rights. There are some fundamental values we will want to uphold, such as democracy, freedom, equality and solidarity. The "rules of the game" include civility and a respect for minorities. All Christians will be committed to the public good because the Creator poured out His common grace on all the cosmos as part of His care for it.

But our task will include entering into dialogue with other partners in the diversity of today's educational system. We are not suggesting a mere exchange of ideas with those of various points of view, nor are we promoting some polemical engagement that would result in accusations of proselytism. Dialogue in today's pluralistic environment is a serious no-hands barred interaction between competing truth.

Such a dialogue is rooted in the development of full, mutual, intellectual understanding and a respect for differences of nuance and subtlety, particularly in the area of those diversifying "lived values" within a culture of many ethnic groups. It includes the development of attitudes and mentalities within the common public culture, which will welcome the variety of different cultures and lifestyles within a society and sees this as an enrichment of human life. But this dialogue is a process where respectful exchange about differences will take place, not merely a tolerant intellectual assent of opinions shared. In the years ahead, dialogue will be the operative form of evangelism.

4. A Protestant Initiative for the 1960s

The growth of the Church in the period 1950 to 1997 is illustrated in Tables 36 and 37.[62] Wesley Peach[63] and Donald Lewis[64] have done the most thorough studies, documenting the reasons for the growth.

First, there are several summary statements that can be made about the praxis of French Protestantism during this third wave. Although the efforts to be described document a high degree of cooperative evangelism, there has been an increasing sectarianism among the movement over the past 30 years. It is obvious that the success of the years 1976 to 1983 allowed each denomination to content itself with its own endeavours. This is most obvious in an examination of the theological institutions of the movement. Prior to 1970 there were two schools reflecting a theological point of view on the charismatic gifts. By the mid-1980s, within a movement that represented perhaps 35,000 francophones, there were 12 evangelical schools with a total full-time equivalent student body of less than 200 students. This, in large part, reflected the incredible amount of money that came from outside Québec to fund these denominational schools. By 1997 only four schools remained but were more viable.

Second, the growth of the movement has been principally in the rural areas of the province. By 1987, 67% of the French-Protestant churches were in areas representing 33% of the population. This was seen in the Peach study undertaken by *Christian Direction* with *Vision 2000*. Only 28% of the respondents came from urban areas of 100,000 people or more. By 1997 the percentage of urban churches was to grow to 46%.

Third, although the movement has become more Québécois in leadership in the past 30 years, particularly at the pastoral level, at the present time the vast majority of denominational leaders are still males from outside the province. Although this leadership does have an increasing tenure (turnover seems to be decreasing at this level) and a growing sensitivity to the needs of the context (which was described in the previous section), it is obvious that we are still working on the Standard Missionary Model[65] described by Robert Burrows in his text, *New Ministries—The Global Context*. This will probably be reversed in the next decade unless nationalism disappears.

Finally, through the help of Wesley Peach's research, we have an accurate profile of the Protestant movement at this time. Better than 54% of the French-Protestant church is female, 10% having completed a university degree (in

Table 36
French-Protestant Churches Primarily in Québec

	1950	1960	1970	1975	1980	1984	1986	1993	1997
Alliance Chrét. & Mis.	---	2	5	7	10	11	9	10	8
Armée du Salut	---	---	---	1	1	1	5	7	10
Assemblées de la P. du QC	5	10	19	40	80	100	2	---	86
Conférence française PAOC	---	---	---	---	---	---	37	49	---
Ministères franc. PAOC	---	---	---	---	---	---	42	49	---
Conv. bapt. du sud	---	---	---	---	---	5	9	9	9
Assemblées des frères	6	16	20	28	37	46	50	47	44
Assoc. C. La Bible Parle	---	---	---	---	---	1	1	1	5
Assoc. de Dieu Indép.	---	2	4	6	6	10	9	---	16
Assoc. d'Ég. bapt.	5	18	21	27	37	48	55	63	60
Assoc. d'Ég. évang.	2	2	3	44	5	6	10	14	7
Assoc. gén. d'Ég. bapt.	---	---	---	---	---	---	---	---	1
Ég. Presby. du C.	25	3	3	4	5	6	6	2	5
Eg. Réformée	---	---	1	2	3	3	4	7	6
Église anglicane (épis.)	---	---	1	1	2	2	2	20	2
Ég. bapt. indép.	---	---	---	2	6	8	13	7	6
Église de Dieu	---	---	---	---	---	---	11	6	2
Ég. des frères menno.	---	---	3	4	6	12	12	9	8

Table 36, Cont'd

	1950	1960	1970	1975	1980	1984	1986	1993	1997
Ég. du Nazaréen	---	---	1	3	7	7	3	6	6
Ég. év. libre	---	1	2	3	4	4	4	5	4
Ég. Italienne de Pent.	---	---	---	---	---	---	2	5	5
Ég. Luthérienne	---	---	---	1	2	2	1	1	3
Ég. méthodiste libre	---	---	---	---	1	3	5	3	2
Ég. mennonite	---	2	2	2	2	2	2	3	3
Ég. missionnaire	---	---	---	---	---	---	2	2	2
Ég. missionnaire bapt.	---	---	---	---	---	---	---	1	2
Ég. mis. bapt. Landmark	9		1	3	6	13	5	---	---
Ég. Unie du Canada	---	10	8	8	9	10	12	8	8
Ég. Vie et Réveil	---	---	1	2	3	4	1	1	1
Ég. Wesleyenne	---	---	---	---	2	2	2	1	1
Élim Fellowship	---	---	---	---	---	---	---	4	10
Féd. des Ég. Cen. Inst.	---	---	---	---	---	---	2	1	2
Mission bapt. Internat.	---	---	---	---	---	---	1	1	1
Non identifiées	2	2	2	2	2	2	2	36	22
Union d'Ég. bapt.	13	9	7	8	13	16	18	22	22

Source : Rapport annuel, Direction Chrétienne inc.

Table 37
English-Protestant Churches in Québec

	1950	1960	1970	1975	1980	1984	1986	1997
Anglican	280	275	257	246	234	231	256	202
Apostolic	---	---	1	1	2	2	1	3
Assemblies of God	---	1	1	1	2	2	---	---
Associated Gospel	3	3	3	3	4	5	5	6
Assoc. of Regular Baptist	---	---	---	---	---	---	---	1
Baptist Convention of Ontario & Québec	21	20	20	20	19	19	18	15
Brethren Assemblies	14	14	14	14	14	14	14	12
Christian & Missionary Alliance	1	1	1	1	1	1	1	2
Christian Reformed	1	1	1	1	1	---	1	1
Church of the Nazarene	---	1	2	3	3	3	3	4
Fellowship of Evang. Baptist	2	3	4	5	6	15	10	14
Free Methodist	2	2	2	2	2	2	2	2
Independent Baptist	---	---	---	---	---	1	1	---
Lutheran	10	10	13	13	13	12	13	9
Mennonite Brethren	---	---	---	---	---	1	1	---
Mennonite	---	---	---	1	1	1	1	1
Missionary Church: Canada Est	---	---	---	---	---	---	---	1
Pentecostal Assoc. of Canada	5	6	7	8	10	10	10	20
United Pentecostal	---	---	---	---	---	---	3	1
Presbyterian	60	60	59	57	53	54	42	36
Salvation Army	5	5	6	6	7	7	8	5
Unidentified or Independent	---	---	---	---	---	---	---	7
United Church of Canada	240	250	225	220	210	205	210	164
Wesleyan	---	1	2	3	4	4	4	1

comparison with 15% provincially). The occupation profile indicates the movement is largely blue collar. As we have already seen, it is a small city/rural phenomenon. The average person came to faith at the age of 30, having been baptized Roman Catholic as an infant. The vast majority were influenced in their spiritual pilgrimage by a close friend or relative (36% and 47% accordingly). It took an average of some eight presentations of the plan of salvation before a decision for Christ was made.

The rise of this third wave is closely linked with the Sermons from Science '67 pavilion. This particular form of outreach was the result of the vision of a group of lay persons who had a keen desire to have a clear presentation of the evangelical Gospel made at the International Exposition to be held in Montréal for Canada's Centennial Year, 1967. From the date of incorporation, November 24, 1964, until the day the Fair opened, April 29, 1967, a series of crucial decisions and events took place that brought to fruition this vision. In addition to raising the necessary finances to build the pavilion and to translate the Moody Science Films into French (a first for that organization), this strategy became the project of Québec and Canadian evangelicals during Canada's centennial. Over 60 local committees were formed across the country to train people to be counsellors and to do follow up, and over 8,200 people took the courses. During the years leading up to the Exposition and through 1967, $737,000 was raised.[66]

The pavilion showed a film 17 times a day, averaging for the six months of the Fair 5,000 people a day. Besides the films, there were four live scientific demonstrations a day. The purpose of the mission was clear, "Sermons from Science is a contemporary proclamation of the Good News of God for modern man. It is an evangelical outreach of the Church, non-denominational and non-sectarian, pointing men and women, boys and girls to Jesus Christ."

From late April to October 1967, 840,538 people saw one of the films and 261,308 went into the counselling room. But in the context of the Québec we described, it would be important to add the effect that this had on the city and the province. Initial estimates foresaw that 70% of the attendance would be anglophones, representing the some 50 million people that Mayor Jean Drapeau estimated would visit the city for Expo '67. The remaining 30% visiting would be francophones, native Québécois. This reflected the harsh realities of little dialogue between Roman Catholics and Protestants at this time and the extreme ultramontanist theology of Québec Catholicism that was only beginning to evolve by the mid-60s. But in God's providence, those percentages were inverted. It is estimated that one in four French Québecers visited the pavilion. In the climate of post-Vatican II, the pavilion became a context for dialogue and spiritual renewal.

An intricate part of the Directors' vision was a desire to equip Christians with the basics of Christian life. The thought was to both equip as many Christians as possible to serve through this form of evangelism and to then educate those who desired to grow in spiritual life as a result of a decision made at the Fair. As noted, 8,000 people received counsellor training, 1,500 served as hosts and hostesses, 19,000 Bible correspondence courses were distributed and 150 Home Bible Study leaders were trained.

Three remarkable things happened. After Expo closed, the mayor offered to buy the Sermons from Science '67 Pavilion, thereby saving Christian Direction the $12,000 demolition costs. He requested that the Board of Directors consider showing the films in the coming summer of 1968 as part of a new *Man and His World* festival. This decision was to give birth to a new organization, to be named on November 19, 1969, Christian Direction, Inc.[67]

As Table 36 indicates, there was immediate growth (the author attends a church that was planted as a result of the follow-up of the pavilion). This included a new excellence in materials. The French films, Bible courses and documentation were to bring a new calibre of instruction to the movement. Finally, new avenues of evangelism were suddenly available. French Roman Catholic schools and institutions were suddenly open to receiving Sermons from Science '67 personnel, films and materials for use in their classes. These arenas of ministry were to immediately expand the work of an organization that by its charter was to have wound down by the end of 1967.

Within a short period of time, the structure and purpose of the new organization was formed. Yet the summer outreach remained central to the mission. In the nine years that this specific dimension of the ministry went on, 2.5 million pepole saw the films, 500,000 went to the counselling room and 160,000 met for individual counselling.

The new openness in Roman Catholic sectors was to have a significant impact on the province and Christian Direction. Father Jean-Paul Regimbald marked his spiritual renewal at the pavilion in 1967.[68] During the succeeding years, he repeatedly invited Christian Direction personnel to present Biblical programs to the institution he directed, a home for delinquent boys, called École Mont-St-Antoine. Within two years, the ministry was involved in active ministry with the new Catholic Pentecostal Movement that swept Québec under Regimbald's leadership. By the mid-1970s, several rallies were jointly organized by Catholic charismatics and Christian Direction.

The reaction from the evangelical movement was quick and strident. Christian Direction was accused of compromise and lost the support of many people who had worked with it during the 1960s. By 1977, the Catholic Pentecostal Movement was able to attract 60,000 Québecers to the

Olympic Stadium. By 1980, the movement had been eclipsed and Father Regimbald had retired to Mexico. With control by the archdiocese it lost its evangelical reformation spirit.

During the years 1974 to 1976, Christian Direction was actively involved in a new outreach planned for the Summer Olympics to be held in July 1976. *Aide Olympique* was born as a vision of Keith Price, Executive Director of the ministry, and Uli Kortsch, Québec Director of Youth With A Mission. It received the full support of the Canadian delegation at the World Congress on Evangelism in Lausanne, Switzerland, in 1974. On November 1, 1975, *Aide Olympique* became a subsidiary of Christian Direction because of funding problems. Eventually, over 50 denominations and organizations sent 3,900 people to do evangelism, to provide social services among the visitors to the Games and to serve the Church in Montréal during a summer of extensive outreach.

This initiative added a new dimension to the essential ethos of Christian Direction. The executive director was now an internationally recognized evangelical Bible teacher. Extensive travel and influence allowed him to speak across Canada and the globe on the needs in Québec. The ministry was called on to add to its purposes of evangelism and education a facilitating dimension, whereby it was helping agencies interested in work in Québec. *Aide Olympique* was the first example of this. Subsequently, Christian Direction organized the broadcast of several Billy Graham crusades on French television, organized a Leighton Ford Outreach for English Montréal and planned six French pastors' conferences that brought together over 50% of the Protestant ministers and their wives from across Québec.

In 1983, when Keith Price chaired the Commission on Cooperation for the Lausanne Committee for World Evangelization, he cited the example of this dimension of the work of Christian Direction:

The Christian activities of the 1976 Montréal Olympics were coordinated by an ad hoc organization known as "Aide Olympique." Some 55 evangelical denominations and organizations worked together in the areas of witness and service to make a much-felt impact on both the Games and the City of Montréal. It was no flash in the pan. At the time of writing this paper, six years later, several organizations with offices in the same building not only still meet together almost daily for prayer and sharing, but work like different departments of the same sodality.[69]

The autumn of 1976 was a crucial moment for the ministry for two reasons. First, on September 7, 1976, the Program Committee submitted a report that incited the ministry to consider its future now that the focus was away from "store-front ministries" like the pavilion and *Aide Olympique*. It resulted in very serious re-evaluation. Second, on November 15, 1976, the *Parti Québécois* was elected as the first separatist government in Canada. This event had immediate results on the province. In the following two years, 100,000 English Québecers left the province, including 350 companies. The social climate was charged with emotion. But, as Table 36 indicates, this was to be a time of unprecedented growth for the evangelical movement. Meanwhile, the Québec Assembly of Bishops reported that of the 5.6 million Roman Catholics in the province, only 25% now attended mass regularly, a drop from 60% in 1960. They added that only 18% of students in Catholic high schools attended mass.

5. The Protestant Church in Québec's 16 Regions

The province of Québec is divided into three administrative structures. Across the province there are 1,637 municipalities,[70] 102 *municipalités régionales de comté* (MRC)[71] and 16 administrative regions. The map at the conclusion of this chapter outlines those regions. Table 38 gives specific data for each region.[72]

Table 38
Data on Québec's 16 Regions

Regions	Municipalities	Total Pop.	Surface km²	Churches Fr.	Eng.
Bas Saint-Laurent	152	211,146	22,405,067	14	1
Saguenay-Lac-St-Jean	70	294,337	104,035,544	16	2
Québec	94	647,497	19,285,710	17	15
Mauricie -Bois-Francs	181	486,737	46,739,372	34	14
Estrie	115	278,703	10,112,600	18	53
Montréal	29	1,799,254	503,760	64	142
Outaouais	89	306,210	32,859,280	14	43
Abitibi-Temiscamingue	105	155,170	64,879,200	12	1
Côte Nord	57	106,674	300,281,630	7	13
Nord-du-Québec	48	36,832	840,178,090	3	2
Gaspésie - Îles-de-la	70	108,536	20,447,348	8	21
Chaudière - Appalaches	171	382,420	15,116,820	25	4
Laval	1	335,009	245,400	12	6
Lanaudière	83	371,649	13,510,040	13	4
Laurentides	110	415,258	21,554,170	26	36
Montérégie	218	1,273,452	11,066,959	65	83
Population		7,208, 884		348	440

The Quiet Revolution touched the very spiritual fibre of cities. If the urban scenario was discouraging to Edwin Orr in 1935, it is alarming on the eve of the 21st century. The most recent Canadian Census distinguishes five major metropolitan areas in Québec: Montréal (including Laval and the South Shore), Québec (the provincial capital), Chicoutimi/ Jonquière, Sherbrooke and Trois-Rivières. These five urban centres are the home of more than 60% of the 7.2 millions of Québecers. Today, more than 80% of Québecers live in cities of 10,000 and more— it's the highest percentage in all the Canadian provinces.

In light of this recent urbanization, coupled with the nationalist crisis, cities today in Québec show a great spiritual vacuum. Table 39 reveals this in part. In the five cities already mentioned, we find 157 French-Protestant churches. In other words, only 46% of French churches serve 62% of the French population. The other 182 churches are found in cities of less that 100,000.

Table 39
French and English Evangelical Churches in the
Five Major Urban Centres of Québec: 1997

City	1991 Population			Evangelical churches		
	F*	A*	E*	F*	A*	E*
Montréal \ Metropolitan	2,200,000	400,000	500,000	115	180	109
Québec	585,320	10,750	5,425	16	3	
Chicoutimi \ Jonquière	154,240	1,725	485	8	1	
Sherbrooke	119,395	8,610	1,500	10	8	
Trois-Rivières	126,410	1,620	650	8	1	
F* = francophone; A* = anglophone; E* = ethnic						

The English-speaking population of Montréal, the third-largest English population in Canada, are not churchgoers. Despite the numerous churches that embellish the architectural scenery of the city, the English evangelical community of Montréal is one of the smallest of all the urban centres in North America. Moreover, we find 530,000 people from different ethnic groups in Montréal, representing 168 different linguistic and ethnic groups. Less than 30 of these groups have a church that serves them in their mother tongue. A ray of hope is, however, shining among the 50,000 Haitians—there are 75 Haitian churches, of which many have 200 to 300 members.

For over 25 years, Christian Direction attempted to study the state of the Church in Montréal. Table 40 illustrates the progression of the French-Protestant movement in the greater Montréal region.

Table 40
**French-Protestant Churches in the Montréal Area
from 1980 to 1997**

	1980	1984	1993	1997
Island of Montréal	37	50	66	60
South Shore	12	26	29	23
Laval	8	7	11	12
North Shore	7	13	18	20
Total	**64**	**96**	**124**	**115**

A definite growth has been registered in the number of churches of the region. In the suburbs, the growth rate surpassed the 100% mark. On the Island of Montréal, though, the rate was less with only 78%; it is much lower on the Island of Laval. On both islands, the attendance remains low (for example, less than 1,400 persons in the 11 churches in Laval, of which 80% of the attendance is found in two of these churches). In the research, we found an average of 80 adults in the churches on the Island of Montréal. Also seen, a definite movement of closing down small churches (less that 30 persons) to be able to have more stable groups where the services offered will be more efficient. This trend exists also because a change in leadership has occurred. More and more, there is a growing need for a well-trained leadership for ministry in the urban context.

Today's largest Protestant and evangelical movements in Québec trace their roots to the post-World War I era. The *Union d'Églises baptistes françaises au Canada*, the descendants of Madame Feller's work and the *Grande Ligne Mission* is the only denomination from the 19th century that has seen significant renewal. As one of the branches of the Canadian Baptist Federation, today it counts 24 churches, with 1,200 members and adherents. Although the denomination began to decline at the end of World War II, like all French denominations life returned in the 1960s and 1970s, when the social climate brought new questioning from the population at large. From six churches in 1963, the Union had 16 congregations by 1980.

The three largest French denominations—the Pentecostals, the Fellowship Baptists, and the Christian (Plymouth) Brethren—also have their roots in the post-World War I era, but find their greatest growth beginning in the 1960s.

The Eastern Ontario and Québec division of the Pentecostal Assemblies of Canada (PAOC) has a long history of English work in Montréal. In 1921 ministry in French began and by 1941 the first French language Bible School *(Institut biblique Bérée)* was born. Although church growth was terribly slow, faithful workers plodded on. By 1970 there were 19 congregations. In 1974 a difference of opinion over strategy took place and the denomination split along administrative lines. Today the PAOC has reconciled these differences and has a new school, called *l'Institut biblique du Québec.*

The *Association d'Églises baptistes évangéliques* (Fellowship Baptist) traces its work to the 1950s. More than one Baptist pastor was jailed in the 1950s for door-to-door evangelism and church planting efforts. By 1980 there were 31 congregations. The Association launched a school of theological education by extension *(SEMBEQ)* in 1973. Today there are 70 churches with some 7,000 adherents.

The Christian Brethren have a rich history in Québec. The first French assembly began in 1927. Through the gentle, quiet leadership of people like Dr. Arthur Hill in Sherbrooke, steady growth took place. By the 1960s there were 12 French Brethren assemblies and 12 English Brethren assemblies. Today there are still 12 English congregations but over 40 French assemblies. The lay initiatives of the Brethren were also seen in the parachurch ministries in Québec. They provided leadership in helping launch ministries like *Inter-Varsity, Groupes Bibliques Universitaires, Christian Direction* and the first interdenominational Bible school, *Institut biblique Béthel*, in Sherbrooke.

As Table 36 illustrates, the surge of French churches took place in the early 1970s at a time of great social upheaval, marked by the events of the October 1970 crisis and the election of the *Parti Québécois* in 1976. Church growth in the 1970s exploded as groups like the Christian and Missionary Alliance (begun in the 1950s), the Mennonite Brethren (started in 1963), the Associated Gospel Churches and the Evangelical Free Church planted scores of new churches.

The 1980s saw the arrival of French churches affiliated with the Nazarene Church and a renewal of French work with the Salvation Army.

Three very interesting trends began to take place. First, the mainline denominations saw a renewal in their French ministries. In 1988 the *Église Réformée de Québec* denomination was formed of various congregations affiliated with the Presbyterian Church and the Christian Reformed Church. The Anglican Diocese of Montréal, with five ethnic French parishes, has prioritized French mission for the 1990s.

But this data leaves one major question unanswered. What is the internal state of the Church? As we have not attempted to determine the size of these churches, is there anything we can learn about the inner dynamics of Protestant church life in urban ministry in the French western world?

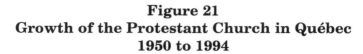

Figure 21
Growth of the Protestant Church in Québec
1950 to 1994

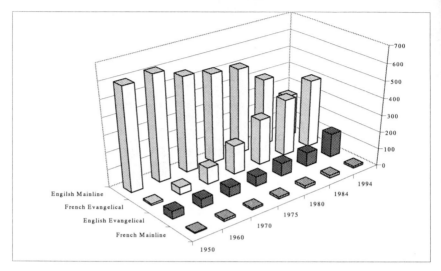

From personal visits to each of these cities and interviews with over 100 urban practitioners, six themes constantly resurface in work across Québec.

1. Monumental doctrinal tensions divide the Church in each of these cities. These divisions follow traditional parameters, yet are a major obstacle to joint initiatives in reaching the city. A major effort organized by the Billy Graham Evangelistic Association sought to bridge these issues. History will record if there was any long-term effect.

2. A diligent search for relevant evangelistic strategy dominates many discussions. There is a definite desire to rethink what evangelism is in Québec. French mission over the past decades has been dominated by traditional forms of evangelism that have had little effect on reaching people in a post-modern context. Most of the strategy has come from the English world.

248

3. There is a growing consensus of the need for a renewal of lay ministry. In discussion after discussion pastors complain about *"how they are forced to do everything"* and lay people feel disenfranchised from the work of service.

4. There is a massive dissatisfaction with the state of theological education. Very few people feel equipped to deal with the realities of the urban world or understand Biblical perspectives of the city. Theological education in the French world has been very traditional, unrelated to an orthopraxis.

5. Rising costs in Québec cities make renting space and finding property dominant concerns for church planting.

6. There is an increasing concern to understand the role of culture and the Gospel. To use Richard Neibuhr's paradigm, much of Protestantism in the French urban world has been "Christ against culture." For example, in reaction to Roman Catholicism, many church buildings are bare, if not ugly. Somehow, one is able to celebrate the dead from wars gone by on the walls of church structures, but not art.

In conclusion, let us look briefly at the religious landscape of Montréal and the greater Census Metropolitan Area. Québec's most populated region is the Island of Montréal. Table 41 and Figure 22 describe the region. There are 72,690 people who are not found in the linguistic data because they speak more than one language in the home.

Montréal represents one of the most unchurched populations in North America. We previously described the ongoing, rapid decline of the social significance of religion in a city that has deep Christian roots. This secularization is one of the greatest obstacles to the evangelization of the city. Today, it is estimated that less than 10% of residents of the island go to church once a month. This decline has resulted

Table 41
List of Municipalities

Municipalities	Linguistic Statistics			Religious				Churches	
	French	English	Other	Catholic	Prot.	Other	None	Fr.	Eng.
Anjou	30,450	2,570	2,695	33,005	1,770	535	1,360	1	1
Baie-d'Urfé	685	2,945	135	1,370	1,650	290	535	—	1
Beaconsfield	3,425	14,385	1,200	9,285	6,725	1,565	1,960	—	3
Côte St-Luc	3,050	21,100	3,425	3,280	7,985	23,110	1,000	—	1
Dollard-des-Ormeaux	8,270	29,455	6,605	20,030	7,985	16,005	2,620	1	6
Dorval	5,125	10,375	1,030	10,280	4,675	900	1,260	—	4
Hampstead	735	5,880	320	885	375	5,720	240	—	1
Kirkland	4,410	11,395	1,095	10,750	3,870	1,800	1,050	—	1
Lachine	21,425	10,375	1,985	26,705	5,435	1,215	1,495	2	5
Lasalle	35,050	26,495	9,250	55,305	10,825	3,995	3,190	2	4
Montréal	630,650	156,595	169,325	736,160	74,370	111,280	76,240	42	54
Montréal-Est	3,215	330	20	3,260	235	0	165	1	1
Montréal-Nord	63,060	5,890	11,325	74,810	4,955	1,910	2,380	6	1
Montréal-Ouest	305	4,285	470	1,805	1,640	1,205	530	—	3

Note: Cat. - Catholic Prot. - Protestant Fr. - French Eng. - English None – No religious affiliation

Table 41, Cont'd

Municipalities	Linguistic Statistics			Religious				Churches	
	French	English	Other	Catholic	Prot.	Other	None	Fr.	Eng.
Mont-Royal	7,760	7,450	2,035	9,155	2,410	5,390	990	—	4
Outremont	15,670	3,245	3,010	13,895	900	4,695	3,170	—	1
Pierrefonds	17,855	23,370	4,990	29,970	9,290	6,155	3,040	3	7
Pointe-Claire	5,185	20,235	1,300	13,065	10,180	1,615	2,610	—	10
Roxboro	2,295	2,900	460	3,435	1,520	465	460	—	2
Senneville	245	665	50	500	275	10	175	—	—
St-Laurent	27,105	20,875	18,755	35,085	7,835	23,745	5,210	2	8
St-Léonard	34,580	12,865	21,375	65,170	3,040	3,105	1,785	1	—
St-Pierre	3,490	995	145	3,795	595	125	315	—	—
Ste-Anne-de-Bellvue	1,485	1,615	125	2,010	745	150	405	—	2
Ste-Geneviève	2,140	780	80	2,510	235	150	160	—	—
Verdun	40,415	15,190	2,730	47,050	7,045	2,135	3,680	2	11
Westmount	3,345	14,835	1,100	6,185	5,430	5,545	2,785	—	8

Note: Cat. - Catholic   Prot. - Protestant   Fr. - French   Eng. - English   None – No religious affiliation

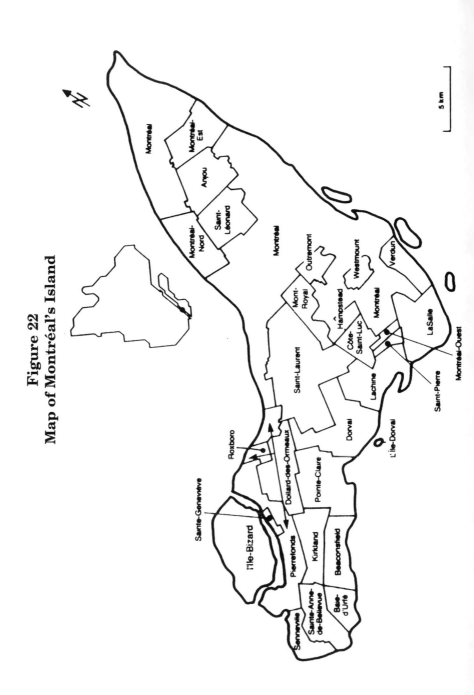

Figure 22
Map of Montréal's Island

in a massive privatization of belief. The result is that Montréalers are pursuing alternative spiritualities. For example, twice a year some 15,000 people attend the New Age Expositions held in a downtown convention centre. Interestingly, over 5% of residents on the Island of Montréal claim they have no religious affiliation. This is one of the lowest percentages for a Census Metropolitan Area in the country. The ongoing exodus of anglophones from the province is a crucial factor in evangelism among this population.

At present there are 60 French-Protestant churches for the French-speaking population of 971,425 and 142 churches for the 427,095 English-speaking population of the island. The state of ethnic churches is described in the description of the Census Metropolitan Area on the next page.

It is obvious that the renewal of the Church in the city and instilling a vision for holistic ministry when only 50% of the active population (15 years of age and older) is employed is a challenge. For the whole area, Outreach Canada estimates that Montréal needs 1,346 new churches. Populations that can be targeted include:

1. **Outremont.** The francophone population of this elite part of the city is largely unchurched.

2. **St-Henri.** This low-income part of the City of Montréal has seen many attempts at church planting, but the results are negligible.

3. **Single-parent families.** Some 20% of the families on the island are led by single mothers. Good initiatives have been launched by French and English congregations, but much needs to be done.

4. **People living alone.** It is estimated that one Montréaler in three lives alone because of divorce, death of spouse and an increasing social acceptance of this reality.

5. **The vulnerable.** The incredible number of people on some form of social assistance underscores that concrete action must be taken to bring the whole Gospel to the whole city.

6. **Youth.** Only a handful of Montréal's full-time workers in Protestant churches minister to university, CEGEP and high school students. These populations represent some 500,000 people living in this region.

Increasingly, the Census Metropolitan Area of Montréal is being considered a city/region by urban geographers and the residents of the area. At the present time, the provincial government is attempting to put structures in place to facilitate policy making and execution. But there is resistance to this from several sectors. Does the rest of the province want to see 48% of the population in one region? This region is presently divided into five administrative regions. Do those regions want to lose their population and power to the Greater Montréal region? Finally, do the residents of Greater Montréal want a city of 3.3 million people created?

The Montréal metropolitan census region includes 102 municipalities with a population of over 3.3 million people. Using socio-demographic criteria we have used for each administrative region, we learn the following information:

- Catholic   2,398,960
- Protestant   252,760
- Other religions   272,330
- No religious affiliation   167,065

There are 115 French churches and 182 English churches in this city/region. Using criteria established by Outreach Canada, this means that there is one (French) congregation for every 18,176 people. It is the same ratio for francophone Protestant churches in the five largest metropolitan areas of the province.

According to the 1996 census this city/region is home to 586,395 immigrants. Table 42 compares the populations for the major language groups in the census region.

Table 42
Mother and Spoken Tongues at Home Other Than French or English in 1986 and 1996 for the   Island of Montréal (Unique Answers)

	Mother Tongue		Language Spoken at Home	
	1986	**1996**	**1986**	**1996**
Italian	115,895	126,820	81,345	62,105
Greek	39,545	41,970	30,400	27,695
Spanish	22,465	60,035	18,015	43,800
Portuguese	20,815	28,420	16,075	16,470
Chinese	15,770	38,565	14,035	32,425
German	14,020	13,070	3,920	2,410
Polish	12,490	16,570	6,100	9,315
Arabic	12,340	53,665	7,300	33,275
Vietnamese	10,080	19,980	11,135	18,890
Hungarian	7,685	7,750	3,410	3,000
Ukranian	7,095	5,840	3,600	2,275
Others	66,770	168,855	44,735	230,350

Island of Montréal only
Source: Statistics Canada (1986 and 1996)

As we saw previously, cultural plurality refers to the presence in society of an increasing nucleus of peoples from other countries or ethnic backgrounds. Québec has historically been known for its two "founding nations." Today the mosaic image reigns. Some 168 countries are represented among the some 200,000 students in the eight school boards on the Island of Montréal. Tables 43, 44 and 45 illustrate this immigration over the past 50 years.

Identifying and counting ethnic churches in the city is not easy. According to the most recent study, the following churches per language and ethnic group have been identified. Its obvious that a concerted effort in evangelism and church planting among all these people groups is a priority in the years ahead. Defining need is difficult.

First, we are comparing the number of congregations per population. But second, certain ethnic groups are more resistant to the Gospel. Special attention must be given to:

1. The Asian population of the city. Some of the highest rates of religious disaffiliation are seen in these ethnic groups. Although Protestant Chinese churches celebrated their centennial in 1996, much still needs to be done among the Vietnamese, Laotian, Cambodian and Chinese population;

2. The Portuguese population. Recently, new efforts have been launched. In spite of census figures, it is estimated that there are 65,000 Portuguese living in Montréal and three Protestant churches with about 100 members;

3. The Italian population. The Pentecostal Assemblies are doing fine ministry here but much is needed; and

4. The Arabic population in the city/region. It has a population of 100,000 people. Ninety percent of people speaking this language are Muslim. But there are another 10,000 Muslims in the Greater Montréal area who come from non-Arabic countries, mostly French-speaking countries in Africa.

Table 43
Churches Per Language and Ethnic Group

Arabs	3	Armenian	3	Cambodian	1	Chinese	7
Cree	4	Estonian	1	Filipino	1	Finland	1
German	1	Greek	3	Haitian	70	Hungarian	2
Italian	7	Jamaican	4	Japonnese	1	Corean	4
Latvian	1	Native	6	Portuguese	3	Romania	1
Spanish	80	Thailand	1	Tamil	2	Ukranian	1
Vietnamese	1	West Indies	3	Zairian	1	Sri Lanka	1

Table 44
Immigrants According to Country of Birth Québec 1990-1993

Country	Number	%
Lebanon	20,049	10.8
Hong Kong	11,713	6.3
Haiti	10,083	5.4
France	9,566	5.1
China	8,852	4.7
Vietnam	5,360	2.9
El Salvador	4,880	2.6
Morocco	4,610	2.5
Sri Lanka	4,560	2.5
Philippines	4,465	2.4
Total of ten countries	**84,138**	**45.4**
Other	**101,173**	**54.6**
Total	**185,311**	**100.0**

Table 45
Québec's Immigration 1946-1989

Rank	Landed Immigrants in Québec According to the Ten Major Ethnic Origin, 1946-1961		
	Ethnic Origin	Number	%
1.	Italian	77,497	18.4
2.	British	75,815	18.0
3.	German and Austrian	47,834	11.4
4.	French	32,001	7.6
5.	Jewish	28,495	6.8
6.	American *	25,582	6.1
7.	Greek	19,579	4.7
8.	Polish	18,384	4.4
9.	Hungarian	13,608	3.2
10.	The Netherlands	9,419	2.2
Sub-total		348,214	82.7
Other Origins		72,640	17.3
Total		420,854	100.0

*Immigration from the United States with ethnic origin non-specified.

Rank	Landed Immigrants in Québec According to the Ten Major Country of Last Residency, 1962-1969		
	Last Country of Residence	Number	%
1.	Italy	39,261	15.9
2.	France	36,041	14.6
3.	United Kingdom	30,629	12.4
4.	Greece	19,699	8.0
5.	United States	17,492	7.1
6.	West Indies	12,115	4.9
7.	Egypt	9,691	3.9
8.	Portugal	9,447	3.8
9.	Germany	9,324	3.8
10.	Switzerland	7,653	3.1
Sub-total		191,352	77.4
Other Origins		55,989	22.6
Total		247,341	100.0

Table 45, Cont'd

Landed Immigrants in Québec According to the Ten Major Country of Birth, 1970-1979				Landed Immigrants in Québec According to Their Birth Country, 1980-1989*			
Rank	Country of Birth	Number	%	Rank	Country of Birth	Number	%
1.	Haiti	21,509	9.3	1.	Haiti	21,530	9.9
2.	United States	19,165	8.3	2.	Vietnam	36,041	7.0
3.	France	16,366	7.1	3.	Lebanon	12,451	5.8
4.	United Kingdom	13,518	5.8	4.	France	11,179	5.2
5.	Portugal	12,366	5.3	5.	Kampuchea (Cambodia)	7,157	3.3
6.	Greece	11,963	5.2	6.	Poland	6,365	2.9
7.	Italy	10,685	4.6	7.	Unites States	6,300	2.9
8.	Vietnam	9,662	4.2	8.	India	6,023	2.8
9.	India	6,999	3.0	9.	Portugal	5,968	3.6
10.	Lebanon	6,575	2.8	10.	Morocco	5,684	2.6
Sub-total – 10 major countries		**128,808**	**55.7**	**Sub-total – 10 major countries**		**97,724**	**45.1**
Other Countries		**102,546**	**44.3**	**Other countries**		**118,779**	**54.1**
Total – all countries		**247,341**	**100.0**	**Total – all countries**		**216,503**	**100.0**

*Preliminary data for 1989.

Action Points

✓ How can the rest of Canada come to better understand Québec and that which is needed to help its peoples come to be fully devoted followers of Christ?

✓ The divisions between English and French Canada, from the Plains of Abraham to the present, seem so great as to constitute a spiritual stronghold. Would you join in repenting for this historic division and praying for God to bring down this stronghold so as no longer to be a barrier to the evangelization of Québec?

✓ With 6 million people at less than .5% evangelical, French Québec is the largest unreached people group in North America. What can your denomination do to challenge this great need?

✓ How can French communities in New Brunswick and other parts of Canada assist in evangelizing their countrymen through church planting?

Chapter Notes

[1]For an excellent overview of the question on how to define "evangelical" see Alister McGrath, *Evangelicalism & The Future of Christianity* (London: Hodder & Stoughton) and D.W. Bebbington, "Evangelical Christianity & The Enlightenment" in *The Gospel in the Modern World*, ed., M. Eden and D.F. Wells (London: IV Press, 1991), pp.66-78.

[2]A study undertaken by the polling firm, Angus Reid, using a 10 item evangelicalism scale based on Bebbington's four criteria, placed 13% of Québecers as adherents to those beliefs but only 2% who identified themselves as Protestant evangelicals.

[3]For a short but clear presentation of the Roman Catholic Church in Québec during this period see Gregory Baum, *The Church in Québec* (Ottawa: Novelis, 1991) and F. Dumont, *Une foi partagée* (Montréal: Bellarmin, 1996).

[4]F. Dumont, *Genèse de la société québécoise* (Montréal: Boréal, 1993), pp.46-54.

[5]C. Dufour, *Le défi québécois* (Montréal: Hexagone, 1989), p.38.

[6]Mirowsky and Fortin, *Urbanization of Poland and Québec, a Comparative Perspective* (Montréal: INRS-URBANIZATION, 1980).

[7]A. Lachance, *La Vie urbaine en Nouvelle-France* (Montréal: Boréal, 1987).

[8]L. Dechêne, *Habitants et marchands de Montréal au XVIIe siècle* (Paris: Éditions Plou, 1974).

[9]Dechêne, p.494.

[10]Kenneth Scott Latourette, *A History of Christianity* (New York: Harper & Brothers, 1953), p.1281.

[11]Dufour, p.66. In the book, *Histoire du Québec contemporain Tome I, de la Confédération à la crise 1867-1929* (Montréal : Boréal, 1989, page 36) the authors note that net immigration from Québec from 1840-1930 was 925,000 people.

[12]Statistics Canada, *Census Canada 1871, 1901, 1931, 1961, 1986, 1996*.

Chapter Notes

[13]D. Thomson, *Jean Lesage and The Quiet Revolution* (Toronto: MacMillan, 1984).

[14]D. Monière, *Développement des idéologies au Québec* (Ottawa: Québec-Amérique, 1977).

[15]M. Rioux, *Les Québécois* (Montréal: Hexagone, 1965).

[16]F. Dumont, *Le sort de la culture* (Montréal: Hexagone, 1987), p.269.

[17]Dufour, p.65.

[18]J.S. Moir, *Canada and The Huguenot Connection 1577-1627* -in *Canada's Huguenot Heritage 1685-1985* (Toronto: Huguenot Society of Canada, 1987).

[19]Louis Rousseau, "Le va-et-vient entre le centre et la marge: trois siècles et demi de catholicisme franco-montréalais." Lecture given at the conference: *Société, culture et religion dans le Montréal métropolitain*, on May 20-21, 1992.

[20]René Hardy, "La rébellion de 1837-1838 et l'essor du protestantisme canadien-français", *Revue historique de l'Amérique française, 29.2* (September 1975), p.166.

[21]Hardy, p.156.

[22]J.M. Cramp, *A Memoir of Madam Feller* (London: Elliot and Stock s.d.), p.120.

[23]Richard Lougheed, "The Controversial Conversion of Charles Chiniquy," doctoral thesis at *Université de Montréal*, 1994, p. 435; "A Major Stimulant for both Québec Ultramontanism and World-wide Anti-Catholicism: the Legacy of Chiniquy," *Canadian Society of Presbyterian History Papers*, 1994, pp.36-55.

[24]Whatever doctrine Chiniquy denounced, Mgr. Bourget the Bishop of Montréal upheld.

[25]Richard Strout, "Advance Through Storm Being the Story of French Evangelical Protestantism in Roman Catholic Québec 1930-1980," course paper, Bishop's University, Lennoxville, 1980, p.48.

Chapter Notes

[26]C. Marcil, "Le schisme de la Saint-Valentin," *L'Actualité*, (February 2, 1977), pp.33-34; *News of Québec*, spring 1986, pp.19-24.

[27]*News of Québec*, Spring 1985, pp.22-23 and Summer 1987; *L'Aurore*, June 1950.

[28]Leslie Tarr, *This Dominion, His Dominion* (Willowdale: Fellowship of Evangelical Baptist Churches of Canada, 1968), p.158.

[29]J. Edwin Orr, *Times of Refreshing* (London, Edinburgh, Grand Rapids: Zondervan Publishing House, 1936), p.45.

[30]At the time, other events stirred up Québec more: the Asbestos strike in 1948 and the riot at the Forum de Montréal in 1955 about hockey player, Rocket Richard. Without any doubt, the television program *Point de Mire*, with host René Lévesque, played a major role as early as 1956, as it allowed international events, explained by a dynamic personality, to come into the homes in Québec. The first two volumes of Lévesque's biography, *L'enfant du siècle et Héros malgré lui*, are an excellent description of the period.

[31]Pierre Trudeau, *Cité Libre*, March 1961, p.3. (Author's translation).

[32]For an excellent analysis see David Lyon, "Post-Modern Canada," *Ecumenism*, June 1997, pp.12-14.

[33]Fernand Dumont believes that the Quiet Revolution was in large part inspired by technocratic rationalism.

[34]J.F. Lyotard, *Le postmodernisme expliqué aux enfants* (Paris: Les Éditions Galilée, 1988), p.32. (Author's translation).

[35]E. Gellner, *Postmodernism, Reason and Religion* (New York: Routledge, 1992), p.24.

[36]F. Dumont, "Quelle révolution tranquille?" in *La société québécoise après 30 ans de changements*, éd. F. Dumont (Québec: INRC, 1990), p.14.

Chapter Notes

[37]Jean-Bernard Racine, *La ville entre Dieu et les hommes* (Genève : PBU, 1993), pp.296-297.

[38]For a more detailed analysis of method, read Glenn Smith, "Doing Theology in the Canadian Urban Context: Some Preliminary Reflections," in *Studies in Canadian Evangelical Renewal - Essays in Honour of Ian S. Rennie* (Toronto: FT Publications, 1996), pp.81-103. Also see note 24 on p.225 of *Espoir pour la ville: Dieu dans la cité*. (QC: Éditions de la Clairière, 1994).

[39]The author would suggest supplementary reading of this section with two works by F. Dumont: *La genèse de la société québécoise* (Montréal: Boréal, 1993) and *La société québécoise après 30 ans de changements*, éd. F. Dumont (Québec: INRC, 1990).

[40]*How Unique is Québec's Religious Climate Anyway?* Study published by Christian Direction, Summer 1997.

[41]J. Moody, *Rechristianization of Religion in Modern European History* (New York: MacMillan, 1964), p.89.

[42]Os Guinness, *The Gravedigger File* (Downers Grove: IVP, 1983), p.59.

[43]See the series of articles in *La Presse*, "Les catholiques de Montréal," August 9-12, 1997.

[44]The study in St-Laurent included an actual head count of people attending all Protestant and Catholic weekend services during the month of February 1990.

[45]Québec Assembly of Bishops, *Towards a Fraternal and Communal Church* (1987), p.28.

[46]Dumont, p.259.

[47]Peter Berger, *A Far Glory* (Toronto: The Free Press, 1992), p.36.

[48]Gilbert, *The Making of Post-Christian Britain* (London: Longman, 1981).

Chapter Notes

[49]P. Quek, *The Promise or Peril of Religion in Modern Society: An Examination of the Secularization Theory*, Crux. June 1987, pp.26-36.

[50]Ibid., pp.26-27.

[51]I think that this definition of the process goes a long way to respond to the questions of Harvie Conn in his article "Any Faith Dies in the City," *Urban Mission 3:5*, May 1986. Also see F. Dumont, "Du catholicisme québécois," *Une foi partagée* (Montréal: Bellarmin, 1996), Chapter 12 for an insider's view of the question of marginalization.

[52]Paul Tillich, *The Protestant Era* (Chicago: University of Chicago Press, 1948), p.57.

[53]Thomson, p.290.

[54]P. Gérin-Lajoie, *Les combats d'un révolutionnaire tranquille* (Anjou: Centre éducatif et culturel, 1989), p.29 (Author's translation).

[55]Ibid., p.51.

[56]Ibid., pp.341-342.

[57]J. Bertin, *Felix Leclerc, le roi heureux* (Paris: Arlea, 1987), p.31.

[58]G. Desplangues, "La population francilienne", *Données sociales Île-de-France* (Paris: INSEE, 1989), p.8.

[59]M. Behiels, *Prelude to Québec's Quiet Revolution* (Montréal: McGill, 1985), p.14.

[60]Québec Assembly of Bishops, p.28.

[61]Michael Greene and Alister McGrawth, *How Shall We Reach Them?* Nashville: Nelson, 1995, p.175.

[62]This research was done by Christian Direction with the help of Edward Hoyer and Richard Lougheed, professor of Church history at the *Faculté évangélique théologique*. Beginning in 1984, Christian Direction asked each denomination to submit a list of

Chapter Notes

congregations for the annual Christian Directory. Confirmation of all information was then done. This chart represents trends, exactitude especially prior to that date is virtually impossible.

[63]W. Peach, "Evangelism - Distinctly Québec," *Reclaiming a Nation*, edited by A. Motz (Richmond: Church Leadership Library, 1989), pp.153-176.

[64]Donald Lewis, "Evangelical Renewal in French Canada," *His Dominion*, Fall 1982, pp.3-11.

[65]Burrows defined this as, ".. a technical term describing the almost universal evangelization pattern utilized by Euro-American churches in the nineteenth century missionary movement. The centre of that model is an ordained clergyman who directs a mission 'station,' the basic unit in the organization of the conversion process. The source of inspiration is the standard and rural, European parish, either Protestant or Catholic; it is this parish structure which is modified for missionary purposes." p. x.

[66]All figures used in this analysis come from the archives of Christian Direction, Inc.

[67]See amendment to letters patents of Sermons from Science '67.

[68]Personal correspondence to Christian Direction.

[69]Keith Price, *Cooperating in World Evangelization*, (Wheaton: Lausanne Committee for World Evangelization, 1983), p.42.

[70]For a complete list of these municipalities including population see, *Répertoire des municipalités du Québec*, 1996, tableau 3.3.3, pp.77-92.

[71]See list on page of *La situation démographique au Québec*, Édition 1995.

[72]*Répertoire des municipalités du Québec*, 1996, p.40.

Section Four

Our Mission Context

"While Paul was waiting for them in Athens, he was greatly distressed to see that the city was full of idols" (Acts 17:16).

Chapter Eight
The Ten Key Findings[1]

Dr. Reginald Bibby

I frequently come across people who tell me that they have "heard something" about my religion research, and then ask, "What have you found?" At first such a seemingly innocent question was somewhat annoying—after all, how does a person sum up 25 years of research in a few sentences? Increasingly, however, I have come to side with the person asking the question. There now is so much data and so many articles and books out there that I occasionally ask myself, "So, in short, what have you found?"

My initial response is, "A lot." The adult surveys since 1975, the teen surveys since 1984, the *Anglitrends* study of the Toronto Anglican Diocese in 1985 and the *Unitrends* national study of The United Church in 1994, the research on evangelicals in Calgary that began in 1971—those add up to a tremendous amount of information that represents a rich and invaluable resource for churches.

I consequently am committed to laying out the highlights with more clarity than ever before. So here's what I consider the **ten most important findings of my research for religious leaders**.

1 – Participation is Down—Sharply

Since at least the late 1940s there has been a pronounced drop in weekly church attendance in Canada. The earliest poll data available, provided by Gallup for 1945, indicate that some 60% of the population maintained that they were attending services on close to a weekly basis at that time. The 60% figure fell to around 50% by 1960, to about 30% by 1980 and now stands at just over 20%.

- Religious group differences are striking: the greatest decreases between the mid-'50s and mid-'90s have been experienced by the Roman Catholic Church in Québec (from 90% attendance to 25%) and the United Church (from 40% to 20%).

- Roman Catholic attendance outside Québec has dropped significantly over the past four decades yet still stands relatively high, at about 40%.

- Conservative Protestant attendance has risen since the mid-'70s and now is the highest of any group, at close to 60%.

Table 46
Church Attendance in Canada: 1957-1993

% indicating attending "almost every week" or more			
	1957	1975	1993
Nationally	53	31	23
Roman Catholic	83	45	30
Outside Québec	75	49	42
Inside Québec	88	41	27
Anglican	24	24	16
United	40	28	20
Conservative Protestant	51	40	59
Source: Bibby, *Unknown Gods*, 1993:4-6; for 1993, *Maclean's*, April 12, 1993: 33ff.			

As service attendance has declined, so has personal religious commitment—although not to the extent of group involvement. In 1975, for example, some 65% of Canadians indicated that religion was very important to them. As of the 1990s, that figure has slipped to about 55%. The drop has been about 10 percentage points for both women (69% to 60%) and men (60% to 52%).

These trends are understandably disturbing to most religious leaders. **The fact of the matter, however, is that the worst is yet to come.** A simple analysis of current weekly attendance by age reveals that churchgoers are disproportionately old: weekly attendees come in at 37% for those 55 and over, 23% for people 35 to 54 and only 14% for those between the ages of 18 and 34.

It doesn't take a brilliant demographer to project the obvious: with the aging of the Canadian population over the next 20 years or so, a dramatic drop in attendance is going to take place—barring some equally dramatic, unforeseen developments.

- Many of today's 55-and-overs—the group most supportive of Canada's churches—will disappear from the scene.

- They will be replaced by current 35- to 54-year-olds, meaning the level of involvement for Canada's oldest churchgoing group will drop from almost 40% to about 25%.

- That middle-age group will be replaced by today's under-35 crowd—meaning involvement for 35- to 54-year-olds will decline from about 25% to a mere 15%.

- And today's adults under 35 will be replaced by today's teenagers and their younger sisters and brothers—the group with possibly the lowest amount of exposure to organized religion in Canadian history.

It's not exactly a pretty projection. There is good reason to believe that **in only 20 years—by approximately the year 2015—the proportion of people attending weekly will drop from today's 23% level to around 15%.**

Translated into actual numbers of people, in just 20 years' time:

- Nationally, the number of weekly attendees will fall from today's 4.5 million to 3.5 million.

- Regular Roman Catholic churchgoers in Québec will decline by one-half—from 1.2 million to 600,000.

- Anglican weekly attendees will drop from today's 220,000 to 100,000.

- The United Church will see its weekly attendees cut in half—from about 400,000 to 200,000.

- The mixed news for Roman Catholics outside Québec is that the church will lose about 200,000 regular attendees, but will still have over one million people attending weekly—easily the most of any Canadian group.

- The most positive news is associated with conservative Protestants, but it's not as positive as many people think. These evangelical groups will experience growth but it will be fairly modest. Evangelicals will add some 200,000 weekly attendees in the next two decades, bringing their weekly total to some 1.3 million people. The downside is that this kind of growth will fall far short of the hopes of "Vision 2000," and may be seen as a failure.

By the year 2015, on an average Sunday there will be three Canadians in a conservative Protestant service for every one person attending United, Anglican, Presbyterian and Lutheran services combined. Outside Québec, the Roman Catholic worshiping total will be about the same as that of the conservatives.

Obviously there are some geographical and congregational exceptions to these national patterns, both positive and negative. All mainline congregations are not declining, just as all conservative Protestant congregations are not growing. Collectively, however, the news is not very good for Canada's religious groups.

2 - Few People are Actually Leaving

The drop in weekly attendance has led many leaders to assume that people are literally being "lost" to the churches. If they are not showing up, the assumption is that, at best, they have dropped out and have simply become inactive. At worst, they have defected to some other group, possibly of the grassroots evangelical variety.

Most of the consternation about dropout and defection, however, is not warranted. As of the 1991 census:

- Some 8 in 10 Canadians continue to view themselves as Roman Catholics or Protestants—in 1971, the figure was about 9 in 10.

- Only 4% of Canadians identify with other faiths—essentially the same as 50 years ago.

- While 12% of Canadians currently say that they have "no religion," many appear to be younger, "temporary nothings" who frequently will turn to religious groups for marriage and birth rites—often "reaffiliating" with their parents' religion in the process.

- Intergenerational retention rates remain high:

  ✓Approximately 90% of Canadians from Roman Catholic homes continue to identify with Roman Catholicism;

  ✓ 85% for mainline Protestants (United, Anglican, Presbyterian, Lutheran);

✓ 65% for conservative Protestants ("evangelical groups" such as Baptist, Pentecostal, Salvation Army, Mennonite, Alliance, Nazarene, Reformed); and

✓ 75% for other faiths (such as Judaism, Islam, Hinduism, Buddhism).

Regardless of their participation levels in religious groups, Canadians are still including religion when they define themselves. They may not be showing up all that much, but they're still out there and they still are thinking that they are Roman Catholic, United, Anglican, Lutheran, Presbyterian, Baptist, Mennonite, Jewish and so on. The more "historic" the faith group, the more likely it seems that people continue to define themselves by it.

Think I'm exaggerating? Frankly, I've considered that possibility myself. Consequently, one corrective I've tried to use is to tell people what I've had in mind and ask them how well they recognize themselves in the descriptions I've been giving of them.

Specifically, in both the 1985 and 1990 national surveys, I asked Canadians who said that they are not regular churchgoers to respond to this statement:

Some observers maintain that few people are actually abandoning their religious traditions. Rather, they draw selective beliefs and practices, even if they do not attend services frequently. They are not about to be recruited by other religious groups. Their identification with their religious traditions is fairly solidly fixed and it is to these groups that they will turn when confronted with marriage, death and, frequently, birth. How well would you say this observation describes YOU?

In both surveys:

- Close to 90% of people who still identified with a religious group but were not attending regularly said that the statement described them either "very accurately" or "somewhat accurately;"

- The "accuracy" figures were just over 90% for inactive Roman Catholic, United and Anglican affiliates; and

- Around 85% for inactive conservative Protestants, Lutherans and Presbyterians.

For all the alarm about defection, these findings suggest that the vast majority of Canadians are "still at home." As I have pointed out in *Unknown Gods*, even when groups would like to delete some of these inactive types from their membership rolls, the truth of the matter is that these people are hard to shed. They can be chastised, ignored and removed from church lists—and they frequently are. But they don't really leave. Psychologically, emotionally and culturally they continue to identify with their religious traditions.

The research is decisive: **defection from the group of one's parents is relatively uncommon.** People may not be highly involved in their group, but most retain psychological and emotional ties.

3 - Religion a la carte is Rampant

Canadians are fussy customers. We have a wide range of choices in virtually every area of life. We can take our pick from an array of possibilities when it comes to day-to-day shopping, entertainment, education, medicine, finance and politics, not to mention lifestyle, family structure, sexuality and morality.

Simultaneously, we keep saying that we have two primary personal concerns—we don't think we have enough money and we don't think we have enough time.

The combination of unlimited choices on the one hand and the perception of limited resources on the other has resulted in people practicing **selective consumption.**

When Canadians as a whole turn to religion, they don't change their posture. They approach religion with the same "pick and choose" mentality that they show pretty much everything else. For starters, they attend when they want. **But sporadic attendance is merely the tip of the religion a la carte iceberg.**

Other results are familiar to church leaders—Canadians tend to accept "the party line" when it comes to believing in God, the divinity of Jesus and life after death, but they essentially ignore teachings concerning sexuality, gambling and capital punishment. People want some services that groups provide, notably rites of passage. But they frequently prefer to pass on preparation classes, Sunday schools and study groups. And, of course, they are prepared to give religious groups only so much time and money. As one United Church board member in Calgary bluntly informed her colleagues in a consultation a few years back: "You people need to understand that I'm prepared to give this church two hours a week. If there's a board meeting on Wednesday night, don't expect to see me at church on Sunday morning!"

The selective consumption approach to much of Canadian life is not just the result of limited resources. **It has its roots in an accelerated amount of individualism.** As I have pointed out in some detail in *Mosaic Madness*, since the 1950s there has been a growing tendency for people from British Columbia to Newfoundland to emphasize the individual over the group or their group over the collectivity. The emphasis on the individual may have been important as a corrective to an excessive emphasis on the group in the pre-1960s. Still, as American sociologist Robert Bellah has pointed out in his book, *Habits of the Heart,*[2] individualism taken too far can make social life at all levels—relationships, family, community, nation and world—extremely difficult. It's no accident that Canada has experienced considerable social fragmentation in recent years; individualism in excess can contribute to a socially debilitating style of "all for one and none for all."

Individualism has also been accompanied by an emphasis on relativism—the idea that "truth and right" exist only in the eye of the beholder. Make no mistake about it: relativism is pervasive. In 1990, the *Project Canada* national survey asked adults to respond to the statement, "What's right or wrong is a matter of personal opinion." Some 50% agreed. In 1992, among teenagers, the figure was considerably higher—65%. **External authority is out; personal authority is in.**

So Canadians interact with religious groups as fussy customers who want to pick and choose according to their consumption whims and personal sense of what is right. They tend to want only fragments of what the country's religious groups have to offer.

The problem is not that people seem to want so much; it's rather that they seem to want so little. Fragments are relatively unimportant consumer items, chosen over systems because they are more conducive to life in our present age.

4 - Religion Continues to be Relational

There is little mystery as to why most people are involved in mainstream religious groups in Canada and elsewhere. **Religious involvement and commitment are learned like anything else. Relationships, led by the family, are religion's centrally important transmission lines.**[3]

- My ongoing research of evangelical churches in Calgary with Merlin Brinkerhoff, for example, has found that, to the extent that "outsiders" are recruited, they invariably come through friendship and marriage links with members.[4]

- It's no different for other groups. The 1994 *Unitrends* survey found that some 75% of today's active members in the United Church come out of United Church homes, with many of the remainder "marrying in."[5]

- Recent Baby Boomer research findings have provided some of the latest and strongest evidence of the strong tendency of parents to pass religion on to their children.[6]

Conversely, **disaffiliation also tends to have social sources.** People whose family members and friends are not involved tend to follow suit. A fairly reliable rule of thumb is this: "the devout beget the devout; the non-devout beget the non-devout."[7]

The research is conclusive for both conservative and mainline churches: **religious groups grow their own, primarily through their members' families.**

Such family sources of religious commitment are readily evident in Canada, whether we are looking at identification, attendance or commitment. What's more, little has changed from the 1970s through the 1990s:

- Almost 90% of Canadians in 1975 and again in 1990 were identifying with the same Protestant, Catholic, Other and None groupings as their parents, with little difference in the tendency to identify with the tradition of one's mother versus one's father.

- Over 80% of current weekly attendees in both 1975 and 1990 maintained that they had attended weekly when they were growing up; all but 5% accompanied by their mothers, 8 in 10 by both parents.

- About 85% of those who viewed themselves as "very religious" in 1975 indicated that their mothers also see themselves as very devout; some 70% of those who were "very religious" said the same designation applied to their fathers.

- In both 1975 and 1990, attendance and commitment were highest for respondents whose mother and father attended weekly and were strongly committed.

Parents are playing the key source role in imparting participation and commitment. The old cliché that "young people represent religion's future" needs to be supplemented with a centrally important socialization point: parents are the key to the religious future of young people. Anyone who doubts such a conclusion needs only to reflect on the relationship between their faith and that of a mother or father—and the relationship, in turn, between their faith and that of a son or daughter.

Precisely because religion is "transmitted" through significant relationships, Canadians—like people elsewhere—do not readily abandon the religions of their childhood. And in those cases where they do, a relationship with someone, such as a friend or a marriage partner, is invariably involved.

Table 47
Intergenerational Identification: 1975, 1990 (in %s)

	1975		1990	
	Women	Men	Women	Men
Identify with mother's religion	86	87	87	87
Identify with father's religion	88	87	82	86
Attended weekly as a child	86	81	81	81
Source: *Project Canada* series.				

This tendency for religious identification to be grounded in family and friendships brings us to religious memory.

5 - Religious Memory is Everywhere

Almost 90% of adults and 80% of teenagers identify with one religious group or another. That's an important finding. At minimum, such identification means that **millions of Canadians—well beyond the 20% to 25% who currently are weekly attendees—have psychological, emotional and cultural ties with the country's religious groups.**

Consider these additional facts concerning people who do not attend services regularly:

* Almost 80% say that they attended monthly or more when they were growing up; close to 7 in 10 were accompanied by their mothers, more than 5 in 10 by their fathers.

* Approximately one-half of those who don't attend on a regular weekly basis nevertheless say that both religion generally and their own religious group heritage specifically are "very important" or "somewhat important" to them; fewer than 1 in 5 indicate that they are "not important at all."

The cultures of those religious traditions include symbols such as family Bibles, family pianos and family burial plots; in those cultures we learn certain choruses and hymns, worship styles, language, theological ideas; we are exposed to particular role-models and lifestyles.

Canadians subsequently feel familiarity in certain religious cultures and discomfort in others.

* A Protestant in a Roman Catholic service isn't sure what to do and when to do it.

* A Roman Catholic in some Protestant services looks in vain for candles and statues, and wonders why the service ended without the Eucharist being celebrated.

- A journalist who has long since thrown over the evangelical faith of her childhood acknowledges that she finds herself wanting to cry when she hears the sounds of *Amazing Grace*—like Kris Kristofferson, she finds that it takes her "back to something that she lost somewhere, somehow along the way."[8]

Obviously those feelings are not always positive. For some, the religion of their parents may be associated with memories and emotions that are unpleasant, sometimes painful.

Yet, even among the disenchanted, what is "normal" in a religious sense is hard to shake. Many are inclined to view the ideas and styles of other religious groups through the eyes of the group in which they were raised. Accordingly, even in wedding and funeral situations, for example, these Canadians feel more comfortable or less comfortable with certain hymns and prayers, words and phrases, symbols and rituals.

Canadians who attend sporadically simply don't wake up on a given Sunday morning and make a random decision as to where they will catch a worship service. **They head in the direction of what is religiously familiar.**

In the 1990 national survey, we asked adults who do not attend services regularly where they or their children turn for occasional services or other activities, such as Sunday schools. We found that:

- 85% of inactive mainline Protestants rely on mainline churches;

- 76% of inactive conservative Protestants turn to conservative churches and

- 97% of inactive Roman Catholics look to Catholic churches.

The vast majority of Canadians continue to have psychological, emotional and cultural links to their parents' religious groups. These links appear to be sustained not so much by religious content as by family history and rites of passage. This is why denominational walls are still in place, in both the United States and Canada, despite common claims to the contrary.

Because of the importance of the point, let me elaborate a bit. I'm well aware of the claims of people such as George Barna, Leith Anderson and Lyle Schaller, along with Don Posterski and Irwin Barker, that denominations have lost much of their importance to people today.[9]

However, two issues have not been sufficiently resolved:

1. If one thinks not of denomination but of "religious families"—mainline Protestants, conservative Protestants, Roman Catholics and other faiths—switching typically involves fairly short theological and cultural trips.

   - While Dean Hoge and his associates, for example, have recently suggested that denomination is not very important to people who were raised as Presbyterians, their own data show that some 70% of their sample retained the "Presbyterian label" as adults.[10]

   - Highly-regarded researchers Kirk Hadaway and Penny Marler have concluded that "the majority of church members (in the U.S.) never change denominations...when Americans do switch, they often remain within the same broad denominational family."[11]

   - Wade Clark Roof and William McKinney similarly have noted that, although at least 40% of American Protestants have switched denominations at one time or another, the figures for those remaining within "denominational families" come in at about 80% for conservative Protestants and 70% for mainliners. They maintain that such findings point to "levels of stability for the larger religio-cultural traditions in America today."[12]

- Consistent with U.S. findings, data collected by Don Posterski and Irwin Barker in 1992 on some of Canada's most active church members show that about 70% of current mainliners and 65% of conservative Protestants were raised in those "families." Further, less than 20% give denomination a "low" ranking as a factor to be considered when switching congregations.[13] My own research pegs the Roman Catholic retention level at almost 90%.[14]

2. Researchers might be confusing **tolerance zones** with **comfort zones.**

- Dean Hoge and his team have found that the tolerance zones of American Presbyterian Baby Boomers, for example, have expanded over the years, but personal comfort zones "are surprisingly narrow and traditional," extending for the great majority "no further than mainline Protestantism," and for many "no further than Episcopalians!"[15]

- Similarly, the *Unitrends* national survey found that although about 95% of United Church members say they would feel comfortable in an Anglican worship service, the figure drops to 70% for a Roman Catholic mass and 35% for a Pentecostal service.

Some of you are undoubtedly saying, "But I know for a fact that there are people in my congregation who come from other traditions." Maybe. Or maybe not.

First, ask yourself if their previous group was actually **outside, not just your denomination, but also your "religious family"**—mainline Protestant, conservative Protestant, or Roman Catholic?

Second, **don't assume that current involvement means that a permanent switch has taken place.** People may attend a given church for highly practical purposes, such as location, children, friendships, a minister and so on. Some Roman Catholics, hurt by their church's attitude toward women priests or divorce, may be attending the local United Church. That's not to say they have switched their affiliation. They're "just attending somewhere." If the home church changes, these temporary residents may well move back.

The distinction is more than an academic one. If people feel no lasting attachment to a denomination or faith "family" beyond a given congregation, their "fickleness" has important implications for their future involvement in the denomination. Their apparent "switch" may be only a temporary stopover en route back to the group of their childhood.

As of the 1990s, this pattern of "involvement without actual identification" characterizes:

- Only about one in 50 people who worship in Roman Catholic churches;

- One in four who attend mainline Protestant congregations; and

- One in three people who attend conservative Protestant churches.

Religious memory typically has strong family roots. As such, it is not easily erased.

6 – Receptivity to Spirituality is Extensive

Ironically, precisely at a time when interest and involvement in organized religion seems to be hitting unprecedented lows, there is considerable evidence to suggest that fairly large numbers of Canadians are highly receptive to the very things that religion historically has addressed.

People across the country—both young and old—continue to be intrigued with mystery. Many have experiences that call for answers that often are not readily available.

- Some 50% think that they have personally experienced an event before it has happened (precognition).

- About 40% believe that we can have contact with the spirit world.

- More than 90% find themselves asking what happens after we die. One in four adults and one in three teenagers think that they, themselves, will be reincarnated.

- Over 80% maintain God exists, but there's more—some 45% of adults and 35% of teens maintain that they, themselves, have experienced God. And remember, for the teenagers that's only "so far"—they haven't even hit 20 yet!

Such beliefs and experiences suggest that significant numbers of Canadians who are not involved in a church are anything but closed to the mysteries of life and death.

Canadians also indicate that they are searching for meaning. It's not necessarily an everyday, pressing thing but, from time to time—perhaps when facing a birth, an illness or the death of a relative or friend, perhaps when coming to grips with a career or marital change, maybe when hitting "a decade birthday" of 30, 40, 50 or 60, the questions are raised.

- Nine in 10 people say they find themselves asking questions such as, "What is the meaning of life?" "Why is there suffering in the world?" and "How can I find real happiness?"

- Some 50% report that the question of life's meaning and purpose is something that concerns them "a great deal" or "quite a bit."

- About 80% or more indicate that they anticipate turning to religious groups for ceremonies relating to birth, marriage and death. Sure, some are responding to family pressures and tradition and are in reality customers shopping for churches with wide aisles and air conditioning. But, as many a minister has reminded me over the years, at least some of these people have a sometimes poorly articulated sense—yet a sense, nonetheless—that "God needs to be brought in" on these events.

- Although fewer than one in five teenagers attend services regularly and only 10% say they place a high value on religious involvement, about 25% report that spirituality is very important to them and 60% explicitly acknowledge that they have spiritual needs.

Organized religion may be in trouble, but large numbers of Canadians who are not highly involved in a church show a remarkable openness to the supernatural and to spirituality.

Given the reality of selective consumption, the obvious question that arises is "how much" and "what kind" of religion do Canadians want...and need?

The "consumer report" I offered in *Fragmented Gods* about fussy customers seems to fly in the face of those who maintain that religion should speak to all of one's life. But then again, maybe not. Perhaps an important reason why people "pick and choose" is because they aren't sure what churches have to offer. Maybe some people aren't aware that some of their interests and needs can be addressed by churches.

Equally serious, **it may well be that the groups themselves have incomplete menus.** Their ministries do not provide a balanced emphasis on God, self and society.

Table 48
Perceptions of Spirituality

"When you think of someone who is genuinely spiritual, how important do you consider the following characteristics to be?" (% indicating "Very Important" or "Somewhat Important")	
Living out one's faith in everyday life	78
Having a basic knowledge of one's faith	76
Believing in a supernatural being or higher power	69
Raising questions of purpose and meaning	69
Engaging in private prayer	69
Struggling to find a faith to live by	64
Engaging in public practices such as worship services	59
Spending time with people who have similar beliefs	54
Telling others about one's beliefs	46
Experiencing the supernatural	26
Source: *Project Canada Survey series*	

7 - Most People are Not Looking for Churches

I find that church leaders are often preoccupied with the question, "What will it take to get people back in the churches?" It's the wrong question to ask.

The research is clear: **the majority of Canadians are not in the market for churches.**

- Only about 20% of adults and teenagers attend every week—and the level is dropping.

- When it comes to sources of enjoyment, religious group involvement is ranked last nationally by both young people and adults.

Canadians are also not "in the market for religion."

- While interest in meaning and mystery is widespread, only about 25% of adults and 15% of teenagers say that they place a high value on "religion" as such.

287

- The teen research, for example, finds over and over that young people express an openness to things spiritual and disinterest in things organizational.[16]

Canadians are, however, in the market for the things that religion historically has been about.

- They are more than interested in "a product" that speaks to the unexplained and the unknown by offering answers that lie beyond the human plane. They are open to—in fact, are fascinated by—explanations of a supernatural variety.

- They are trying to make sense of what life is for and to find out how to make their own existence more meaningful. Many find that their lives do not add up to particular significance.

- One in three explicitly acknowledge that they should be getting more out of life.

- Canadians also want to feel good about themselves, to have solid self-esteem and a sense of personal worth; they want to be able to minimize personal strain and pain; experience happiness and fulfillment, new beginnings and life-invigorating hope.

- And besides staying alive and living well, there is nothing that Canadians young and old say they value more than good relationships. They want to love and be loved and to experience good ties with the people they associate with.

No, most Canadians are not looking for churches—or religion. **But they do express spiritual, personal and social needs.** Therein lies religion's "great opportunity." It's almost an ideal match-up.

- Canadians indicate that they have spiritual needs; the churches have much to say about God and spirituality.

- Canadians indicate that they have personal needs; the Judeo-Christian tradition, for example, says much about personal dignity and fulfillment, resources and joy, new beginnings and hope.

- Canadians indicate that they have social and relational needs; a religion like Christianity attempts to teach people how to experience optimum relationships that start with family and friends and extend to outsiders, to the enhancing of social life regionally, nationally and globally.

Unfortunately, the obvious connection is not taking place.

Many observers assume, in a naïve, matter-of-fact manner, that if increasing numbers of Canadians are not having their spiritual, personal and relational needs met by the country's religious groups, they must be having them met in other ways. Academics, for example, have spoken of "privatized faith," while the media have given considerable attention in the post-1950s to a variety of new religious expressions. *Maclean's* devoted a front cover story to "The New Spirituality," with writer Marci McDonald telling the nation that "a massive quest for a new spirituality [is] currently gripping mainstream North America," and proceeded to discuss how it possibly is being met—everywhere but in traditional churches.[17]

The research to date, however, provides little evidence that Canadians who are no longer turning to churches for needs pertaining to God, self and society are automatically turning elsewhere.

- While some are curious about new religious ideas and may explore and adopt some New Age offerings, for example, most are extremely reluctant to abandon their traditional religions. The result is that large numbers of people are failing to have their spiritual needs met.

- Personal issues such as the need for positive self-esteem, new beginnings and hope for better things have been central religious themes; but they appear to remain elusive goals for many Canadians. While self-worth, forgiveness and hope can be instilled without religion's help, religion nonetheless has been an important ally whose contribution is being sorely missed.

- Interpersonally, churches have at minimum aspired to and encouraged values such as compassion, generosity and respect. It is not at all clear that the task of instilling such basic civility values has been assumed by any alternative source such as school, media or home.

No, Canadians are not looking for churches. But there is good reason to believe that they continue to be very much in need of the God-self-society themes that churches are about.

8 - Most Churches are Not Looking for People

It's not easy to say, but needs to be said: the research suggests that **one of the main reasons why Canada's churches are not ministering to a larger number of people is because they typically wait for people to come to them.**

Look at the data:

- More than 80% of today's weekly attendees were, in fact, attending that often when they were growing up; just 4% of the people who were attending "yearly or less" now are attending regularly.

- As many as seven in ten additions to congregations are active members of the congregations in the same "denominational families." Two in ten are the children of members, and only about one in ten have come from other religious families. When outsiders do appear, friendship and marriage seem to be the key links.

290

Quest in Search of God

Novelist Don DeLillo's bestseller Mao II characterizes our culture as crowded with lonely, isolated individuals and controlled by religious cults and terrorist groups. The book begins with a mass marriage of thousands of young couples by the Reverend Sun Myung Moon, leader of the Unification Church. The event actually occurred in Madison Square Garden in 1982. In DeLillo's account the stadium is filled with anxious, confused parents straining to identify a son or daughter in the swirling mass of anonymous couples. One father muses over the event and reflects: "When the Old God leaves the world, what happens to all the unexpended faith?"

For many, the "Old God" has left the world, but faith and the need to believe have not disappeared. So unexpended faith is swirling about looking for somewhere to root itself, some new "god" to satisfy its hunger. The Church is not seen as a credible alternative.

-Alan Roxburgh, minister and former Director of the Center for Mission and Evangelism at McMaster Divinity College.[18]

- Canada's religious groups continue to have considerable cultural homogeneity: some 85% of Anglicans, along with 80% of United Church and Presbyterians, still have British roots; about 85% of Lutherans come from a limited number of European countries.[19]

- Many congregations and denominations appear to exist primarily to provide services for their active members; consistent with such an argument, congregations, for example, tend to "rise and fall" in accordance with their attractiveness to members who change residences.

Figure 23
Sources of Additions to Congregational Membership

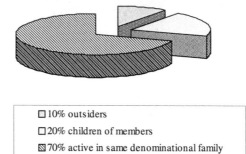

☐ 10% outsiders
☐ 20% children of members
▨ 70% active in same denominational family

I've maintained in *Unknown Gods* that, from an outsider's point of view, many religious groups look very much like "religious clubs," with fairly predictable clienteles and cultures.

If you have any doubts about such conclusions, do what I occasionally do—randomly attend the services of a variety of congregations. You'll discover the troubling reality almost everywhere. **Many churches function as if they are oblivious to the possibility that a stranger could be present.** They call people by first names. They discuss finances. They show no respect for the clock. Of course, if one assumes that only the initiated are present, there's no need to use surnames, to play down dollar problems, or to worry about punctual starting and closing times.

The problem I personally have with "the club" concept is that such churches run the risk of failing to reach out beyond the initiated, in terms of either membership or ministry. Homogeneous churches are not especially appealing to outsiders who, because of ethnicity or class or religious culture, do not "fit in."

But there is still more that needs to be said. **It's not at all clear that outsiders are always wanted.** As one United Church minister put it in a recent conversation with me,

"People in my congregation say that they want more members. If they were really being honest, what they'd say is that they want more money but not more members."

Overly harsh? Perhaps. Still, ethnically, theologically and culturally, a disturbing number of congregations and parishes constitute what amount to "religious clubs" and "family shrines." Their appeal to outsiders is limited, their enthusiasm for the uninitiated in question. In the pointed words of theologian Letty Russell, "Christian communities fear difference sufficiently that they usually spend a considerable amount of time tending the margins or boundaries of their communities, not in order to connect with those outside, but rather to protect themselves from strangers."[20]

There is another way some churches have found themselves not looking for people. Ironically, some mainline Protestant congregations have made a virtue of not recruiting people, celebrating their paucity of numbers. They pride themselves on being—to use a bit of business jargon—"lean and mean." Once in a while, they have even taken explicit shots at yours truly, relegating him to something of a—gulp—mindless bean counter.

To minimize the reality of declining numbers is to minimize the more serious issue: **declining numbers suggest the very real possibility that fewer and fewer Canadians are having their spiritual, personal and social needs met**. Muriel Duncan, the Editor of *The United Church Observer*, puts things this way:

> *Many of us are still repenting a history of forcing our beliefs on those with less power. So how do we now share our joy in Jesus in a just and positive way? Can we go humbly to those outside our churches...who are open to mystery? Can we open our churches to them so we can search together for answers and community, for faith?*[21]

Many of Canada's churches are not doing a particularly good job of aiming their resources at Canadians who need to be involved and/or require ministry. Locked doors, inaccessible stairs, cold shoulders and private gatherings too often send a less-than-subtle message to outsiders. The disparity between the needs of the population and the numbers touched by the churches suggests that far too many congregations are not "looking for people."

People not looking for churches, churches not looking for people. These two realities sum up the tragedy of the current situation: **many Canadians are not associating their needs with churches and many churches are not associating what they have with what Canadians need.** Churches and Canadians are badly in need of connection.

9 - Part of the Problem is Culture

In retrospect, I think that *Fragmented Gods* drew our attention to a basic but very important point: **a major reason why Canadians respond the way they do to organized religion is culture.** The sharp decline in church attendance since the 1940s is directly tied to the inclination to:

- Adopt a belief here and a practice there;

- Want religion to speak to some areas but not others;

- Resurface for baptisms, christenings, weddings and funerals; and

- Not really come, but not really leave.

In short, Canadians today tend to selectively draw items from increasingly diversified religious smorgasbords, reflecting broader cultural developments.

"Don't take it personally," was my message to clergy at the time. "What's happening to religion is happening in every other sphere of Canadian life. Selective consumption,

People Who Need to be Reached

I recently read your book, *Unknown Gods.* I am a member of that huge group of ex-church members you feature in your book—one of the Baby Boomers who withdrew from church life in utter confusion, at the age of 19. Apparently I have never been missed. Nevertheless, I cannot escape from the feeling that I AM a spiritual being, with spiritual needs.

I found myself wondering just what you could tackle as your next topic. Possibly you could look at WHY so many people have spiritual needs, but stay away from the churches. Could it be that my friends and I are not unusual or abnormal in feeling unwanted by, unwelcome at and unacceptable to Christian congregations? Maybe you would like to do some research and publish a book called, *Rejecting Gods,* for most of the people I know who are ex-church members seem to have experienced just that—judgmental attitudes, rejection, condemnation.

I am still confused by church teachings, still haunted by the questions, still yearning for answers that are useful to me.

-A December 1994 letter from a reader.

pluralism, individualism and relativism are being felt everywhere. Just ask retailers, or educators, or the media, or politicians."

There was, and is, much truth to such a position. There's no doubt about it: religion's effort to claim Canadians' time and money, beliefs and outlook, values and behavior, encountered some formidable competition in the late 20th century. Cultural developments, including the proliferation of choices, the increase in exposure to higher education and the rise to prominence of electronic media as the major source of reality creation, have all had a dramatic impact on religion's role and influence.

Still, it would be a serious error to equate culture's impact on religion as totally negative. Culture is only partly to blame. To place undue emphasis on culture's negative role is to invite—it seems to me—at least three inappropriate responses.

1. Those who value faith can in effect **give up**. They can sit back and proclaim that the real problem is the era in which we live. Depending on their theological and historical outlooks, they will use phrases, such as "last times," "post-Christian era" or "post-modernism," to depict the bleak situation. After all, if it's culture's fault, it's not their fault. In fact, it's not apparent to such people that much can be done at all. It might be wise not to fight the inevitable too tenaciously, but rather accept the reality of the times and function as faithful remnants.

2. Perhaps worse, some might unconsciously **give in**, bowing to the selective consumption tendencies of the populace. Believing that "times simply have changed" and that "expectations have to be lowered," such people might make the organizational adjustments necessary to cater to a la carte-minded customers, further fragmenting the gods in the process.

3. Or they can **take too little** from culture—assuming that culture and its creators, including media, education, government and business, have only a negative impact on religion. Here culture becomes something of an relentless enemy. This view overlooks the extent to which culture actually predisposes Canadians to religion, by stimulating, for example: their interest in the supernatural; their quest for more fulfilling lives; their

questions about living and dying and about the possibility of healthy and satisfying relationships; and the importance of justice and fairness, values and ethics.

In short, the problems of organized religion in Canada lie only partly with culture. Certainly culture defines the environment in which the churches "live and move and have their being." But that's only part of the story. Culture does not dictate the outcome of the game. Equally important—perhaps far more important—is how churches themselves function in cultural environments.

10 - The Heart of the Problem is Churches

If the opportunity and need for ministry to larger numbers of Canadians is there, yet the number of people that are being touched by religious groups is actually decreasing, it's hard to escape the obvious conclusion: **churches today are collectively failing**. What makes the situation so disturbing is they are failing at a time when conditions suggest they should be flourishing.

Let's not mince our words: religious groups **are** organizations. If they are to function effectively, they have to operate as sound organizations. No one should act surprised to find that organizational efficiency makes efficient ministry possible, while organizational ineptitude makes ministry difficult.

We don't show such bewilderment when we reflect on the ups and downs of the corporate sector—be they Cadillac-Fairview or the Canadian Football League. When companies succeed or fail, we assume that such outcomes have something to do with their performances. We further assume that, even in difficult times, the best companies find ways to stay alive and even thrive. **Survival and success are not organizational accidents.**

If Canada's religious groups are not ministering to significant numbers of Canadians at a time when large numbers of people are exhibiting both openness and need, then a number of organizational questions need to be raised. In *Unknown Gods*, I focused on four lines of inquiry:

1. Structural Issues

- Religious groups are typically top-heavy with volunteers. This can seriously jeopardize organizational efficiency. Perhaps insufficient attention is being given to optimum use of such unpaid workforces.

- Coordination between national bodies and local congregations appears to be a problem for many religious groups, frequently making the implementation of effective programs very difficult.

- Considerable attention and energy is devoted to ongoing issues relating to social and cultural change. These include considerations of the role of women, sexual orientation, worship practices and theological reflections. In the process, large amounts of time and energy that could be used to minister to others are instead turned inward.

- The image of religious groups in Canada has been severely tarnished in the '80s and '90s by televangelist scandals, sexual abuse cases and controversies over homosexuals and homosexuality. Further, women—in many instances—have continued to feel highly marginalized. The churches, in the eyes of many Canadians, are not associated with openness, generosity of spirit and sheer joy. Such negative perceptions have made ministry to Canadians all the more difficult.

2. Product Issues

Historically, religion has had much to say about three centrally important areas: **God, self and society**. Ideally, the three themes are interwoven, with God first and foremost, giving the other two themes of self and society a unique tone.

- The finding that Canadians are fascinated with supernatural ideas, yet often don't associate that interest with churches, suggests that the God emphasis is sometimes missing.

- Although many Canadians are searching for personal meaning, hope and fulfillment, the fact that they frequently don't associate those kinds of quest with what churches have to offer suggests that the combined God and self emphasis is not always readily apparent.

- Canadians young and old value nothing more highly than relationships. That they often don't associate enhanced social life—from immediate ties to global concerns—with what churches have to offer suggests that the combined God, self and society emphasis is not obvious in some settings.

3. Promotion Issues

The three-dimensional product of God, self and society is potentially powerful. But it is not at all clear that Canadians are aware of that integrated "product."

- Many Canadians, looking at church buildings from the outside, literally do not know "what they do in there." Architecture typically reveals little to the uninitiated onlooker—the guideline for church signs, for example, seems to be "keep it inconspicuous." Most churches in Canada are better known by the buildings, businesses and parks around them than by what goes on inside.

- Advertising is usually limited to "the church pages," read by "church people" who are looking for "their churches." It is not exactly an ideal way to expand clientele.

- Efforts to "get the word out" to outsiders—through means such as visitation and the distribution of brochures, books and videos—tend to take the largely outdated "total market approach," aiming at the entire population. The results, unfortunately, tend to be predictably poor.

Signs of the Times

SIGN. An attention-getting device for the local church. Usually presents to the public the name(s) of the resident clergy, the times of worship and the subject of last week's sermon. Signs are commonly placed in highly visible locations, after which some church group or other plants a bush or tree in front of them.

Andrew Jensen, *GOD: (n) The Greatest User of Capital Letters. A Modern Churchgoer's Dictionary,* (Wood Lake Books,1994:73)

---

4. Distribution Issues

Groups that think they have something to offer Canadians who express spiritual, personal and social needs have to develop ways of connecting with those people. They have to make sure they are getting "the product out of the warehouse to the customer."

- It seems clear that much alleged ministry to Canadians is being done from the safety of sanctuaries.

- Ministry to the world, nation and outsider is frequently delegated to the denomination or "national church."

- Many congregations seem to have become ends in themselves. They exist for each other and become preoccupied with themselves and their way of "doing" religion. Lay ministry means nothing more than getting involved in running the church.

In sum, cultural conditions are making ministry in the '90s tough. But cultural conditions also are such that much can be done by well-run religious organizations.

Some critics invariably protest that I am overestimating both the need and the opportunity. Perhaps. But it surely is incumbent on those who value faith to do everything they can to respond, **before setting limits on what they can and need to accomplish.**

No, not everyone will respond to churches that seek to reach out and minister. Maybe, even with solid, well-planned efforts, the pool of people receptive to what churches have to offer spiritually, individually and relationally will turn out to be only 50% of the population, or perhaps 40%—maybe only 30%.

But my point is that **churches are well positioned— indeed probably best positioned—to respond to the central God-self-society requirements of Canadians**. And there's no doubt that the number of people who have such needs easily outnumbers the people who currently have contact with the churches. What is needed, and needed urgently, is for Canada's churches to do a much-improved job of making contact with Canadians and addressing their spiritual, personal and social concerns.

As things stand, to the extent that religious groups are failing to respond to the needs at hand, the real losers are not the churches. The real losers are Canadians.

Change is needed. It also is possible. That's an understatement. The key pieces of the connection and ministry puzzle have been uncovered by research. What is required now is the assembly.

Action Points

✓ Bibby suggests that churches today are collectively failing and survival and success are not organizational accidents. How do you respond to this statement? What changes to the Church are needed to effectively touch Canadian spiritual needs in your community? How long has it been since your congregation made deliberate changes in worship style, policies or programs to reach your community?

✓ Finding 8: "One of the main reasons Canada's churches are not ministering to a larger number of people is because they typically wait for people to come to them." This being the case, the ratio of "population-to-church" referred to in Chapter 2 is relevant only to the degree the churches in a given neighbourhood reach out rather than wait for people to come.

✓ Count the "go" structures and programs active in your church and those structures and programs designed for people to come to. What will be your next step?

✓ If Canadians are inclined to pick and choose the aspects of their faith they will allow to affect their lives:

a) Which aspects of historic interest in "religion a la carte" can best be used to reconnect with unchurched Canadians in your community?

b) How can you then lead such persons to understanding Christian discipleship more fully and becoming devoted followers of Christ?

Chapter Notes

[1] This chapter has been reprinted by permission of author Dr. Reginald Bibby and the publisher Wood Lake Books Inc., 10162 Newene Road, Winfield, BC V4V1R2.

[2] Ward, 1994:96-97.

[3] See, e.g., Nash and Berger, 1962; Parsons, 1963; Kotre, 1971; Hunsberger, 1983; Kirkpatrick and Shaver, 1990; Bibby and Posterski, 1992.

[4] See, e.g., Bibby and Brinkerhoff, 1994.

[5] See Bibby, 1994:16.

[6] See, e.g., Roozen, McKinney and Thompson, 1990; Roof, 1993; Bibby, 1993:12-22.

[7] See, e.g., Mauss, 1969; Hunsberger, 1980; Ozorak, 1989; Hoge, Johnson and Luidens, 1993:243.

[8] Cited in *Fragmented Gods,* 1987, p.5.

[9] See, e.g., Barna 1991; Anderson 1991; Schaller 1994; Posterski and Barker, 1993, p.53.

[10] Hoge, Johnson and Luidens, 1994.

[11] Hadaway and Marler, 1993, p.97.

[12] Roof and McKinney, 1987, p.167.

[13] Posterski and Barker, 1993, pp.53-54.

[14] Bibby, 1993, pp.33-36.

[15] Hoge, Johnson and Luidens, 1994, p.120.

[16] Bibby and Posterski, 1992, p.53.

[17] *Maclean's,* October 10, 1994.

[18] Roxburgh, 1993, pp.125-126.

[19] Includes "North American".

[20] Russell, 1993, p.176.

[21] Muriel Duncan, *United Church Observer*, November 1993, p.8.

Chapter Nine

Striving for Relevance in a Changing Nation

Dr. Gary Walsh

Introduction

It will be woe to us if we preach religion instead of the Gospel ...Woe to us if we preach inner piety [that] does not relate our faith to the world around us ... And woe to us if we fail to hand on to future generations the unsearchable riches of Christ which are the very heartbeat of the Church and its mission.
- Archbishop George Carey, 1991.

A unique period in the world's history is about to unfold as we approach the third millennium. For many individuals, groups and organizations this occasion is being used to mark a time of reflection and a renewal of purpose. It is a time to look to the past and acknowledge the endeavours that have brought us this far. It is a time to develop new strategies and mechanisms for overcoming challenges. It is a time to renew our commitment to the things that are most important to us.

The Body of Christ is no exception. As we stand on the threshold of the new millennium, the Canadian Church faces unique challenges to carry out its purposes. In recent years,

Christianity has, to a great extent, been pushed to the sidelines to accommodate secular philosophies that exclude God from daily life. Growing numbers of Canadians who would typically classify themselves as Christians now view the Church or Christianity as obsolete or irrelevant to their daily comings and goings.

In addition, the growing diversity of cultural and religious groups in Canada has given rise to a dominant pluralistic mentality that now views Christianity as just one religion among many. There is no special or "exclusive" status granted to Christianity because of its historical or traditional influence on Canadian culture. In fact, in many cases, Canadians may be even less open to Christianity than other religions because of its insistent claim to absolute truth.

How then can the Church of the '90s pass on "the unsearchable riches of Christ" to a society that is determined to exclude any recognition of an ultimate spiritual and moral authority? How can the Church exert a positive influence on a culture that has become deaf to its voice? The ideas that dominate our culture have exerted a powerful influence on the Church, and the growing trend to have a nation that tolerates diversity, even at the expense of truth, has profoundly complicated the ability of the Church to succeed in its mission of preaching the Gospel.

These challenges are significant and must be acknowledged. But they cannot, and should not, be considered without recalling the sovereign reign of God and without remembering how the mighty hand of God has moved among shifting cultures in the past to carry out the Divine intention.

The Church stands at a crossroads and must undergo a major transformation if it is to have a transforming impact on Canadians and their culture in the next millennium. This is the time for the Body of Christ to stand united in God's empowering presence. We need to reflect on the past, create new strategies to accomplish our goals and renew our commitment to live a genuine life of faith in the midst of an unbelieving culture. As stated by Archbishop Carey, our challenge is to preach the Gospel and to relate our faith to the world around us. That must be the primary mission of the Church as we enter the new millennium.

Background on Canadian Culture and Religion

Historically, Canada has never had a strong national identity. From its inception it has been a nation under the influence of the aboriginal culture and cultures beyond itself. Over the years, large numbers of people from other cultural groups have immigrated to Canada, thereby further increasing the diversity of Canadian life. This "cultural mosaic" that is our society has not only encouraged the development of many subcultures, but has also served to nurture the growth of religious pluralism (the presence of different faith groups with distinctive values and practices) that is prevalent in Canada today.

As a result, Canada has become a nation with no dominant religion and, in the past decade, a rising mood of secularism pervades the land—a worldview that excludes God from daily human life. The secularist lives for the present and evaluates his/her life and choices without any reference to God or to divine moral and spiritual absolutes. As such, it appears to be a fitting philosophy to guide the lives and serve the needs of a materialistic, "me-oriented" society.

In the 1990s, secularism and pluralism have dominated the views and attitudes of Canadians. Although Canadians are encouraged to "celebrate" diversity of perspective, people with a secular outlook on life are not only indifferent, but sometimes even hostile to the Christian message.[1] As a consequence, Christians are increasingly being forced to keep their message of truth out of the public realm and within the confines of their churches. This struggle with secularism and pluralism is constantly being played out in our public institutions, such as schools and hospitals.

For example, the Lord's Prayer is no longer viewed as appropriate for a multi-cultural society and has been removed from most schools and classrooms in Canada. Many of the religious references to Christmas, as well as Christmas carols that mention the name of Jesus or Christ, have been banned from public settings. Public displays of the manger and Jesus' birth have been pushed out of the public square in the name of tolerance and multi-culturalism. Even the name, "Christmas," has been deemed inappropriate and, in many cases, schools and public institutions refer to the season simply as the Winter Celebration or Winter Holiday. Christians accustomed to an historic Christian presence in Canadian life find this new circumstance uncomfortable.

Canada's Quest for Spirituality

In spite of these challenges, there is mounting evidence that secularism is failing to provide an adequate answer to the inner search for meaning that exists within each of us. Surveys show that there has been a massive upsurge in "spiritual interest" in the 1990s, even as the vestiges of organized or traditional religion have been forced from the public square.

In a *Macleans*/CTV poll at the end of 1997, 75% of Canadians said that developing their spiritual life was important to them. This response is relatively comparable to its 1995 poll, in which 82% of Canadians said they considered themselves to be "somewhat or very spiritual."

These are rather astounding statistics for a society that is committed to a philosophy of secularism. Yet they serve as a practical demonstration of the truth found in St. Augustine's words, "Thou hast made us for Thyself and our hearts are restless until they find their rest in Thee."

Spirituality gives much-needed meaning to life, and it holds great allure for members of a society facing widespread uncertainty about the unity of their country, economic hardships, political uncertainty, family breakdown, and social problems. The sense that things are going wrong and spinning out of our control naturally leads many to search for an answer that lies outside our physical existence. However, it is clear from the rising interest in spirituality that secularism cannot provide an answer to the deep-seated need to find meaning in our daily lives.

Unfortunately, for many people, this search for spirituality has little to do with truth and rarely amounts to more than an unfocused quest for meaning. It is often difficult to even get people to define what is meant by the term "spirituality." In general, it is considered to be an individual search for the truth. It does not deal with the question of whether God or truth exists, but rather is a search for gods or other divine forces or truths that can be found in such diverse or obscure places as nature or in the community of a self-help group. Spirituality is essentially a personal faith journey that has little to do with a commitment based on the existence of God, special revelation, objective truths or a community committed to faithful obedience. In 1995, Canadian researcher, Dr. Reginald Bibby, compared the importance of spirituality and religion among Canadians and documented that the group that is the most interested in spirituality is also the least interested in organized religion.

This finding suggests a clear distinction between religion and spirituality in the minds of those who are interested only in "spiritual things." The exact nature of that distinction remains unclear. One wonders whether such a distinction is related to a reluctance to submit to any organized form of religion or to doctrinal beliefs.

Figure 24[2]
Importance of Spirituality Vs. Religion

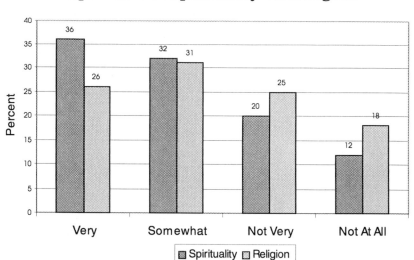

Canadians and the Church

This privatization of spiritual belief may be the underlying factor explaining why 81% of Canadians say they believe in God and 68% of Canadians identify themselves as Christians (Angus Reid poll, 1996). The 1991 Census shows that 46% of Canadians are Roman Catholic, 36% are Protestant and 5% say they have some other religious affiliation, while 13% claim to have no religion.

In spite of the high degree of association that Canadians have with particular religious affiliations, only 21% of Canadian adults claim to attend a church or religious meeting of any kind regularly (Angus Reid, 1994), and this number appears to be dropping at about 1% per year. In fact, Dr. Bibby hypothesizes that weekly attendance at church will eventually drop to about 15%. This compares to the 1945 census data, which showed that 60% of Canadians attended religious services on a weekly basis.

The Canadian church is not only generally drawing smaller percentages of Canadians, but those attending are older. Polls show that older Canadians attend church much more frequently, feel closer to God and are more spiritually satisfied than younger Canadians.[3] Dr. Bibby's research also confirms that younger adults are less likely to be involved in religious groups and that religious groups are getting older.[4] Since Canada's population is aging, this problem will likely get worse unless challenged by a bolder and more relevant Canadian church.

Table 49 compares the weekly service attendance by major religious groups in 1975, 1985 and 1995 confirming that for the majority of Canadians there has been a decreasing emphasis on the importance of weekly church attendance. The most significant reduction in church attendance has occurred within the Roman Catholic faith, while the most positive indication of hope—a sharp increase in attendance over the past two decades—comes from within the conservative Protestant groups (Baptists, Pentecostals, Alliance, Mennonites, etc.). One reason suggested for this continued growth in attendance is that young people are more likely to stay involved in evangelical churches than in mainline churches.

Table 49[5]
Weekly Service Attendance 1975 Through 1995

	1975 %	1985 %	1995 %
Nationally	31	28	25
Roman Catholic	45	37	30
Québec	49	31	24
Outside Québec	41	40	38
Mainline Prot	23	16	19
Anglican	24	16	17
United Church	28	13	20
Conserv Prot	40	60	64

According to Dr. Bibby, the best demographic evidence available from Statistics Canada suggests that Protestant mainline churches (United, Anglican, Presbyterian and Lutheran) and the Roman Catholic Church inside Québec, will experience dramatic losses in terms of attendance over the next 20 years. In fact, by the year 2015, it is predicted that there will be a drastically revised religious landscape in Canada. Churches currently considered to be the "mainline religions" will become marginalized and the Conservative Protestants, largely composed of evangelicals, will become the new "mainline" and thereby exert the greatest influence on Canadian society. Roman Catholic churches will remain prominent nationally, but will experience significant losses in churches within Québec.

Table 50[6]
Current and Projected
Weekly Attenders (in 1,000s)

	Now	2015
Nationally	**4,600**	**3,500**
Roman Catholic		
Québec	1,200	550
Outside Québec	1,500	1,200
Mainline		
Anglican	220	100
United Church	400	200
Lutheran	80	50
Presbyterian	80	75
Conservative		
Baptist	200	225
Other	740	900
Other Faiths	**200**	**175**

From: Bibby, Unknown Gods, 1993:106.

Although Christians are encouraged to assemble together regularly, it is perhaps a "sign of the times" that church attendance is no longer in public vogue. Modern priorities may echo the words of Bill Gates, the creator of most of our modern computer technology and one of the richest men in the world, who states, "Just in terms of allocation of time resources, religion isn't very efficient. There is a lot more I could be doing on a Sunday morning."

Figure 25[7]
Weekly Attenders in the Year 2015

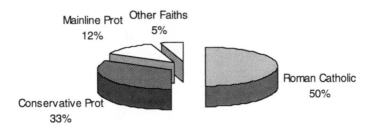

Mainline Prot
12%

Other Faiths
5%

Conservative Prot
33%

Roman Catholic
50%

While a decline in church attendance is not the sole indicator of the health of our Christian culture, it is a primary indicator of Christian commitment and therefore the present situation, unless changed, does not bode well for the future of the churches in Canada. The church represents a primary place of Christian accountability, individual growth, participation in community, worship and intentional focus on God. Yet, a great deal of anecdotal evidence suggests that even "regular" church attenders or members are becoming far more irregular in their attendance habits.

Modern Trends Impacting Church Attendance

The decline in church attendance and the declining emphasis on the exclusive truth that Christianity possesses have undoubtedly been influenced by a number of societal philosophies and factors, some of which have already been noted. However, each of these philosophies or ways of thinking represents a barrier which the Church must recognize and understand if it is to overcome them and play a dominant role in Canadian society in the 21st century:

a) Pluralism

In its broadest meaning, pluralism refers to the existence of people with different beliefs in our society, cultures, races, religions and ancestries. Unfortunately, the term sometimes contains the assumption that all differences are good and should therefore be encouraged or accepted equally.

As has already been described in this chapter, Canada is a cultural mosaic in which "tolerance" is given a much higher value than "truth." Therefore, different cultures and religions are mutually respected, encouraged and even celebrated— whether they are true or not, or more fundamentally, without concern for whether or not truth exists. As a result, no particular religious tradition is given prominence and the concept of absolute truth tends to fall by the wayside.

It makes no sense to take a collection of contrary beliefs and assume that because we live in a pluralistic society each belief must be true. Supporting the pluralistic idea that all religions have the right to exist and be free from discrimination is quite different from saying that we cannot debate and evaluate the claims of each religion to determine if they are legitimate or true. Unfortunately, most Canadians do not distinguish between these two points of view and assume that they have to give up a belief in absolute truth for the sake of participating in a misguided form of tolerance.

Christians can live, and even thrive, in a pluralistic society. We can coexist among all religions. But we must not forget to carry the message that true tolerance does not eliminate the existence of absolute truth and should never be sacrificed for truth.

b) Secularism

Secularism is a philosophy or collection of beliefs that excludes God and the existence of moral and spiritual absolutes. Billy Graham refers to it as one of the most discouraging historical trends that has developed over the last century. Its message of life without God led to the "dechristianization" of former Christian strongholds in Europe and has now become its dominant belief.

Over the past decade, secularism has become a dominant force in Canada as well—primarily because many see it as the answer to problems presented by religious pluralism. It seems highly unusual, if not utterly unrealistic, to expect that secularism should provide a solution to religious differences, but secularists claim that religion must be removed from public life and confined to private life if we are to have harmony in a religiously pluralistic society. In essence, secularism mistakenly preaches that we are only able to give equal respect to all religions by excluding all religions from having a public role.[8]

This situation has been likened to that in which various people are trying to agree on what sport, if any, to play. Some people want to play hockey, some soccer, some basketball and some want to play no sport at all. Finally it is announced that because we can't play a sport that pleases everyone, the only solution is to not play any sport.

In reality, secularism accepts the preference of those who don't want to play a sport and rejects the preferences of all others. We must remember that secularism is not a position that is above all others, it is a position alongside the others; that is, it is one way—not the only way and certainly not the best way—to deal with religious pluralism.

c) Privatization of Faith

In the past decade there has been a broad shift to the privatization of religion. Canadians simply seem to prefer to create their own understanding of God. According to *Evangeltrends*, the private religious practices of Canadians are now far more prominent than their public practices, such as attending church. Sizable numbers of Canadians report that they pray privately (roughly 50%), say grace before meals (approximately 20%) and read the Bible or other Christian writings (also about 20%).

Figure 26
Conventional Practices (Weekly or More)

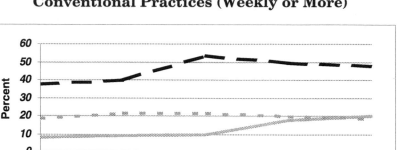

Although many Canadians consider themselves religious or even Christian, and although they may adhere to private religious practices, their actual understanding of faith is cloudy at best. They may state that they believe in God, Jesus, heaven and the Christian faith, yet have little or no evidence of it in their lives because they have little understanding of what the Bible says about the Christian faith. They have little knowledge of their beliefs because they are not worshipping and receiving the spiritual instruction that is required to produce a mature Christian faith.

Unfortunately, privatized religion is often composed of a "mix and match" of various religions and doctrines. It is a faith that is based on the individual's own understanding of God and unmediated by doctrine or the community of faith.

Dr. Bibby comments: "The vast majority of Canadians still call themselves Christian, but they are grasping bits and pieces of the traditional creed—'the fragmented god.' We now see a high level of belief in almost anything imaginable, but there is no rhyme or reason to it. And when we try to measure the sort of guidance these private beliefs play in people's lives, there is really nothing there. There is no moral authority, so it really doesn't add up to anything."[10]

d) Relativism/Moral Ambiguity

The pervasive reality and inescapable problem of our culture is relativism—the idea that absolute truth is non-existent and therefore all claims to truth are considered to be nothing more than "subjective opinions." As a result of this modern belief, truth is essentially up for grabs in Canadian society. This notion of subjective truth is demonstrated in a more practical way by a survey which showed that two out of three young Canadians live with the assumption that right and wrong are matters of personal preference.

But Canadian philosopher and apologist, Michael Horner, states that people seem only to invoke relativism when issues of morality or religion are at stake. "We don't hear people claiming that mutually exclusive statements are true when it comes to the stock market." Further, as Horner argues, the idea that relativism is exclusively and absolutely true shows that it is no more tolerant than any other exclusive claim to the truth. In fact, it is worse—because it hides its claim to be the absolute truth behind the facade of denying the existence of absolute truth.

Relativism has led to an abundance of moral ambiguity in our society. In the past, most families and individuals looked to the church and religion as the primary provider of moral guidance for their lives. But for the past few decades, the Christian belief in absolute right and wrong has been challenged daily by a culture that promotes the notion that any absolute claim to truth is nothing more than mere opinion.

As a result, even many Christians no longer believe that truth and morality are absolute. In fact, many also fail to believe in the authority of Scripture or the deity of Christ, and it is apparent that some orthodox doctrines and central truths of the Christian faith are treated skeptically. A survey done by the Barna Research Group reveals that Christians lack basic doctrinal knowledge about their faith:

- 80% of born-again Christians agreed with the statement that God helps those who help themselves.

- 49% of Christians agreed that the Devil, or Satan, is not a living being but is a symbol of evil.

- 39% agreed that if a person is generally good they will earn a place in heaven.

- 30% agreed that Jesus Christ was a great teacher, but did not come back to physical life after He was crucified.

- 29% agreed that Jesus Christ was human and committed sins like other people.[11]

There is one truth in relativism that must be acknowledged. All of our views are partial, incomplete and fragmentary, and therefore our reasoning occurs within the limitations of our abilities, our history and our culture. But recognizing this does not mean that absolute truth does not exist. Real truth is God's truth.[12]

e) Relevance to Our Lives

The 1994 Angus Reid poll of religion in Canada suggests that people are looking for a personal experience with God and they come to church because they want to learn about the link between their faith and their life. The reasons given for attending church (in order of significance) were to: 1) gain guidance on how to live, 2) have spiritual needs met, 3) get help to instill personal values in their children and 4) worship God.

However, many people in our society see the Church's teachings as meaningless and irrelevant as a result of the influence of pluralism and secularism. Others blame the hypocrisy that exists in the lives of some Christians. A few highly visible failures create a widespread perception of hypocrisy. The result is a "credibility gap" that Christians have to overcome to have their message heard.

f) Urbanization

As we enter the third millennium, the world's population will total 6 billion people—about three times the number present at the dawn of the 20th century. Approximately 50% of them will be under the age of 25. Globally, at least one-half of these people will live in large cities—many of them uprooted from their past, away from their families and experiencing a poverty.

There is a strong relationship between the size of the community and church attendance. People with marginal commitment to the church in a small town, often abandon that commitment in a larger centre where they are free from the peer pressure of participation that would be more evident in a smaller town. As Canada's population becomes increasingly urbanized, it is likely to continue to have a negative impact on church attendance. Table 51 documents the influence of increased urbanization on church attendance.

In addition, churches in large cities have to compete with sporting, shopping, entertainment and other leisure options for people's free time. Some Canadians simply feel that they do not have

Table 51[13]
Attendance by
Community Size

	1975 %	1995 %
Over 400,000	26	22
Catholic	59	31
Protestant	23	22
100,000-400,000	27	19
Catholic	60	22
Protestant	25	28
10,000-99,000	33	21
Catholic	56	29
Protestant	20	20
<10,000	39	31
Catholic	48	34
Protestant	33	37

time to maintain a job and a family and enjoy leisure time plus go to church.

Implications for the Church

In such a diverse nation as Canada, it is a challenge to witness to the truth of the Gospel when few Canadians are willing to recognize the authority of any one particular religion or truth. In the midst of these cultural changes, the Church must address the following questions:

- How can the Church exist and carry out its mission in such a society?

- How do we live as Christians and communicate our faith in a relevant manner in a multi-cultural, pluralistic society?

- How do we as a Church deal with the significant differences that exist?

- How do we exhibit deep religious conviction with an open and tolerant spirit?[14]

To answer these questions, Christians must look to the core of their faith—the unfathomable love of Jesus. His love must shape the way we hold to our faith and the way we present it to others.

The Church of the Next Millennium

In the midst of so many changes in the world, it is the unique function of the Church to declare by word and deed that there are some things that never change. It is the message that God—the supreme, unchanging, omnipotent Creator of the universe—loves humanity and wants us to know Him in a personal way.

- Billy Graham[15]

As the Church enters the 21ˢᵗ century, it is in dire need of seeking a renewed vision of how we can carry out our mission of proclaiming God's love and truth to a secular culture. It is obvious from the evidence that we have just examined that the Church must adapt to the societal changes that are occurring in Canada and discover new ways to overcome these barriers without compromising its message.

The most successful churches in the next millennium will likely be characterized by:

- A commitment to Biblical teaching/principles and to proclaiming absolute truth,

- Unity,

- Community,

- Renewal and

- Engaging the culture.

A Commitment to Biblical Teaching/Principles and to Proclaiming Absolute Truth.

In the midst of uncertain relativism and moral neutrality, people are looking to the Church to affirm what is true—to proclaim and affirm the essentials of the Christian faith. According to Don Posterski, "It represents a sense of stability within a world which is otherwise open to negotiation and uncertainty."[16]

One reason so many people in Canadian culture state that they believe in God, Jesus, heaven and the Christian faith yet have little or no evidence of it in their lives, is because many of them have little understanding of what the Bible says about the Christian faith. According to Dr. John Stott, a mature church is a product of the Word of God and therefore needs to preach it in all its fullness. Therefore, the first task of the Church must be to present God's clear and undiluted message to the world.

In his book, *A Peculiar People,* Dr. Rodney Clapp also argues that in order for the Church to experience renewal and exert a renewed influence in its culture, it must become:

> *A total institution, possessing its own language, its own history, its own practices...When the church understands itself properly, it always has a subversive element. It refuses to be conformed to the dominant ideology of the culture in which it exists. The early Church created and sustained a unique culture. The peculiar people of God manifested a peculiar culture for God.*

Canadian Christians will need to overcome the disappointment over not being the privileged faith community, revise the nature of the Christian mission and get on with the subversive task of witness and service in a needy community.

Unity

Jesus speaks of the power of unity in John 17:21. We have given lip service to unity, but practically speaking have far to go.

Recent vision work by the leaders of the *Evangelical Fellowship of Canada* (EFC) reveal a growing conviction that the medium is the message. Believers from across the land and from across the theological spectrum are calling for unity. Great interest is expressed in accentuating the things we have in common rather than focusing on the things that divide.

Community

Our society is increasingly at a loss for the experience of community. We have become a nation of individualists, obsessed with our own private lives. Yet, there is an inherent desire for community that pervades our lives. The vital Church is a vibrant facilitator of community in the face of the increasingly impersonal forces of society. In fact, according to Charles Truehart, the new Church will likely be the "clearest approximation of community ... that a whole generation is likely to have known or likely to find anywhere in an impersonal, transient nation."[17]

The Church is meant to be a community of support for faith commitments as well as physical and emotional needs. But this fellowship of believers is also expected to meet the needs of others in the neighbourhood or wider community.

Many Canadians are looking for a place to belong—not only to be involved, but to have their emotional and faith needs met. Research from many sources indicates that most people become Christians through friendships. People will enter into a community circle if that community encourages experience with God and offers relevant direction for daily living.

"The Church is a powerful institution in our society because it encapsulates the individual in a community that becomes an essential part of the individual's own identity. ...The community can become," in Dietrich Bonhoeffer's memorable words, "a source of incomparable joy and strength to the believer."[18]

Renewal

"...Not by might nor by power, but by my Spirit, says the LORD Almighty" (Zechariah 4:6).

As the Church seeks a renewed sense of mission and commitment, it is a time for commitment to serious prayer and fasting. We have to remember that every success, every advance, no matter how slight, is possible only because God has been at work by the Holy Spirit. The Spirit gives us the message, leads us to those already prepared and brings both conviction of sin and new life. When we understand that truth, we will realize the urgency of prayer.

Engaging the Culture

God's love and His plan for individuals hasn't changed and neither has the human heart. The Great Commission remains unchanged, as does God's call to the unsaved. Yet evangelism only accounts for 10% of the growth in evangelical churches, something which demonstrates the failure of the Church to carry out its mission of spreading the Gospel.

Churches are challenged to communicate their message to a society that is indifferent—or even hostile to its message. Unfortunately, most Canadian evangelistic efforts are geared to people who already understand the Christian culture, language and basic Biblical concepts. This doesn't work in a culture where people may *think that they know* the basics, yet have no true or accurate understanding of them. Nor does it work in a culture where Christianity is just one of many religious options.

Efforts to engage our culture should be characterized by persuasion, an openness to listen to what others have to say, and an openness to change. We need to listen to others if we want them to listen to us—and we need to listen so that we can learn from them. The good things that are heard when listening to others need to be affirmed. Things that are untrue need to be questioned. Christians must have confidence that the world, history and our present social changes are in God's hands. It is only then that we can be free from fear and completely free to engage those with different philosophies.

In short, the new Church has to be culturally relevant, it must understand people's needs and it must appeal to both the Christian and secular heart and mind. Sunday morning worship must be connected to the realities of everyday life, and leaders must be prepared to address the tough issues, and to present the teachings of Jesus in a way that is relevant to daily life. The Church must also strive to meet the needs of those in the community and to provide community for those who seek fellowship. At the same time, the Church must refuse to conform to the dominant ideologies of the culture in which it exists.

Conclusion

"Any funeral planned for Canadian Christianity is premature."[29]

At the end of the day, the ministering person must evaluate the demographics, check with the political scientists, measure the mood and evaluate the context of Canadian culture in the '90s. But a person called to the ministry of reconciliation will never be satisfied with these factors as a final evaluation of what is going on.

The person who understands the way of salvation and the call of God upon the Church is the person who understands that our God reigns. Governments come and go. Ideologies come and go. Trends come and go. Those who see with eyes of faith see that God is working mightily in the affairs of state, in the changing nuances of culture and through His community of people who choose to trust and obey.

If one looks only from a human perspective, one could easily be discouraged with the prognosis of Christian faith in the land. But people formed in the ways of faith, prayer and salvation are always looking for that higher dimension of reality. When Jesus stood before Pilate, he said, *"My Kingdom is not of this world..."* (John 18:36). Followers of Jesus today are still seeking to see and understand this Kingdom—which is not based in any city or nation.

While certain cultural trends have moved away from the affirmations to which Christians adhere, spirit-led people are moving into new realms of ministry, churches are being planted, groups are learning to partner together in the name of Jesus and the tone of evangelicalism is a note of praise to God. The 1997 Canadian Church Planting Congress marked an historic moment in terms of cooperating across all traditional lines for the good of the Kingdom in the ministry of church planting. What a sacred moment as leaders of denominations, congregations and other ministering organizations accepted challenges to plant geographically accessible and culturally relevant churches everywhere in Canada. It is so easy to let walls develop and to have our most gifted, energetic people pouring energy into projects that perpetuate organizational life but do not represent a Kingdom strategy. Observers were thrilled to see the commitment of these conference participants to Kingdom strategies and a willingness to align organizational life with that larger vision.

The global interface sponsored by EFC's Task Force for Global Mission was another historic event in 1997. Some 90 organizations were represented, and again people who face the tough realities of organizational life were willing to entertain dreams and visions of Kingdom strategies that would stretch around the world.

It is dangerous to identify litmus tests of the health of Christendom. Someone would want to evaluate personal holiness. Another would bring tests for justice and peace. Someone else would say that we are healthy when corporate prayer is a priority. And the list would go on. I value each of these. In addition, we are watching for willing Christian leaders to see beyond the realities of their own organizational lives and to begin to pour energy into strategic alliances for Kingdom purposes. When we see this happen, we begin to believe that we are moving into a season of marvelous renewal within evangelicalism.

The Billy Graham Association is prayerfully considering whether it should plan a millennial conference on evangelism. When Billy Graham asked the EFC what concerns might come to the floor in such a conference, this was identified as the crucial issue in the life of the movement. We must demonstrate a willingness to make our individual agendas the servant of the larger Kingdom agenda.

The struggle may be easier to observe within the world of foreign missions. It does not take much insight to see the folly of transferring contextually-based denominational structures to other places in the world where there is no knowledge of their history and no awareness of the reason why this organization should be distinct from the one next door. This kind of thing has happened and to some degree is still happening.

The good news, however, is that it is happening less frequently than was previously the case. And if the Canadian experience is any indication, we may be walking into a whole new era of partnership, alliances and deferring to each other for the good of the Kingdom.

Every organization participating in the ministry of evangelism is itself experiencing waves of change. Surely this is the moment to join hands and configure our ministries in such a way as to reap the maximum benefit for Christ and His Kingdom as we move forward!

We believe that this is a "kairos" moment within evangelicalism in Canada. Never have the walls been so low. Never have leaders been more eager to co-operate. Never have congregations been more ready to celebrate diversity while respecting the essentials. And never before has the need been greater.

One must believe that the God who reigns is not even nervous about the cultural symptoms that tend to resist faith and salvation. Our God was able to bless and multiply the Church during the Roman Empire, during recent decades in China and under every oppressive regime within which the Church has grown and thrived. Barriers to belief in Canada are more than conquerable, and we are eager to watch the vision unfold!

Dr. Walsh asks a series of pointed practical questions:

"How can the Church pass on 'the unsearchable riches of Christ' to a society that is determined to exclude any recognition of an ultimate spiritual and moral authority, and how can the Church exert a positive influence on a culture that has become deaf to its voice? How can the church exist and carry out its mission in such a society? How do we live as Christians and communicate our faith in a relevant manner in a multicultural, secular society? How do we exhibit deep religious conviction with an open and tolerant spirit?"

✓ Take the questions to your Bible study or informal discussion group and invest a session exploring these important issues.

✓ Take the questions to the Lord of the harvest in a season of quiet, waiting prayer to see if His answers may be different than those we might expect to offer.

✓ Review Dr. Walsh's challenge to be the "Church of the next Millennium" and respond in one concrete way to each calling, (such as):

⇨ *Commitment to Biblical Absolutes*: Affirm and list 10 things you know to be true, not maybe or negotiable, about the Gospel. Share one of these with a non-Christian friend today.

⇨ *Unity:* The next time you meet a Christian for the first time, don't ask which denomination he/she participate in, but turn the conversation to a point of unity such as prayer for the lost.

Action Points

⇨ *Community:* Invite into your home, engage in social activity or express care in a practical way to non-Christians at least as many times as you do to Christians this next month. Keep track!

⇨ *Renewal:* Go out of your way to participate this month in a renewal service or congregation even if you are not entirely sure you will be comfortable with the experience. Further, the next time a Christian associate criticizes an expression of renewal, turn the conversation rather to personal renewal currently needed or recently experienced.

⇨ *Engaging the Culture:* Facilitate a discussion with the leadership of your congregation identifying the felt needs of contemporary Canadian culture. Respond by: (1) changing one aspect of your worship experience to better engage our culture, (2) instituting an expression of "servant evangelism," (3) offering a new service to your community.

Chapter Notes

[1] Billy Graham, "Rediscovering the Primacy of Evangelism," *Christianity Today*, December 8,1997.

[2] Dr. Reginald W. Bibby, *The Bibby Report: Social Trends Canadian Style*. Toronto: Stoddart Publishing Company, 1995, p.134.

[3] Angus Reid Group, reported in *Context* (Mississauga: MARC/ World Vision), Vol. 4, Issue 4, pp.6-7.

[4] Dr. Reginald W. Bibby

[5] Dr. Reginald W. Bibby, p.134.

[6] Dr. Reginald W. Bibby, p.128.

[7] Dr. Reginald W. Bibby, p.129.

[8] *Pluralism in Canada*, a paper of the Social Action Commission of the Evangelical Fellowship of Canada, November 1997. p.6.

[9] Dr. Reginald W. Bibby, p.131.

[10] Dr. Reginald Bibby, *Fragmented Gods: The Poverty and Potential of Religion in Canada*. Toronto: Staddart, 1987.

[11] Barna Research Group reported in *Western Report* "Every Man His Own Church," June 10, 1996, p.35.

[12] Essay on Christian Theology in Secular Culture

[13] Dr. Reginald W. Bibby, *The Bibby Report: Social Trends Canadian Style*. Toronto: Stoddart Publishing Company, 1995, p.127.

[15] Essay on Christian Theology in Secular Culture

[16] "Rediscovering the Primacy of Evangelism," *Christianity Today*, December 8,1997.

[17] Don Posterski, *Healthy Churches, the Canadian Way*.

[18] Charles Truehart, "Welcome to the New Church," *Atlantic Monthly*, August 1996. p.10.

[19] Dietrich Bonhoeffer, *Life Together* New York: Harper & Row, p. 21.

[20] Dr. George Rawlyk, *Atlantic Baptist*, January, 1995.

Chapter Ten

How Current Trends Impact the Church

Dr. Gerald C. Kraft and R. Murray A. Jarman

As we approach the turn of the millennium, it has been natural to use the year 2000 as the focus for church planting and church growth strategies. These have ranged from local church efforts and denominational strategies, to the goal of the *AD2000 and Beyond* movement. Its goal is to have a church for every people group and to share the Gospel with every person by the year 2000. Within Canada, the effort of *Vision Canada* has been to provide every Canadian the opportunity to see, hear and respond to the Gospel by the year 2000. *Church Planting Canada*, a national trans-denominational effort, is working toward planting 10,000 new congregations by the year 2015. This national goal has been broken down into denominational goals for each five-year span. The sheer magnitude of the task has stimulated an impetus for renewed evangelism, church growth and church planting efforts. It has given us renewed cause to evaluate the state of our nation and our world, and commit ourselves to the task of reaching Canada with the Gospel.

If this renewed commitment is to be taken seriously, it will require the cooperation of evangelicals and new innovative ways to reach people. This requires change in the way denominations and churches think about church size and the church planting process. The typical building-oriented understanding of "church" will need to be supplemented by a people-centered philosophy, viewing church less as a meeting facility and more as groups of people joining together for worship, discipleship and caring. There are also new challenges to be faced in raising funds to support these new works and church planters. All of this is taking place against the backdrop of strained conditions economically and shifting moral and religious values culturally. Many of the traditional ways of evangelizing and planting new churches have lost or are losing their effectiveness. How will these efforts be financed? Where will the leaders be found? Who are the unreached people groups or where are the locations needing an evangelical witness? How will the increasingly large proportion of Canadians who have never gone to church be reached with the Gospel? These are the questions facing Canada's Christians in the '90s, as they seek the will of God in reaching their world.

Canada in the Nineties

Canada is undergoing a profound social and cultural restructuring. In the past half-century, Canada's population has moved from a rural orientation to a modern, urban-centric culture. With this has come a shift from the farm to the factory—from the church as a focal point within the community to the community relying on governmental directives and assistance. This process, referred to as the first demographic transition, was the integration of the industrial revolution and its values into the social and cultural fabric of Canadian society. While the focus shifted from rural to urban development, the traditions and institutions that brought meaning to rural society still filled a role, albeit a less important one, within Canadian culture. Cities were the new center of attention, but the rural mindset remained.

During the late 1980s and the 1990s, a further transformation has been increasingly evident. There are a number of trends, taken together, that indicate that Canada is already entering the second demographic transition—a shift from tradition and traditional institutions to greater individualism, secularism and focus on personal development. Canada is following a trend already observed in Europe, in which traditional ways of thinking, along with traditional institutions, are replaced by new, modern and secularized ideas. This shift, although outwardly less noticeable than the initial urbanization phase, has the potential for creating greater tension and stress on the fabric of Canadian society, as many valued traditions and organizations are discarded or marginalized in the paradigm shift.[1] If Canada follows the same path through the second demographic transition as Western Europe, the Church will have little relevance to the majority of Canadians. The challenge for Christians in Canada will be to evangelize the unchurched, and to change many of the externals of how churches function without compromising the message of the Gospel.

The second demographic transition is identified by a confluence of population trends and social changes. Among the indicators are rising age at marriage, rising divorce rates, higher percentages of dual-income families, increased proportions of single-parent families and greater participation in the workforce by women, especially women with young children. There is a tendency toward cohabitation as the prevalent form of partnership and the postponement of families, combined with smaller family sizes. All of these indicators are visible across the Canadian landscape. Some have been evident since the 1970s, but recently a critical mass of factors has been statistically verifiable. Many of the pertinent trends will be discussed in the following sections of this chapter.

Population Trends

Aging of Society

As a long-term trend, the average age of Canadians has been rising steadily since the 1970s. However, in the late 1980s and early 1990s the rate of increase has accelerated, and it shows no signs of reversing its course. Canada's maturing population will have a significant effect on the entire face of our society. Social programs, employment and popular culture will all be heavily influenced.

The median age of Canada's population is rising. In 1997, the median age of Canadians was 35.6 years. Fertility rates (average number of babies born to women of childbearing age) have been below the population replacement level since 1970, and currently stand at 1.59 children per woman (from a peak of 3.8 in 1957). This is almost an all-time low, and it it reflects low birth rates in every province. There is a notable difference in fertility rates for married women compared with women in comon-law unions. Women who are married throughout their reproductive life had twice as many children (2.87) as women in a comon-law relationship (1.44).[2]

We are currently at historic highs for the proportion of workers to total population. Projections show that seniors will comprise 23% of the Canadian population in the year 2030, up from 12% in 1991 and 8% in 1961. This is an increase of 168% over current levels. Comparatively, workers aged 15 to 64 will increase by 28%, while children under age 15 will remain constant at today's level. This points to massive changes in the pension system, to government support for seniors and for large-scale changes in the job market. An exponential increase in the number of seniors' care workers will be required. Also, as the need for workers increases as economic pressures on Canadians to provide for longer retirements increases, and as more people are physically

Figure 27
Age Groups as a Percentage of Population

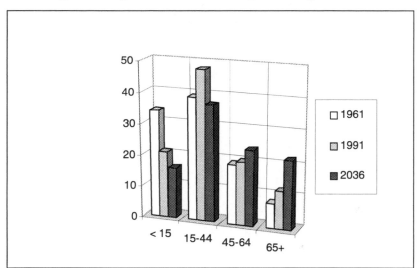

capable of working well beyond age 65, the traditional retirement age of 65 will be challenged.[3]

In addition to age group differences, Canadians will have to cope with ethnic dimensions to the aging question. Currently 75% of visible minorities are aged 15 to 44.[4] This fact suggests that the vast majority of Canada's elderly are Caucasians, while an increasing percentage of workers and younger families will belong to visible minority groups. The shifting ratio of visible minorities will be another factor in the transformation of our society.

The Baby Boomers

Baby Boomers dominate the landscape of the Canadian population. This population group of adults born from 1946 to 1964 is the single-largest age group in Canadian society, accounting for 30% of all Canadians in 1996. On January 1, 1996 the first of the Boomers turned 50. This transition point has signaled a shift in focus from endless consumerism to planning for financial security in retirement. Right now the Baby Boomers are making the transition from a group of spenders in the 1980s and early 1990s to a generation of savers and investors. Contributions to pension and retirement plans are setting new highs each year. Assets invested in mutual funds have grown from $25 billion in 1990 to $143 billion in 1995, with 1996 expected to set even higher totals. Canada's Baby Boomers have recognized that the government will probably not have the ability to support their current lifestyles when they retire, so they are trying to make up for lost time now.[5] The population distribution of Canada is graphically shown in Chapter 3, Figure 7.

After the Boom

Lost in the shadow of the Baby Boomers are the Baby Busters and Generation Xers. Born after 1966, these two age groups have had to struggle to make it in a world oriented toward, shaped and dominated by the Boomers. The Baby Busters are now turning 30, and are struggling with the transition into the world of career and family. As they strive to build their families and careers, they are faced with job markets saturated by Baby Boomers and housing markets boosted beyond single-income affordability by the preceding generations. All the good jobs and cheap housing are gone, while life in general seems to be oriented against them and toward the Boomers.

Generation X has a fundamentally different viewpoint from the Baby Boomers. While the Baby Busters still pursue many of the dreams held in common with Baby Boomers, Generation Xers have a more cynical attitude. They struggle just to take care of themselves, let alone help others. They aim to be different from the Boomers, in everything from dress to music to lifestyle choices. The unique mindset of Generation Xers impacts everything from consumer purchases to housing to church giving.

Baby Busters and Generation Xers, for all their disdain for the Boomers, are about to become the most prolific consumers in society. Just as the Baby Boomers drove the economy of the 1980s, it will be these two groups who drive the economy into the next millenium. They are the first generations to grow up with computers and electronic communications technology. Rapidly evolving technology is natural to them. It is from this group that tomorrow's missionaries, church leaders and supporters will have to be drawn. One of the big challenges facing the Church is motivating and involving the Busters and Xers for church renewal and church planting.

Social and Cultural Trends

Family and Parenthood

Family has always been a central part of our culture. Polls indicate that family ties are still rated as one of the most important parts of the lives of Canadians.[6] There is increasing disagreement, however, about what constitutes a family. Attempts are being made by gay and lesbian lobby groups to redefine "family" to include same-sex couples; the same groups are also pushing to be recognized as legally married with the right to adopt children. Yet even as our definition of family is under attack, the structure of the family has been changing over the last few decades. Families are smaller, reflecting low fertility rates that have been below replacement levels since the mid-1970s. The number of children being born to Canadian families will not be sufficient to replace their parents when they die. Without immigration or an increased birth rate, Canada's population would eventually shrink. Parents are also waiting longer before having children. In the 1960s, the 20 to 24 year old group had the highest fertility rate. That changed to the 25 to 29 age group in the 1970s and before the year 2000 it may be women aged 30 to 34 who have the most babies. Already, more babies are being born to mothers over the age of 30 than ever before. One in three women having their first child in the '90s are over 30 years of age. More women aged 30 to 34 have babies than women aged 20 to 24, the first time that has ever happened.[7]

Marital Status

It is not only the age of parents that is changing, but also the age at which they get married. The Baby Boomers were the last generation to marry early, while in the 1990s, the trend is toward couples getting married later. In 1992, the average age at first marriage was 29 for men and 27 for women, up three years respectively since 1989.[8] This is in contrast to the 1960s and 1970s, when the average age at marriage was stable at 25 for men and 23 for women. Couples are also less likely now than ever before to get married, at least initially. Twelve percent of all families in 1996 were living common-law, up from 6% in 1981. This figure is much higher in Québec, where 21% of all families were living common-law. In 1990, 31% of Canadians who married at age 25 or older had lived common-law before getting married. Among people forming a first conjugal union between 1990-95, 57% chose to live common-law, with the Quebec figure standing at 80%. Although these statistics are unsettling, one positive note is that of common-law unions formed in the 1970s over 50% resulted in marriages between the same partners,[9] and an additional 25% had married someone else. It is also encouraging to note that people who attended religious services weekly were significantly less likely to live common-law. It appears that many couples want to give a relationship a "trial run," and then get married if everything works out.

Figure 28
% of Couples Living Common-Law

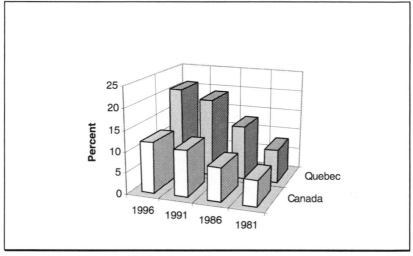

Women in the Workforce

One of the biggest changes in the labor force over the past two decades has been the change in women's employment patterns. Fifty-five percent of women now work outside the home. Mothers of young children are even more heavily involved in the workforce (67% in 1996) than women without children (47% in 1996). Women without children were only slightly more likely to work in 1991 than in 1981, while the likelihood of mothers to work increased by 29% over the same period.[10] Women are almost as likely as men are to have a university degree. Among young women under age 24, more have university degrees and other post-secondary training than men. In 1992-93, 53% of undergraduate students, 46% of masters students and 35% of doctoral students are women.[11] However, wages for women still are only 72% of those for men in the same occupations. There is movement in the right direction, since real wages for women rose 14% in the 1980s compared to 0.4% for men ("real wages" are adjusted to compensate for the effects of inflation, to allow for accurate comparisons in income levels over a period of time).

Although women are more heavily involved in the workforce, they are still just as likely as in previous decades to shoulder the burden of household work. Of women who worked full-time in dual-earner families, 31% of those under age 45 reported being severely "time-crunched," compared to 15% of men,[12] and over 65% of household responsibilities are the sole responsibility of the wife, with another 13% of responsibilities being shared equally. Husbands are only responsible for 15% of household chores. These statistics are even more lopsided in male single-earner families.

Women's involvement in the workforce is also a significant factor in the rise of common-law households.[13] Being employed is the strongest factor indicating likelihood of living common-law for women, although it is not nearly as significant for men.

Urbanization

Canada, for all its vast size, natural beauty and wide open spaces, is a country of city-dwellers. Eight of 10 Canadians live in cities rather than in rural areas. Sixty-two percent of the residents live in only 25 metropolitan areas, each over 100,000 in size and each of them still growing. Thirty-four percent of all Canadians live in three cities—Toronto, Montreal and Vancouver. By itself Toronto makes up 16% of Canada's total population. The narrow strip of developed urban corridor from Windsor to Québec City is home to well over half of all Canadians. It is also the large urban centers that are attracting the surge of immigrants, mostly from visible minority groups. With just over 50% of Canada's annual population growth coming from immigration, and with over 80% of new immigrants moving to the large urban centres, the major cities will be home to an ever larger percentage of the total Canadian population.

Urban living has its economic costs. In Canada's 25 Census Metropolitan Areas (CMAs) over one-third of renters had trouble affording housing (CMAs are the 25 largest cities in Canada, from Toronto at 4.3 million to Thunder Bay at 126,000). Furthermore, fewer people can afford to own housing in the cities. Forty-three percent of all urban households rented their accommodations, but it was only 16% in rural areas. With rising unemployment and little change in real wages, the dream of owning a home, or even of living comfortably in rented housing, is beyond the reach of an increasing segment of our society. On the positive side, however, Canada's large cities are not plagued with as many serious problems as large cities are in the United States. Canada's cities are more ethnically diverse, more stable and have higher average incomes than U.S. counterparts.[14] Family structures, while changing, are typically more "traditional" than in U.S. cities, where divorce, single parenthood, teen pregnancy and drug problems are much more severe. Overall, Canadian cities are "kinder, gentler" cousins to the larger U.S. cities.

Immigration and Ethnic Groups

The changing face of Canada is nowhere more evident than in the increasingly diverse cultural backgrounds of its inhabitants. In 1996, 11.2% of Canada's population belonged to visible minority people groups. Almost two-thirds of visible minority adults have moved to Canada since 1972. Despite stereotypes, Canada's visible minorities (18%) are more likely than the general populace (11%) to be educated, especially at the university level.[15] Many immigrants are highly educated, highly skilled people searching for a higher standard of living and with the resources to leave their country of origin. During the 1980s, over one-third of all immigrants came from visible minority groups, primarily from China, Hong Kong and other Asian nations. In 1994, seven of the top 10 countries of origin were in Asia, and accounted for 51% of the 223,875 immigrants.[16] From 1991-96, the top five countries for recent immigrants were all from Asia, with two more in the top ten. Recent government policy on immigration has set the annual limit on immigration at around 200,000 people, well above rates during the 1980s. The government increased immigration to maintain population growth, since natural population growth is not sustainable. The number of people belonging to visible minority groups increased 62% between 1991 and 1996, from 2 million to 3.2 million.

Large cities are the most ethnically diverse areas, and will become increasingly cosmopolitan well into the next century. Ninety-four percent of visible minorities live in Canada's 25 largest cities. By comparison, only 59% of all Caucasian adults live in those cities. Visible minorities tend to settle in pockets within large cities. Seventy-three percent of all visible minorities live in either Toronto, Vancouver or Montreal. They make up 32% of the population of Toronto, 31% of Vancouver and 12% of Montreal. People in visible

Table 52
Immigration to Canada, 1991 to 1996

Immigration 1991 to 1996	Number	% of Total
Hong Kong	108,910	10%
China	87,865	8%
India	71,330	7%
Philippines	71,315	7%
Sri Lanka	44,230	4%
Poland	36,970	4%
Taiwan	32,135	3%
Vietnam	32,060	3%
United States	29,015	3%
United Kingdom	25,425	2%
Total of Top 10	**539,255**	**51%**
Total Immigration	**1,038,990**	**100%**

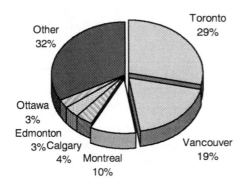

**Figure 29
Immigration to
Cities—1994**

minority groups also tend to be younger than the average Canadian. Around 75% of each ethnic group is between the ages of 15 and 44, a much higher percentage than the 44% average for all of Canada. By the year 2016 visible minorities are projected to increase over 250%, from 2.7 million in 1991 to 7.1 million in 2016. During that time, the population of Canada is projected to grow by 25%.[17] As a percentage of total population, visible minories would move from the current 11% to 20% in 2016. Based on the current situation, by 2016 it is likely that visible minorities in Toronto and Vancouver will be over 50% of the total population, and Montreal will be around 30% of total population. Increases through immigration will also be supplemented by the higher fertility and larger family sizes of visible minority families.

Technological Change

As we approach the turn of the century, the pace of technological change is growing increasingly rapid. Whirlwind change seems everywhere. Traditional fabrication and manufacturing industries are in decline, while service sector, life sciences and high technology companies are booming. Many companies, and also government at all levels, are going through the pains of downsizing and severe cost cutting.

Convenience and timesaving technologies are in high demand, seen in everything from drive-through coffee bars to telephone and computer banking, mega-stores and proliferating fast food choices. Increased choices, options and new possibilities are a defining feature of this decade.

Nowhere is the pace of change more apparent than in the world of computers and the Internet. New computers, new programs and new technology are constantly being introduced. The number of people connected to the Internet has topped 60 million worldwide, and is growing rapidly. Growth of the World Wide Web, a graphical combination of text, sound and images on virtual "pages," is estimated at 10% per month! E-commerce, or the selling of goods and services over the Internet, is growing by leaps and bounds, and is already measured in the billions of dollars annually. According to estimates, within five years over three-quarters of Canadians will have electronic mail (e-mail) addresses. According to the 1996 federal budget, every school and library in the country will be "wired" for Internet access by 1998. One thousand rural communities will have Internet connections provided through government funding, as will 50,000 small businesses. Our world will be much more interconnected and remotely accessible. Some are even predicting the demise of phone books and directories, these items being replaced by websites and special "net phones" that can look up new information in them without needing a computer.

Income and Donations

It is not news to anyone that we live in hard times economically. During the 1990s, for the first time since World War II, real incomes (after adjusting for inflation) declined. With actual wage increases of 0 to 2%, and inflation of 2 to 3%, spending power of the average person has declined since 1990.

In order to get by, most Canadian families have moved to both husband and wife working to support the family. In 1967, the husband was the lone wage earner in 58% of all households. That figure dropped to 19% in 1991 and stayed the same through 1996, with 61% of households being "dual-earner" families. Dual-earner families are the only group in society whose real incomes (after adjusting for inflation) have risen over the past decade.[18] Dual-earner families tend to be younger couples with smaller families, which they tend to start later in life than single-earner families. Forty percent of dual earners are under the age of 40.

Figure 30
Real Wage Increases by Decade

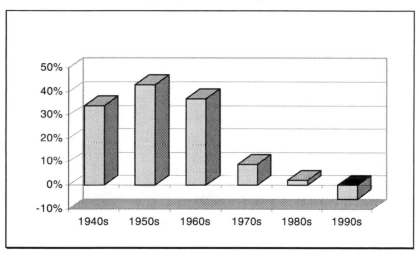

In 1996 27% of Canadian taxfilers reported making a charitable donation, down from 29% in 1990. The average age of these donors has been steadily increasing. In 1990, the average age was 47. By 1996, it had reached 50. The average donation was $730 in 1996, up from $544 in 1990, an increase of 5.0% annually. The median donation (the median is the point at which half the amounts are higher and half the amounts are lower—half of all donors contributed more and half contributed less) rose from $120 to $150.[19] Average donations by age group in 1996 increased from $364 for those under 35, to $612 for those 35-44, to $757 for those 45-54, to $872 for those 55-64, to $1,034 for those over 65.

Table 53
1996 Charitable Donations by Province

Region Figures 1996	Avg. Age	Ave. Donation	% of Taxfilers	Median Donation	Median income
Canada	50	730	27	150	35,200
Newfoundland	49	600	22	260	27,700
Prince Edward Is.	49	640	30	230	28,000
Nova Scotia	51	630	26	200	32,000
New Brunswick	51	750	25	230	30,900
Québec	50	370	25	100	34,000
Ontario	50	810	29	180	37,400
Manitoba	51	810	30	190	31,200
Saskatchewan	53	840	29	240	30,600
Alberta	48	970	27	170	35,700
British Columbia	51	940	24	180	36,500
Yukon	45	760	18	160	47,200
N.W. Territories	42	790	15	190	57,300

Figure 31
Donations by Age Group (1990)

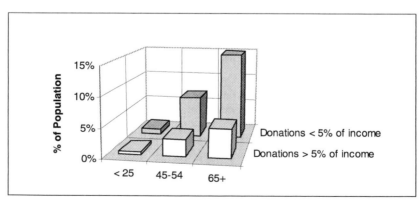

348

There is a disturbing disparity in donations between the young and old, as seen in Figure 31. While the vast majority of taxfilers contribute less than 1% of their total income to charity, the proportion donating more than 1% tends to increse with age and income. A large percentage of young families are dual-earner families. Single and dual earners contributed, on average, equal dollar amounts to religious organizations, but dual earners had over 50% greater income. Discretionary spending of dual earners was over 50% higher in many categories (clothing, recreation, entertainment), and dual-earner families saved or invested $4,700 on average, compared to $200 for single-earner families.[20] It is clear that dual-earner families, while having higher incomes, are less likely to increase their giving to religious organizations. This is not, however, for lack of financial resources. They do have money, but they have raised their lifestyles and spending habits to match.

Change Within the Church

The Church is not immune to the changes taking place in society. The same forces that are shaking Canadian society affect churches and mission organizations. Aging, family trends and spending patterns have an impact on how churches grow, reach their communities, fund their ministries and recruit and develop both volunteer and vocational workers. Speaking particularly on the financial giving side of current trends, James Engel writes: "Unless radical changes are made by mission agencies and local churches, Christian Baby Boomers will not provide the human and financial resources needed for accelerated evangelism in the 1990s."[21]

Trends in financial giving toward churches and missions are partially explained by the attitudes of the Baby Boomer generation. The 1990s are a pivotal decade for the funding of mission enterprises. To date, the generation that grew up during the Great Depression and the war years has been the

Table 54
1992 Family Expenditures

Category 1992 Figures	Single Earners (with young children)	Dual Earners (with young children)	All Households
Food	$6,843	$8,350	$5,686
Shelter	$9,128	$11,678	$8,102
Household expenses (incl. childcare)	$2,042	$3,841	$1,974
Furnishings	$1,642	$2,224	$1,372
Clothing	$2,405	$4,030	$2,222
Transportation	$6,450	$8,022	$5,640
Personal Care	$987	$1,316	$844
Recreation	$2,481	$3,683	$2,300
Education	$433	$774	$430
Alcohol & Tobacco	$1,199	$1,587	$1,410
Miscellaneous	$1,191	$1,852	$1,322
Taxes	$11,190	$17,187	$9,378
Security	$2,750	$4,696	$2,289
Gifts & Contributions	$898	$1,207	$1,464
Total Expenditures	**$50,928**	**$72,067**	**$45,548**

financial backbone of many churches. These people, though, are aging and stretched to the limit in their ability to support new ministries, or even to maintain current support. Increasingly the burden for financial support for church and mission organizations needs to be drawn from the Baby Boomers and subsequent generations. Moreover, Boomers have different priorities and interests that must be addressed in order to convince them to support a new generation of church and mission activities. Baby Boomers have a "prevailing entrepreneurial spirit and desire for immediate gratification. While distrust of traditional institutions is common, Boomers view themselves as problem solvers who, if given an appropriate challenge, are likely to rise to meet it."[22] They are willing to commit time and funds when they have ownership of the cause, and prefer being involved in projects where they can have direct, hands-on participation. Because these traits have not been identified and catered to, the Baby Boomers are "largely immune to the cause of world missions as it has been traditionally practiced and presented."[23]

Churches are faced with many challenges in raising funds and recruiting workers. As Canada's social structure changes, churches will need to adapt to meet the needs of their communities. New strategies will have to be implemented to reach a generation of young people who have grown up largely without church ties. Churches will have to be planted to reach the unchurched areas of our cities. Programs will have to accommodate the diversity of language, cultural and family backgrounds that Canada's cities increasingly represent. This is a massive undertaking, especially considering the lack of robust health within Canadian evangelical churches.

Table 55
Growth Stages of Evangelical Churches

Stage of Growth	% of Evangelical Churches
Initial Formation	10
Maximum Efficiency	10
Plateaued	65
Declining	10
Disintegration	5

On a national level, almost two-thirds of evangelical churches have plateaued.[24] They have become inward-focused and maintenance-oriented, having lost their mission-driven focus. They are not experiencing any significant growth beyond the population growth rate. No effective outreach is taking place. An additional 15% of evangelical churches are either declining or dying.

The health of existing churches has a profound impact on the capacity of the Canadian church to engage in significant church planting efforts. According to the latest research compiled by *Outreach Canada*, the current church planting rate of 1.5% annually is only slightly above the annual population growth rate of 1.2%. Effectively, the number of new churches, after population increases are taken into account, is 0.3% every year. In light of the fact that two-thirds of churches have no growth, another 15% are in decline, and 10% are still in the stages of formation, only 10% of churches are in a life stage which accommodates planting a daughter church. It would seem self-evident that for any significant change to occur in the rate of church planting, a corresponding positive change in the general health and ministry effectiveness of existing churches would also have to take place.

It is also apparent that churches' budgets for local ministry and missions will come under increasing pressure in future years. Staff salaries, as a percentage of church budgets, have remained fairly constant over the years.[25] With increased debt loads for buildings, ministry funds will be squeezed. Church and mission organizations will have to find new, creative ways to finance their outreach activities into the next century.

Table 56
Church Spending by Category

Budget Category	1992	1994	1996
Staff Salary	47%	51%	49%
Debt Service	11%	11%	7%
Local Ministry	26%	22%	27%
Missions	12%	12%	14%
Evangelism	4%	4%	3%

The challenge presented by the Canadian Church Planting Congress held in October 1997 included a vision for 10,000 new gatherings of believers by the year 2015. For this to become a reality there will need to be a significant increase in the present rate of church planting. Currently our evangelical church planting rate is 1.5% per annum nationally. Our current population growth rate is 1.2% annually. The currently reported world rate of church planting is 4.5%. For Canadians to meet the challenge of having a witnessing congregation within the reach of every person will require aggressive changes in the way we plant and support new groups meeting to worship.

Implications

The challenges facing church and mission organizations in Canada are daunting. Waves of change are rippling through churches, denominations and parachurch ministries constantly. Canada's social fabric is being redefined. Shifting demographics indicate that Canada's future population will be older than today's, highly urbanized, and composed of more diverse ethnic groups. Families will be smaller as people are waiting longer to have children, and most families will have both parents working outside the home. Real wages will probably continue to see little growth, so the only way for families to increase their spending power will be to work more.

Christians in Canada must respond to these trends by taking action now. Church and mission organizations will need to begin changing their perspectives on promoting, funding and staffing their ministries, or risk becoming further removed from their cultural context. It may be argued that what is not broken does not need to be fixed. However, in light of the lack of progress in planting new churches, and the high percentage of evangelical churches that are either plateaued or declining, it is clear that something must change.

Continuing ministry using the models of the past will not work effectively in the Canada of the 21st century. Eckard Pfeiffer, CEO of Compaq Computers, has stated that "small incremental changes block your vision of doing something fundamentally different." Minor modifications to the present ministry model will not be sufficient to face the challenges of the next century. What is needed are new ideas, new directions, new supporters, new sources of funding and new vision for ministry.

Creative partnerships and involvement between churches, denominations and parachurch organizations are vital in affecting significant change in the church planting and evangelization rates. Cooperative ventures and strategic alliances between organizations have the potential to reduce the duplication of services and competitive spirit that often characterizes the church planting scene. New channels of communication would need to be opened, allowing specialized staff within diverse organizations to collaborate on a wide variety of initiatives. Churches would focus more on the results than on the organizational processes involved. Decisions would be made that have the best interest of the outreach project in mind, rather than those of individual churches or denominations. Church, denomination and mission organizations would partner together to share resources and expertise.

One vehicle for sharing information and coordinating activities is the World Wide Web. It has become apparent that the information highway will be a central part of the 21st century world. The Internet is here now, and it is not just a passing fad. Computer communications open up new horizons for individuals and organizations to explore. The World Wide Web provides quick access to immense volumes of information, while e-mail allows virtually instantaneous contact around the globe at little or no cost. Enormous potential exists to creatively use electronic communication to network church leaders and share strategies and progress reports. Mailing lists and e-mailed newsletters have the potential to rally immediate prayer and financial support for challenges as they arise. New technology even allows video-conferencing across the Internet, allowing two users to exchange video and audio signals without paying long distance charges. Technology like this could be put to creative use in training meetings and networking centers for church planters and church leaders.

Canada as a Mission Field

The first obvious implication of the pervasive social and cultural change underway in Canada is that our nation is a vast unreached mission field. The needs are enormous for new churches, for revitalizing older plateaued churches and for re-evangelizing the cities. Since most Canadians live in cities, and the cities are becoming more and more diverse in their ethnic mix, new ways of reaching the cities must be found. Religious groups that are resistant to the Gospel, such as Muslims and Sikhs, have to be targeted for intensive efforts in evangelization, church planting and discipling.

An example of targeting specific unreached people groups would be the Sikh community. If past trends continue second- and third-generation Sikhs should be much more receptive to the Gospel than the immigrants who were born and grew up in India. Since the second generation was born and raised in Canada, many of the ties to Sikh religion and culture are not as strong. Many second-generation Sikhs follow western cultural patterns, and do not place heavy emphasis on their religious heritage. These changes are even more pronounced among third-generation Canadians from visible minority people groups. This does not mean that efforts should not be made to reach these people groups immediately after they immigrate, but recognize that certain people groups have a higher readiness and openness to the Gospel message. It is those groups that should receive the focus of our attention.

Global Partnerships

A further implication that arises from Canada's status as a needy mission field is forming global partnerships to reach people groups. Church and mission agencies need to join together to reach people groups all over the world. An approach that reaches only immigrants in Canada or only an overseas people group is limited in its strategic effectiveness. Take an example of a metro Toronto church trying to reach a neighborhood of West African Muslims. Rather than struggling to discover how to reach African Muslims who emigrated from Nigeria, church and mission organizations can form partnerships with sister organizations in Africa. Leaders and ministry teams can visit churches in Africa that are effectively reaching those people groups. Leaders could be exchanged for a few weeks or months. Evangelists and leaders from African churches can be brought over to help the church understand the culture, needs and effective methods of reaching that people group. Global partnerships share the burden and stimulate creative outreach both within Canada and internationally.

Investing in the Future

To reach Canada's burgeoning immigrant population, missionaries can be sent overseas to invest in leadership training to reach those people groups. As part of the missionary's development of national leaders, he/she can intentionally develop leaders who would be willing to come to Canada as missionaries to work among their own people group. To follow our previous example, missionaries could be sent to West Africa to assist with the training of national leaders. African pastors and evangelists could be brought to Canada to develop strategies to reach African immigrants in

Canada. This arrangement could be either with one church or denomination, or with a mission organization, or even a combination of the two. There is plenty of scope for creative sharing of resources and funding, in addition to the sharing of global missions responsibility between the Canadian Church and the Church in other nations.

Churches can also invest in their own future through creative church planting. Many existing churches, particularly those that are plateaued or declining, have been overwhelmed by change and have not been able to continue to change with society. Rather than encouraging these churches to make radical changes to better reflect their communities, a more appropriate action might be to plant a daughter church. Rather than forcing changes that could cause strife and be a major burden for the church, planting a daughter church could have significant rewards for the mother church. It would benefit from the birthing process, seeing another group of believers reaching their community, and would accumulate a small win. Over time, with other opportunities to reach out to the community, the mother church can build a culture of change that will allow it to better minister to its own community.

Cultivate New Funding Sources

One of the primary tasks for church and mission agencies in the 1990s is finding new ways to develop their financial support bases. Most Christian organizations are heavily funded by people over age 55. As these people move toward retirement, their ability to continue to support missions will be curtailed. Special attention must be given to increasing the level of support from younger families. In particular, dual-earner families have financial resources available. They make up the majority of younger families, and despite higher family incomes they only give as much as single-income families. If they can be convinced of the need to support and given a creative project to be involved in, dual-earner families can become a major financial asset to missions into the next century.

New sources of funding will also be needed if the church planting rate is to be substantially increased. Most churches and denominations are near their financial resource limits in planting churches at the present rate. If this rate is to be increased, new models both for organizing church plants and for funding them will be needed.

Churches Partnering with Mission Organizations

Greater responsibility for the church planting enterprise can and should be extended to the local church. One method of increasing the number of new churches planted is to encourage churches to daughter churches more regularly. The larger role would include churches more as partners rather than just spectators and financial contributors. Churches will be the primary leaders, with denominations and parachurch organizations acting in close support and as equippers of local church leaders. Some large churches already function in this capacity, planting churches and sending out missionaries entirely from their own resources.

Partnerships would allow grass-roots involvement within the church to support church plants and the workers sent out for ministry. Ownership by the local church of the church planting process also increases the level of funding given. Denominations would have to shoulder less of the burden of supporting each church plant, which usually is a major limiting factor in the number of churches planted. The potential for involvement should also appeal to younger church leaders, who are more accustomed to an inclusive style of management.

New Models for Recruiting Leaders

If the church planting rate is to be significantly increased, new methods will be needed to train and prepare church planters. Already there are times when the lack of qualified personnel holds back the start of a new church plant. Often it is the least-experienced church leaders recently graduated from seminary who make the jump into church planting. Increased numbers of experienced, well-trained church planters will be needed. Recognition of the risks involved, proper training and support of church planters, and adequate financial support are important factors in increasing the success rate of new church plants.

Effectively Harness Communications Technology

Modern communications technologies, especially the Internet and e-mail, have great potential to be used effectively in the cause of evangelizing Canada. Church planters can rally immediate prayer support for urgent needs that would otherwise not be made known for weeks or months. A network can be set up between churches, denominations and mission organizations to better communicate and channel help and resources between each party. Denominations can increase communication and information-sharing capabilities while reducing costs by using e-mail to send materials to churches. A number of denominations in the United States already require each pastor to have a computer and e-mail account and to file monthly reports on ministry progress electronically.

Conclusions

If we are to be effective in mobilizing Canadians for church planting into the 21st century, we will need to make some dramatic changes in how we approach the task. We will have to advance innovative, even radical, ways to establish new relationships between churches and support organizations.

The paradigm needs to shift. Denominations have to move from being intermediaries between churches and church planters, to supporting and resourcing the local church to accomplish its mission directly. We will need to focus on unreached people groups wherever they live around the world. This will help to bring missions closer to home for most churches and organizations, while focusing more on effectiveness than on organizational concerns. Partnerships, strategic alliances and collaboration on church planting projects will be key components to building the Body of Christ in the 21st century.

Action Points

✓ What changes in the social and cultural trends will challenge the Church the most?

✓ What will the Church need to do in order to maximize its ministry?

✓ Who should be targeted as new leaders for the workforce?

✓ Where will we need to look for the financial resources to accomplish our ministries?

✓ How can churches and denominations work together in planting new churches?

✓ What role do mission organizations play in the church planting enterprise? How will they be engaged in the challenge?

✓ How can churches at all stages of growth be involved in planting new churches?

Chapter Notes

[1] *Canadian Social Trends* 39, p. 13.

[2] *Canadian Social Trends* 46, p. 36.

[3] *Canadian Social Trends* 29, p. 4.

[4] *Canadian Social Trends* 37, p. 4.

[5] *Maclean's*, Jan 8 1996, p. 3 of Investment Advertising Supplement.

[6] *Canadian Social Trends* 35, p. 3.

[7] *Canadian Social Trends* 39, p. 14.

[8] *Canadian Social Trends* 33, p. 5.

[9] *Canadian Social Trends* 33, p. 7.

[10] *Canadian Social Trends* 36, p. 25.

[11] *Canadian Social Trends* 39, p. 18.

[12] *Canadian Social Trends* 31, p. 9.

[13] *Canadian Social Trends* 47, p. 10.

[14] Glenn Smith, "Reaching Canada's Cities for Christ," *Urban Mission*, September 1990, pp.30-31.

[15] *Canadian Social Trends* 37, p. 6.

[16] Citizenship and Immigration Canada, *Citizenship and Immigration Statistics 1994* , Minister of Public Works and Government Services Canada, 1997, p. x.

[17] *Canadian Social Trends* 37, p. 8.

[18] *Canadian Social Trends* 35, p. 7.

[19] Statistics Canada's *The Daily*, November 27, 1997.

[20] *Canadian Social Trends* 32, p. 23.

[21] James F. Engel, "We are the World," *Christianity Today* Sept. 24, 1990, p. 32.

Chapter Notes

[22] Engel, "We are the World", p. 32.

[23] Engel, "We are the World", p. 33.

[24] Outreach Canada research findings. Based on Ministry Assessment results and interviews with denominational leaders.

[25] Outreach Canada research findings from annual statistics. Table shows one particular denomination with over 500 churches.

Epilogue

Epilogue

God's Call to the Church

Dr. Arnell Motz

Two young boys were in the principal's office—in trouble again. The principal called the first boy in and to impress him with the bigger issues of life asked in his most serious voice: "Where is God?" The boy's stare was blank even after a second attempt. Exasperated the principal called the other boy in. The first boy whispered as he passed his friend: "Apparently God is missing and they're trying to hang it on us."

As we reflect on Canadian society the appropriate question is: "Where is God?" Our society has said it is okay for women to go topless in public. Pornography is accessible on cable TV, the corner store and the Internet. So where is God in our thinking, in our morals and in our values?

Canada is waiting for an answer. Is God relegated to being a back-bencher in the halls of government, a relic in the museum of education, a faded shadow in the corner of our homes?

When Charles Templeton published his "Farewell to God," he expressed in open terms where many Canadians are headed in their thinking, God is either a distant memory or a a question that cannot be answered. Where is God? They don't know—or they don't care.

If *Vision Canada* accomplishes anything, let it be a call to the Church to try to answer that question. The fact is that society has replaced God with empty answers. Hedonism and narcissism, the philosophies of our day, are ringing hollow. So we try to escape the drudgery of life with sports, "suds" and the silver screen. But our emptiness shows itself in the rise of broken families and a mood of despair. The Church must ask the question, "Where is God?" And then it must try to provide answers that can be understood. If we don't, we will have nowhere to go but this abyss of agnosticism and hopelessness.

Where is the Church?

Instead of asking, "Where is God?" we should ask, "Where is the Church?" Where is the incarnate witness of who God is?

So many times we focus on the question, "Was Canada ever a Christian nation?" as if to legitimatize our presence in society. The Church does not get its mandate from the history books, but from the book that claims to be the Word of God. As followers of Christ we are called to be light in a dark world. Where there is more darkness, we are to be there with more light. We enjoy being part of "light conventions," but our calling is to find a dark place in this world and let our light shine.

Canada has a great heritage in Christian values. Sir Leonard Tilly called upon the framers of our nation to make its foundation a firm belief in God, and so our motto was taken from Psalm 72:8—*He shall have dominion from sea to sea.* The fact that the Fathers of Confederation used the term, "dominion of Canada," was a direct inference taken from this verse. William Westfall reminds us that the Psalmist is holding up values of justice and righteousness in "triumph over the selfishness and wickedness of men." He states the motto was chosen to reflect "a new type of society on the earth when the wilderness of sin and injustice will become the dominion of the Lord."

In 1905 Canadian Prime Minister, Sir Wilfred Laurier, spoke to the House of Commons about the need for Christian morals to be taught in our Canadian schools.

Against a backdrop of his description of American society, he said:

When I observe in this country of ours a total absence of lynchings and an almost total absence of divorces and murders, I thank heaven that we are living in a country where the young children of the land are taught Christian morals and Christian dogmas.

Many of the one million British Loyalists who headed north after the American War of Independence were devout Anglicans, Presbyterians, Methodists and Baptists. Many of the settlers who came from Europe brought their Reformation and Pietist beliefs. Our leaders of the past, such as Wilfred Laurier, John Hamilton Craig, John Diefenbaker, Tommy Douglas and others, had their political beliefs shaped by strong Christian convictions.

In a sense, the Church has a political right to have its voice heard, but the Church must rise above the din of politics. The Church must speak in terms that are not confused with political opinions. The Church must speak to issues of truth and righteousness. The Church must bring a message of hope into the hopelessness of society.

So where is the Church at this point in our history? Is it growing or has it lost its vision? This book has detailed various descriptions. On one hand we could say that religious conviction has lost its foothold in society at large. While 81% still claim religious affiliation, what that really means is a recognition of their religious roots rather than ownership of religious beliefs. In an Angus Reid poll only 58% consider religion an important part of life, and church attendance on a monthly basis (of all religious groups) now stands at 21%, which indicates the majority will only turn to the Church for weddings or funerals.

Where is the Church? If buildings of brick and mortar were to define the Church, then the largest number would be Mainline denominations such as United and Anglican. If it were responses to the pollster on "religious affiliation," then the largest group would be Catholic. Yet if you were to measure it by actual church attendance in your community, most communities across Canada would have the largest numbers in evangelical churches on any given Sunday (about one of every ten Canadians would claim to be evangelical, the only number that has been growing). But is being evangelical enough? Is holding to the essentials of what the Bible claims as Biblical truth fulfilling the mandate of the Church? No! Christ also calls us not to be adherents but proclaimers of the truth. And where truth is not heard, then we should ask, "Where is the Church?"

What is truth?

Pilate tried to ask Jesus that same question, "What is truth?" Jesus had said, "for this I came into the world to testify to the truth. Everyone on the side of truth (literally *of the truth*) listens to me." Pilate didn't know how to respond, so he tried to sideline the issue with the question that we often hear today, "Yes, but what is truth? How can you claim to have 'the truth?'" The answer came, not in a great apologetic, although the Bible gives a good basis for its truth claims, but in a demonstration of the incarnate Christ. It came in a model of self-denial and self-giving love.

As Christians in this great nation called Canada, we may not be able to provide all the answers to society's questions, but we cannot sit back and let society say farewell to God. We must incarnate a witness of who Jesus is in the middle of all the despair and hopelessness that society may feel.

Sociologist, Dr. Reginald Bibby, has said:

There is a tremendous need for what religion has to offer. We're finding that Canadians are continuing to raise questions of meaning and purpose, and it seems to me that in this instance religion has an awful lot to say to Canadians.

Our history shows us leaders, such as Egerton Ryerson, who shaped Ontario's system of public education and wrote the textbook, *First Lessons in Christian Morals.* He and his evangelical colleagues sparked a vision for building hospitals, libraries and homes for unwed mothers—all because of a belief that a commitment to God meant incarnating that message into the very being of society.

Making truth claims does not mean imposing religious institutions or creating a theocracy. The education system of today seems to fear this and has imposed a valueless system on our children. The warning of Dr. Bibby's words may be the result. He says:

Religion in Canada is in serious trouble. Canadians are into religion a la carte. They're into select beliefs and practices. They want professional services from the churches by way of weddings, funerals and baptisms, but they are not embracing religion as a way of life. It's not something that is informing the everyday existence of the average Canadian."

Rabbi Dennis Prager wrote:

Liberals (whom we have called secularists) are always talking about pluralism, but that is not what they mean. They mean "melting pot." Pluralism (properly) means that Catholics are Catholics, Jews are Jews, Baptists are Baptists, etc. That's what pluralism means—everyone affirms his values and we all live with civic equality and tolerance. That's my dream. (But) in public school, Jews don't meet Christians. Christians don't meet Hindus. Everybody meets nothing. That is, as I explain to Jews all the time, why their children so easily inter-marry. Jews don't marry Christians. Non-Jewish Jews marry non-Christian Christians. Jews for nothing marry Christians for nothing. They get along great because they both affirm nothing. They have everything in common—nothing. That's not pluralism. But that is exactly what the liberal world wants. They want a bunch of secular universalists with ethnic surnames.

Paul Marshall uses this quote of Rabbi Prager to say our Constitution should:

...enhance the place of religion in Canadian society. Our religious values should provide an interpretive framework as we seek to develop and interpret the Constitution, especially the Canadian Charter of Rights and Freedoms.

His point is not just political. It is not just because our social structure is "rooted in our religious inheritance," but because the destruction of society results when we hold to nothing. It is the "nothingness" imposed on the youth of our nation that results in hopelessness.

I belabour this because it points to our mandate as the Church living in a pluralistic society. Christian values must be upheld at a foundational level. The Church must speak to issues of truth and righteousness to a society that seems to be losing its memory of those values. Then it must go beyond that. It must incarnate Christ in society. It cannot impose a Christian religious system that everyone must adhere to, but it can demonstrate a Christian compassion to the hurts of society. It can be something they can *see* and something they can *hear* in terms that they can *understand*.

But they must hear. We may be one of many voices, but we must speak clearly the truth claims of Christ that are relevant to every person in our nation. We must speak in a strong voice that calls men and women, boys and girls, to become followers of Christ. But in the intimidation of losing our right to be a voice in society, have we lost our will to speak the good news of Christ?

What Should We Do?

Why do we find ourselves in this condition? Why is there a spiritual desert not only in our culture but also in our churches? Could it be the result of bringing "empty offerings" to God? Could we be like the Israelites in the Old Testament, who performed their religious duties but presented their offerings empty of devotion and whole-hearted commitment to God?

So then what should we do? The answer is not first or only in coming up with a new program of research and strategies for reaching our nation. While these have great value for calling God's people to do what Christ calls us to do, we need to be careful that they do not become just another well meaning intention. Rather our reply should be like David's in a similar situation. He had called for research that would shape strategies dependent on his own strength. It was at that point his motives were wrong and God called him into account for his empty offerings.

What did David do? What we should do, also, if we expect God to move in our nation. We see it in 1 Chronicles 21:8. Note that God responds because of his **repentance.** David did not try to hide his sin. We should not try to hide ours. Could our lack of effectiveness be a lack of commitment or lack of Christ-centredness to our lives? Could divisiveness in the Body of Christ, wrong priorities or the lack of integrity in our lives be the barrier to a move of God? God's call is still: *"...if my people, who are called by my name, will humble themselves and pray and seek my face and turn from their wicked ways, then I will hear from heaven and forgive their sin and will heal their land"* (2 Chronicles 7:14).

The emphasis of His words is not on the greatness of a nation but on the heart of His people. God desires repentance so that He can revive—put life back into His people. It is for us to call out, *"Will you not revive us again, that your people may rejoice in you?"* (Psalm 85:6).

But in the example of David, God also responded because of his **sacrifice.** In 1 Chronicles 21:24 he offers to buy everything from Araunah so as to make a sacrifice to the Lord. Araunah offers to give it to David. David replies: *"I will not* (offer that which) *costs me nothing."* This was not an empty offering. He knew it had to cost him something! Are we willing to let our service to God cost us something?

We long for God to grow His Church through revival as He has done in China, Ethiopia or other places in the world today. When I tell accounts of the Wolayatta church in southern Ethiopia baptizing between 15,000 to 20,000 people each year, my Canadian listeners usually say wistfully: "If God would only do that here." Yet in those places the Church has grown through adversity and a sense of sacrifice on the part of believers. During my time in Ethiopia, I heard many stories of Christians being imprisoned during the Communist years, yet what shone through was the sense of their life being expendable for Christ. I saw evangelists willing to leave their families for a year so as to go into some of the hard places and establish a church.

Would I be willing to do the same? To be honest, I'm not sure. I like the comforts of home, the sense of being cloistered in my family room by the warm glow of the electronic hearth. Am I really willing to be inconvenienced? Am I willing to give up something to have a witness, to get involved with people? What am I really willing to sacrifice for Christ? As we look at ourselves should we say, "No wonder the Canadian Church is losing its effectiveness in society?" Are we one of those bringing empty offerings in our prayers for revival?

Eva Barrows, of the Salvation Army, reminds us that great revivals never began in a big way but with one life given up. Sometimes it was with martyrdom. Other times with personal sacrifices. She pierces the issue by saying, "...and a cross-bearing Savior should not have cross-evading disciples." We might not be asked for a sacrifice of martyrdom, but we might be called to a sacrifice of personal convenience—to give up something or to do something that pushes us out of our comfort zone and gets us into His commission zone. As with the account of David, when there is true sacrifice, then God answers "with fire from heaven."

The Prophetic Message for the Year 2000

The prophetic voice of *Vision Canada* should echo the call for repentance and sacrifice if we want to see God move through our land. But it can also raise a prophetic message of what the Church could be if God were to respond to our prayers. It is not presuming on God, but giving us a challenge to believe God for something only He can do.

In 1990 we published the first edition of *Reclaiming a Nation,* in which I wrote:

Research should lead us to a "prophetic message." It should not only describe our present condition and what has happened, but should suggest our future condition and what could happen. It should challenge us to ask: "What will we ask God to do through us?" and "What will we look like if we do?"

These could be the most important questions of the whole book. It is helpful to look at trends in our society to know how to contextualize our communication. It is wise to examine how the Holy Spirit is working today as we desire to become more effective. We need to understand our strengths and weaknesses if we seek to build vision. But the articulation of what we could become is really the apex of our work.

The point of saying "What could happen?," is not an earthly kingdom building for those who call themselves "evangelicals." Nor is it a triumphalism—"let's go take the hill." Rather this is holding out a vision of what could happen through God's kingdom if we are true to His mandate.

If the harvest force is represented by 8 to 10% of our nation, or approximately 9,000 congregations, and if we were to grow through evangelism at just **3% per year,** then the harvest force would **double in the next 18 years.** Evangelicals worldwide are growing at a rate of 4.5% per year.

More specifically, one of the primary challenges of *Vision Canada* and this book is church planting, because it presents effective means of mobilizing for evangelism and ensuring the Gospel can be within reach of every person.

So let us focus the prophetic message of what we could become on church planting and say—If each denomination were to add 3% annually to their corporate number of congregations, this is what could happen to the Church in Canada. (see Table 22 in Chapter 4)

Could the Holy Spirit do more through us? What if each congregation were to plant or co-parent a daughter church each 3 to 5 years, simply as a commitment of its evangelism program along with Alpha and other purposeful evangelistic efforts? What if new churches were to build plans to daughter again into their philosophy of ministry DNA from the outset? What if new churches were birthed in every high-density housing complex, among every people group and by every congregation?

What if a majority of congregations in Canada were to grow—on campus and on new sites—by 7% per year? (Some are in fact growing well beyond that.) A church could double in a decade with a 7% growth rate—a rate combining on site evangelistic growth and church planting. Based on this rate, a church of 100 would have a net growth of seven people the first year, nine the next and thirteen the following year. Envision what could happen to that church in ten years.

Figure 32
Congregational Growth at 7% per Year

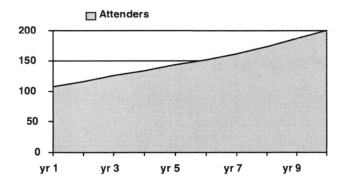

We asked before and we ask again—can it be done? Not without a renewed commitment to vision and a willingness to make sacrifices. But we must echo the words of D.L. Moody: "It can be done, it must be done!"

The fact is—the *Canadian Church Planting Congress '97* declaration *is* possible. And when we ask the question in terms of each congregation, we can see that this is a reasonable faith goal. Churches can plant churches which in turn will plant churches. Will every evangelical congregation accept this challenge? No, not every congregation—but does that change our own commitment to the task? The issue is not what others will do, but what will you do? What will your church do? God always holds the individual responsible first, and then the nation. Revival comes the same way.

Valley of Decision

In the film, *Valley of Decision,* a country church that is oblivious to the threat of a prairie fire becomes a metaphor for what could be happening to the Canadian Church today. We can act as if nothing is wrong and ignore signs of danger. The late Robert Thompson speaks in the film from his 18 years as a member of parliament and warns that Canada could become "another burned-over area of Christianity." As a great Canadian statesman who gave his years of service not only in the hard places of Ethiopia but also in the halls of power in Canada, his voice needs to be heard. We cannot assume the future based on blessings of the past. Whatever place Christian values and the Christian message had in our nation in the past is no guarantee that it will continue in the future.

The preacher in the film uses the prophet Joel as a voice to us today. The nations were saying: "Where is their God?" To Canada it could be: "Where is God in a land that claims a Christian heritage or in the churches that claim to be His people? Where is Christ incarnate in a witness to all people?" In Joel's day God withdrew His power because of the sin of His people. Could the same be true today? It is a hard question but one that must be asked.

378

The prophet called out: *"Return to the Lord... weep.... Do not make your inheritance an object of scorn,...Why should they say among the peoples, 'Where is their God?'"* (Joel 2:13, 17).

The message of Joel is one of promise as well as warning. It is the promise *that "I will pour out my Spirit on all people... And everyone who calls on the name of the Lord will be saved"* (Joel 2:28, 32). But then it ends with the picture of His people needing to decide their destiny... *"Multitudes, multitudes in the valley of decision!"* (Joel 3:14)

We too need to decide. If we take the challenge of, *the Gospel for every person and a church for every people,* will it be an empty offering? If we cross over into a new century or a new millennium, what will Canada become? When people ask: "Where is God...in our nation?" could we say, "He is being lived out in the lives of thousands of Christians across this land. His presence is being felt in the schools, hospitals, jails, homes and wherever people are hurting. His 'Body' is being multiplied in every part of Canada as His people respond to His commission with obedience and sacrifice."

Where is God? Let Him be heard in every heart of this land, in every part of this dominion called Canada. Let us respond with witnessing congregations that incarnate the message of Christ to every person and to every people. Let us cry out from the depth of our hearts—*"Will you not revive us again, that your people may rejoice in you?"* (Psalm 85:6).

This is the question for the Church in Canada—the "multitudes in the valley of decision."

Action Points

✓ What is the main issue for your church in keeping vision for accomplishing Christ's Commission? What becomes the greatest distraction?

✓ How do you personally respond to the call for "repentance" and "sacrifice?" Where do you think the Spirit's voice may be challenging you?

✓ Look at the growth rate of your church or denomination in the last five years. If you were to set a faith goal of growth, what would it be?

Appendices

Appendix One

Canadian Non-Christian Affiliation

"North America is now the largest mission field in the English speaking world and the third largest after China and India...we are in a mission situation in our own country."

- Leighton Ford

Census Metropolitan Area	1991 City Pop	Jehovah's Witness		Mormon		Jewish		Buddhist	
Toronto	3,863,110	19,170	0%	5,855	0%	151,115	4%	48,390	1%
Montréal	3,091,110	15,730	1%	2,570	0%	96,710	3%	27,910	1%
Vancouver	1,584,115	12,025	1%	5,750	0%	14,360	1%	31,645	2%
Ottawa-Hull	912,095	4,395	0%	1,455	0%	9,915	1%	6,015	1%
Edmonton	832,155	5,935	1%	6,260	1%	4,040	0%	9,285	1%
Calgary	748,210	4,390	1%	12,285	2%	5,455	1%	8,870	1%
Winnipeg	645,610	3,430	1%	1,200	0%	13,325	2%	5,075	1%
Québec	637,755	1,885	0%	135	0%	155	0%	1,260	0%
Hamilton	593,805	3,435	1%	1,440	0%	4,465	1%	2,305	0%
London	376,720	2,005	1%	1,540	0%	2,190	1%	1,425	0%
St. Catharines-Niagara	359,985	2,805	1%	960	0%	1,150	0%	550	0%
Kitchener	353,110	2,565	1%	1,130	0%	805	0%	2,220	1%
Halifax	317,630	1,365	0%	1,025	0%	1,480	0%	1,170	0%
Victoria	283,630	2,155	1%	1,390	0%	965	0%	1,465	1%
Windsor	259,290	965	0%	430	0%	1,560	1%	1,080	0%
Oshawa	238,030	1,285	1%	700	0%	455	0%	315	0%
Saskatoon	207,825	2,050	1%	580	0%	615	0%	930	0%
Regina	189,440	1,000	1%	940	0%	485	0%	635	0%
St. John's	169,810	780	0%	160	0%	95	0%	85	0%
Chicoutimi-Jonquière	159,595	475	0%	30	0%	0	0%	95	0%
Sudbury	156,120	1,110	1%	375	0%	230	0%	80	0%
Sherbrooke	136,705	465	0%	90	0%	100	0%	315	0%
Trois-Rivières	134,890	575	0%	20	0%	15	0%	120	0%
Saint John	123,600	375	0%	180	0%	180	0%	70	0%
Thunder Bay	122,860	620	1%	230	0%	210	0%	145	0%

Hindu		Muslim		Sikh		Other Non-Christian Groups		No Religious Affiliation		Total Non-Christian Affiliation	
90,140	2%	105,970	3%	41,450	1%	12,965	0%	562,265	15%	1,037,320	27%
13,775	0%	41,215	1%	3,880	0%	3,940	0%	167,065	5%	372,795	12%
14,880	1%	23,335	1%	49,625	3%	9,690	1%	493,215	31%	654,525	41%
4,780	1%	17,585	2%	1,575	0%	3,660	0%	93,290	10%	142,670	16%
5,815	1%	14,815	2%	6,480	1%	2,735	0%	165,910	20%	221,275	27%
4,155	1%	13,895	2%	6,075	1%	2,225	0%	165,635	22%	222,985	30%
3,105	0%	3,235	1%	3,290	1%	2,215	0%	104,505	16%	139,380	22%
80	0%	1,195	0%	155	0%	335	0%	21,785	3%	26,985	4%
2,800	0%	3,815	1%	2,240	0%	1,360	0%	79,955	13%	101,815	17%
990	0%	4,455	1%	560	0%	1,170	0%	54,035	14%	68,370	18%
515	0%	865	0%	170	0%	1,015	0%	35,865	10%	43,895	12%
2,815	1%	3,870	1%	1,180	0%	975	0%	40,000	11%	55,560	16%
755	0%	1,000	0%	230	0%	615	0%	28,620	9%	36,260	11%
510	0%	535	0%	2,990	1%	2,420	1%	84,140	30%	96,570	34%
710	0%	3,545	1%	555	0%	380	0%	19,700	8%	28,925	11%
1,075	0%	1,365	1%	285	0%	425	0%	33,280	14%	39,185	16%
600	0%	455	0%	230	0%	895	0%	29,165	14%	35,520	17%
720	0%	555	0%	210	0%	840	0%	25,805	14%	31,190	16%
320	0%	225	0%	70	0%	170	0%	4,970	3%	6,875	4%
0	0%	105	0%	15	0%	55	0%	2,525	2%	3,300	2%
135	0%	470	0%	55	0%	290	0%	11,230	7%	13,975	9%
60	0%	475	0%	115	0%	80	0%	5,680	4%	7,380	5%
20	0%	110	0%	0	0%	120	0%	2,790	2%	3,770	3%
145	0%	95	0%	10	0%	190	0%	7,450	6%	8,695	7%
120	0%	175	0%	45	0%	465	0%	13,325	11%	15,335	12%

Appendix Two

Church Planting Needs
by City

"In view of social trends, North America faces one of two scenarios in the next five to ten years: moral anarchy or spiritual revival."

- George Barna

Greater St. John's, NF Area

	1996 Population	Reported Evangelical Churches	People per Evangelical Church	New Evangelical Churches Needed to Provide One for Every 2,000 People
English	170,305	23	7,405	62
French	175	0	N/A	0
Chinese	385	0	N/A	0
Vietnamese	90	0	N/A	0
Russian	75	0	N/A	0
Norwegian	75	0	N/A	0
Arabic	65	0	N/A	0

Greater Halifax Area

	1996 Population	Reported Evangelical Churches	People per Evangelical Church	New Evangelical Churches Needed to Provide One for Every 2,000 People
English	317,485	99	3,207	60
French	3,440	0	N/A	2
Arabic	1,640	0	N/A	1
Chinese	1,165	2	583	0
Greek	410	0	N/A	0
Polish	265	0	N/A	0
Italian	240	0	N/A	0

Halifax Proper

	1996 Population	Reported Evangelical Churches	People per Evangelical Church	New Evangelical Churches Needed to Provide One for Every 2,000 People
English	105,420	32	3,294	21
French	820	0	N/A	0
Arabic	1,175	0	N/A	1
Chinese	745	2	373	0
Greek	330	0	N/A	0
Urdu	230	0	N/A	0
Polish	210	0	N/A	0

Greater Saint John, NB Area

	1996 Population	Reported Evangelical Churches	People per Evangelical Church	New Evangelical Churches Needed to Provide One for Every 2,000 People
English	121,030	55	2,201	6
French	2,090	0	N/A	1
Chinese	100	0	N/A	0
Greek	65	0	N/A	0
Spanish	55	0	N/A	0
Polish	50	0	N/A	0
Portuguese	40	0	N/A	0

Greater Chicoutimi-Jonquière Area

	1996 Population	Reported Evangelical Churches	People per Evangelical Church	New Evangelical Churches Needed to Provide One for Every 2,000 People
English	915	0	N/A	0
French	157,265	6	26,211	73
Chinese	30	0	N/A	0
Spanish	20	0	N/A	0
Vietnamese	15	0	N/A	0
Romanian	15	0	N/A	0
Italian	10	0	N/A	0

Greater Québec City Area

	1996 Population	Reported Evangelical Churches	People per Evangelical Church	New Evangelical Churches Needed to Provide One for Every 2,000 People
English	8,155	2	4,078	2
French	645,520	26	24,828	297
Spanish	835	0	N/A	0
Serbo-Croatian	780	0	N/A	0
Chinese	545	0	N/A	0
Vietnamese	435	0	N/A	0
Arabic	320	0	N/A	0

Québec City Proper

	1996 Population	Reported Evangelical Churches	People per Evangelical Church	New Evangelical Churches Needed to Provide One for Every 2,000 People
English	1,920	2	960	0
French	159,605	8	19,951	72
Spanish	405	0	N/A	0
Serbo-Croatian	280	0	N/A	0
Vietnamese	270	0	N/A	0
Khmer	170	0	N/A	0
Chinese	85	0	N/A	0

Greater Sherbrooke Area

	1996 Population	Reported Evangelical Churches	People per Evangelical Church	New Evangelical Churches Needed to Provide One for Every 2,000 People
English	7,990	5	1,598	0
French	132,220	9	14,691	57
Spanish	670	0	N/A	0
Serbo-Croatian	630	0	N/A	0
Arabic	230	0	N/A	0
Serbian	140	0	N/A	0
Polish	105	0	N/A	0

Greater Trois-Rivières Area

	1996 Population	Reported Evangelical Churches	People per Evangelical Church	New Evangelical Churches Needed to Provide One for Every 2,000 People
English	1,130	0	N/A	1
French	135,415	13	10,417	55
German	60	0	N/A	0
Bulgarian	60	0	N/A	0
Arabic	45	0	N/A	0
Lao	40	0	N/A	0
Khmer	40	0	N/A	0

Greater Montréal Area

	1996 Population	Reported Evangelical Churches	People per Evangelical Church	New Evangelical Churches Needed to Provide One for Every 2,000 People
English	555,675	80	6,946	198
French	2,249,925	185	12,162	940
Italian	62,105	5	12,421	26
Spanish	43,800	20	2,190	2
Arabic	33,275	2	16,638	15
Chinese	32,425	6	5,404	10
Greek	27,695	5	5,539	9

Montréal Proper

	1996 Population	Reported Evangelical Churches	People per Evangelical Church	New Evangelical Churches Needed to Provide One for Every 2,000 People
English	153,045	28	5,466	49
French	606,060	79	7,672	224
Italian	30,880	2	15,440	13
Spanish	26,670	13	2,052	0
Chinese	15,065	4	3,766	4
Arabic	13,145	0	N/A	7
Vietnamese	12,720	1	12,720	5

Laval

	1996 Population	Reported Evangelical Churches	People per Evangelical Church	New Evangelical Churches Needed to Provide One for Every 2,000 People
English	33,010	2	16,505	15
French	251,310	18	13,962	108
Greek	8,105	0	N/A	4
Armenian	4,120	0	N/A	2
Italian	3,795	0	N/A	2
Arabic	3,440	0	N/A	2
Spanish	2,485	0	N/A	1

Longueuil

	1996 Population	Reported Evangelical Churches	People per Evangelical Church	New Evangelical Churches Needed to Provide One for Every 2,000 People
English	3,625	0	N/A	2
French	114,140	7	16,306	50
Spanish	1,305	1	1,305	0
Chinese	945	0	N/A	0
Vietnamese	740	0	N/A	0
Arabic	535	0	N/A	0
Italian	450	0	N/A	0

Greater Ottawa-Hull Area

	1996 Population	Reported Evangelical Churches	People per Evangelical Church	New Evangelical Churches Needed to Provide One for Every 2,000 People
English	602,895	95	6,346	206
French	295,175	17	17,363	131
Arabic	12,090	1	12,090	5
Chinese	11,620	5	2,324	1
Spanish	5,195	3	1,732	0
Italian	4,555	1	4,555	1
Vietnamese	4,530	1	4,530	1

Ottawa Proper

	1996 Population	Reported Evangelical Churches	People per Evangelical Church	New Evangelical Churches Needed to Provide One for Every 2,000 People
English	234,605	39	6,016	78
French	32,055	2	16,028	14
Arabic	6,975	1	6,975	2
Chinese	6,215	3	2,072	0
Spanish	3,140	2	1,570	0
Italian	2,775	0	N/A	1
Vietnamese	2,560	1	2,560	0

Nepean

	1996 Population	Reported Evangelical Churches	People per Evangelical Church	New Evangelical Churches Needed to Provide One for Every 2,000 People
English	97,175	17	5,716	32
French	2,115	1	2,115	0
Chinese	2,245	2	1,123	0
Arabic	1,515	0	N/A	1
Italian	1,205	1	1,205	0
Polish	865	0	N/A	0
Vietnamese	805	0	N/A	0

Gloucester

	1996 Population	Reported Evangelical Churches	People per Evangelical Church	New Evangelical Churches Needed to Provide One for Every 2,000 People
English	70,675	11	6,425	24
French	20,870	2	N/A	8
Arabic	1,335	0	N/A	1
Chinese	1,270	0	N/A	1
Spanish	595	0	N/A	0
Vietnamese	530	0	N/A	0
Polish	440	0	N/A	0

Greater Oshawa Area

	1996 Population	Reported Evangelical Churches	People per Evangelical Church	New Evangelical Churches Needed to Provide One for Every 2,000 People
English	251,335	44	5,712	82
French	2,130	0	N/A	1
Polish	2,000	0	N/A	1
Italian	1,350	0	N/A	1
Chinese	865	0	N/A	0
Ukrainian	860	1	860	0
Portuguese	685	0	N/A	0

Oshawa Proper

	1996 Population	Reported Evangelical Churches	People per Evangelical Church	New Evangelical Churches Needed to Provide One for Every 2,000 People
English	123,810	23	5,383	39
French	1,520	0	N/A	1
Polish	1,605	0	N/A	1
Italian	760	0	N/A	0
Ukrainian	610	1	610	0
Portuguese	505	0	N/A	0
Chinese	335	0	N/A	0

Greater Toronto Area

	1996 Population	Reported Evangelical Churches	People per Evangelical Church	New Evangelical Churches Needed to Provide One for Every 2,000 People
English	3,077,400	561	5,486	978
French	19,605	0	N/A	10
Chinese	243,825	64	3,810	58
Italian	95,995	4	23,999	44
Portuguese	68,445	8	8,556	26
Polish	52,520	2	26,260	24
Punjabi	51,270	1	51,270	25

Toronto Proper

	1996 Population	Reported Evangelical Churches	People per Evangelical Church	New Evangelical Churches Needed to Provide One for Every 2,000 People
English	447,855	87	5,148	137
French	4,520	0	N/A	2
Chinese	44,450	12	3,704	10
Portuguese	33,840	5	6,768	12
Vietnamese	10,580	3	3,527	2
Italian	10,325	2	5,163	3
Spanish	8,800	7	1,257	0

North York

	1996 Population	Reported Evangelical Churches	People per Evangelical Church	New Evangelical Churches Needed to Provide One for Every 2,000 People
English	359,550	65	5,532	115
French	2,560	0	N/A	1
Chinese	37,795	14	2,700	0
Italian	30,220	2	15,110	13
Spanish	15,435	11	1,403	0
Russian	9,850	0	N/A	5
Farsi	8,320	0	N/A	4

Scarborough

	1996 Population	Reported Evangelical Churches	People per Evangelical Church	New Evangelical Churches Needed to Provide One for Every 2,000 People
English	363,415	59	6,160	123
French	1,975	0	N/A	1
Chinese	71,215	17	4,189	19
Tamil	21,525	6	3,588	0
Tagalog	8,340	2	4,170	2
Greek	6,705	1	6,705	2
Italian	5,770	0	N/A	3

Mississauga

	1996 Population	Reported Evangelical Churches	People per Evangelical Church	New Evangelical Churches Needed to Provide One for Every 2,000 People
English	394,955	53	7,452	144
French	2,830	0	N/A	1
Chinese	19,525	9	2,169	1
Polish	16,020	0	N/A	8
Punjabi	16,005	0	N/A	8
Portuguese	8,620	0	N/A	4
Italian	6,980	0	N/A	3

Etobicoke

	1996 Population	Reported Evangelical Churches	People per Evangelical Church	New Evangelical Churches Needed to Provide One for Every 2,000 People
English	229,310	45	5,096	70
French	985	0	N/A	0
Polish	12,560	0	N/A	6
Punjabi	8,270	0	N/A	4
Italian	8,230	0	N/A	4
Spanish	5,700	3	1,900	0
Ukrainian	4,830	0	N/A	2

York

	1996 Population	Reported Evangelical Churches	People per Evangelical Church	New Evangelical Churches Needed to Provide One for Every 2,000 People
English	91,820	20	4,591	26
French	345	0	N/A	0
Portuguese	9,050	0	N/A	5
Italian	8,360	0	N/A	4
Spanish	5,780	2	2,890	1
Chinese	3,060	0	N/A	2
Vietnamese	2,825	0	N/A	1

East York

	1996 Population	Reported Evangelical Churches	People per Evangelical Church	New Evangelical Churches Needed to Provide One for Every 2,000 People
English	76,465	14	5,462	24
French	665	0	N/A	0
Chinese	4,470	1	4,470	1
Greek	4,250	0	N/A	2
Tamil	2,025	0	N/A	1
Tagalog	1,735	1	1,735	0
Gujarati	1,385	0	N/A	1

Markham

	1996 Population	Reported Evangelical Churches	People per Evangelical Church	New Evangelical Churches Needed to Provide One for Every 2,000 People
English	117,165	22	5,326	37
French	595	0	N/A	0
Chinese	32,960	6	5,493	10
Italian	1,685	0	N/A	1
Punjabi	1,495	0	N/A	1
Gujarati	1,160	0	N/A	1
Tagalog	975	1	975	0

Vaughan

	1996 Population	Reported Evangelical Churches	People per Evangelical Church	New Evangelical Churches Needed to Provide One for Every 2,000 People
English	96,175	11	8,743	37
French	310	0	N/A	0
Italian	14,270	0	N/A	7
Chinese	4,005	0	N/A	2
Hebrew	1,645	0	N/A	1
Russian	1,575	0	N/A	1
Punjabi	980	0	N/A	0

Richmond Hill

	1996 Population	Reported Evangelical Churches	People per Evangelical Church	New Evangelical Churches Needed to Provide One for Every 2,000 People
English	72,690	14	5,192	22
French	390	0	N/A	0
Chinese	15,905	3	5,302	5
Italian	2,245	0	N/A	1
Persian	845	0	N/A	0
Greek	565	0	N/A	0
Arabic	495	0	N/A	0

Brampton

	1996 Population	Reported Evangelical Churches	People per Evangelical Church	New Evangelical Churches Needed to Provide One for Every 2,000 People
English	216,710	35	6,192	73
French	1,235	0	N/A	1
Punjabi	12,595	0	N/A	6
Portuguese	5,495	2	2,748	1
Chinese	2,640	1	2,640	0
Italian	2,500	0	N/A	1
Spanish	1,880	0	N/A	1

Oakville

	1996 Population	Reported Evangelical Churches	People per Evangelical Church	New Evangelical Churches Needed to Provide One for Every 2,000 People
English	113,850	18	6,325	39
French	1,020	0	N/A	1
Portuguese	1,635	1	1,635	0
Chinese	1,290	0	N/A	1
Italian	1,120	0	N/A	1
Polish	920	0	N/A	0
Punjabi	745	0	N/A	0

Greater Hamilton Area

	1996 Population	Reported Evangelical Churches	People per Evangelical Church	New Evangelical Churches Needed to Provide One for Every 2,000 People
English	546,895	145	3,772	128
French	2,645	0	N/A	1
Italian	9,735	0	N/A	5
Polish	5,970	0	N/A	3
Portuguese	4,590	1	4,590	1
Chinese	4,220	2	2,110	0
Croatian	3,210	0	N/A	2

Hamilton Proper

	1996 Population	Reported Evangelical Churches	People per Evangelical Church	New Evangelical Churches Needed to Provide One for Every 2,000 People
English	267,370	68	3,932	66
French	1,310	0	N/A	1
Italian	7,415	0	N/A	4
Portuguese	4,130	1	4,130	1
Polish	4,045	0	N/A	2
Chinese	3,340	2	1,670	0
Spanish	2,500	5	500	0

Burlington

	1996 Population	Reported Evangelical Churches	People per Evangelical Church	New Evangelical Churches Needed to Provide One for Every 2,000 People
English	128,690	27	4,766	37
French	1,005	0	N/A	1
Polish	950	0	N/A	0
Chinese	455	0	N/A	0
Punjabi	440	0	N/A	0
German	260	0	N/A	0
Portuguese	260	0	N/A	0

Greater St. Catharines-Niagara Area

	1996 Population	Reported Evangelical Churches	People per Evangelical Church	New Evangelical Churches Needed to Provide One for Every 2,000 People
English	337,995	131	2,580	38
French	5,265	0	N/A	3
Italian	5,880	4	1,470	0
Polish	2,460	0	N/A	1
German	1,625	5	325	0
Chinese	1,170	1	1,170	0
Spanish	1,075	2	538	0

St. Catharines Proper

	1996 Population	Reported Evangelical Churches	People per Evangelical Church	New Evangelical Churches Needed to Provide One for Every 2,000 People
English	117,675	40	2,942	19
French	1,355	0	N/A	1
Polish	1,645	0	N/A	1
Italian	1,275	0	N/A	1
German	655	2	328	0
Spanish	610	2	305	0
Ukrainian	500	0	N/A	0

Greater Kitchener Area

	1996 Population	Reported Evangelical Churches	People per Evangelical Church	New Evangelical Churches Needed to Provide One for Every 2,000 People
English	332,165	105	3,163	61
French	1,495	0	N/A	1
Portuguese	6,970	2	3,485	1
German	4,800	2	2,400	0
Polish	3,310	0	N/A	2
Spanish	3,065	8	383	0
Chinese	2,245	3	748	0

Kitchener Proper

	1996 Population	Reported Evangelical Churches	People per Evangelical Church	New Evangelical Churches Needed to Provide One for Every 2,000 People
English	151,505	43	3,523	33
French	705	0	N/A	0
Portuguese	2,395	0	N/A	1
Spanish	2,080	6	347	0
Polish	2,080	0	N/A	1
German	1,835	1	1,835	0
Romanian	1,825	1	1,825	0

Cambridge

	1996 Population	Reported Evangelical Churches	People per Evangelical Church	New Evangelical Churches Needed to Provide One for Every 2,000 People
English	88,905	26	3,419	18
French	445	0	N/A	0
Portuguese	4,335	2	2,168	0
Spanish	635	2	318	0
Vietnamese	425	0	N/A	0
Polish	420	0	N/A	0
Italian	400	0	N/A	0

Greater London Area

	1996 Population	Reported Evangelical Churches	People per Evangelical Church	New Evangelical Churches Needed to Provide One for Every 2,000 People
English	357,700	107	3,343	72
French	1,145	0	N/A	1
Polish	5,265	0	N/A	3
Portuguese	3,085	1	3,085	1
Spanish	2,635	5	527	0
Arabic	2,490	0	N/A	1
Chinese	2,240	2	1,120	0

London Proper

	1996 Population	Reported Evangelical Churches	People per Evangelical Church	New Evangelical Churches Needed to Provide One for Every 2,000 People
English	288,475	63	4,579	81
French	1,060	0	N/A	1
Polish	4,980	0	N/A	2
Portuguese	3,060	1	3,060	1
Spanish	2,605	5	521	0
Arabic	2,445	0	N/A	1
Chinese	2,105	2	1,053	0

Greater Thunder Bay Area

	1996 Population	Reported Evangelical Churches	People per Evangelical Church	New Evangelical Churches Needed to Provide One for Every 2,000 People
English	116,435	32	3,639	26
French	920	0	N/A	0
Italian	1,610	0	N/A	1
Finnish	1,040	1	1,040	0
Polish	695	0	N/A	0
Ukrainian	245	0	N/A	0
Chinese	215	0	N/A	0

Greater Winnipeg Area

	1996 Population	Reported Evangelical Churches	People per Evangelical Church	New Evangelical Churches Needed to Provide One for Every 2,000 People
English	580,105	174	3,334	116
French	13,330	0	N/A	7
Tagalog	9,075	5	1,815	0
Chinese	7,175	3	2,392	1
German	4,910	5	982	0
Polish	4,435	0	N/A	2
Portuguese	3,910	1	3,910	1

Greater Regina Area

	1996 Population	Reported Evangelical Churches	People per Evangelical Church	New Evangelical Churches Needed to Provide One for Every 2,000 People
English	183,165	52	3,522	40
French	820	0	N/A	0
Chinese	1,805	2	903	0
Vietnamese	590	0	N/A	0
Spanish	365	1	365	0
Tagalog	335	0	N/A	0
Greek	320	0	N/A	0

Greater Saskatoon Area

	1996 Population	Reported Evangelical Churches	People per Evangelical Church	New Evangelical Churches Needed to Provide One for Every 2,000 People
English	205,155	86	2,386	17
French	875	0	N/A	0
Chinese	1,805	2	903	0
German	1,040	1	1,040	0
Ukrainian	755	0	N/A	0
Vietnamese	445	0	N/A	0
Spanish	420	1	420	0

Greater Calgary Area

	1996 Population	Reported Evangelical Churches	People per Evangelical Church	New Evangelical Churches Needed to Provide One for Every 2,000 People
English	718,300	192	3,741	167
French	3,110	0	N/A	2
Chinese	28,705	12	2,392	2
Vietnamese	6,445	2	3,223	1
Punjabi	6,040	0	N/A	3
Polish	4,415	1	4,415	1
Spanish	4,355	8	544	0

Greater Edmonton Area

	1996 Population	Reported Evangelical Churches	People per Evangelical Church	New Evangelical Churches Needed to Provide One for Every 2,000 People
English	756,050	212	3,566	166
French	5,465	0	N/A	3
Chinese	25,015	8	3,127	5
Punjabi	5,930	1	5,930	2
Polish	5,490	1	5,490	2
Vietnamese	4,975	2	2,488	0
Spanish	4,170	5	834	0

Edmonton Proper

	1996 Population	Reported Evangelical Churches	People per Evangelical Church	New Evangelical Churches Needed to Provide One for Every 2,000 People
English	517,525	139	3,723	120
French	3,940	0	N/A	2
Chinese	24,690	8	3,086	4
Punjabi	5,845	1	5,845	2
Polish	5,370	1	5,370	2
Vietnamese	4,965	2	2,483	0
Spanish	4,055	5	811	0

Greater Kelowna Area

	1996 Population	Reported Evangelical Churches	People per Evangelical Church	New Evangelical Churches Needed to Provide One for Every 2,000 People
English	129,375	58	2,231	7
French	655	0	N/A	0
German	1,300	3	433	0
Punjabi	705	0	N/A	0
Hungarian	275	0	N/A	0
Spanish	190	0	N/A	0
Italian	185	0	N/A	0

Greater Vancouver Area

	1996 Population	Reported Evangelical Churches	People per Evangelical Church	New Evangelical Churches Needed to Provide One for Every 2,000 People
English	1,370,635	373	3,675	312
French	6,860	1	6,860	2
Chinese	198,695	58	3,426	41
Punjabi	52,235	0	N/A	26
Korean	12,260	18	681	0
Tagalog	11,330	14	809	0
Vietnamese	11,265	7	1,609	0

Vancouver Proper

	1996 Population	Reported Evangelical Churches	People per Evangelical Church	New Evangelical Churches Needed to Provide One for Every 2,000 People
English	322,915	87	3,712	74
French	2,745	0	N/A	1
Chinese	102,165	32	3,193	19
Punjabi	9,925	0	N/A	5
Vietnamese	8,610	3	2,870	1
Tagalog	5,350	8	669	0
Spanish	4,120	7	589	0

Surrey

	1996 Population	Reported Evangelical Churches	People per Evangelical Church	New Evangelical Churches Needed to Provide One for Every 2,000 People
English	236,090	73	3,234	45
French	675	0	N/A	0
Punjabi	28,740	0	N/A	14
Chinese	7,765	1	7,765	3
Hindi	3,330	1	3,330	1
Korean	1,870	3	623	0
Spanish	1,640	3	547	0

Burnaby

	1996 Population	Reported Evangelical Churches	People per Evangelical Church	New Evangelical Churches Needed to Provide One for Every 2,000 People
English	120,550	37	3,258	23
French	680	0	N/A	0
Chinese	27,110	7	3,873	7
Korean	2,945	5	589	0
Punjabi	2,605	0	N/A	1
Italian	1,555	0	N/A	1
Spanish	1,320	4	330	0

Richmond

	1996 Population	Reported Evangelical Churches	People per Evangelical Church	New Evangelical Churches Needed to Provide One for Every 2,000 People
English	92,365	28	3,299	18
French	410	0	N/A	0
Chinese	38,405	10	3,841	9
Punjabi	3,425	0	N/A	2
Tagalog	1,540	1	1,540	0
Japanese	930	0	N/A	0
Spanish	605	0	N/A	0

Greater Victoria Area

	1996 Population	Reported Evangelical Churches	People per Evangelical Church	New Evangelical Churches Needed to Provide One for Every 2,000 People
English	283,090	66	4,289	76
French	1,435	0	N/A	1
Chinese	4,505	2	2,253	0
Punjabi	1,590	0	N/A	1
Portuguese	690	1	690	0
German	595	0	N/A	0
Vietnamese	570	1	570	0

Appendix Three

Church Planting Needs
by Province

Appoximately 82% of Canadians from coast to coast are unchurched —that is, of 30 million Canadians, 24.6 million are not following Christ.

-Murray Moerman

Newfoundland

City / Town	Actual 1996 Population	Reported Evangelical Churches	People per Evangelical Churches	New Evangelical Churches Needed to Have One Church for Every		
				2000 People	1000 People	500 People
St. John's	101,936	15	6,796	36	87	189
Mount Pearl	25,519	3	8,506	10	23	48
Corner Brook	21,893	9	2,433	2	13	35
Conception Bay South	19,265	4	4,816	6	15	35
Grand Falls-Windsor	14,160	5	2,832	2	9	23
Paradise	7,960	1	7,960	3	7	15
Gander	10,364	6	1,727	0	4	15
Labrador City	8,455	3	2,818	1	5	14
Happy Valley-Goose Bay	8,655	4	2,164	0	5	13
Stephenville	7,764	3	2,588	1	5	13
Portugal Cove-St. Philip's	5,773	0	N/A	3	6	12
Marystown	6,742	3	2,247	0	4	10
Torbay	5,230	0	N/A	3	5	10
Placentia	5,013	1	5,013	2	4	9
Channel-Port aux Basques	5,243	2	2,622	1	3	8
Harbour Grace	3,740	0	N/A	2	4	7
Carbonear	5,168	3	1,723	0	2	7
Bonavista	4,526	2	2,263	0	3	7
Bay Roberts	5,472	4	1,368	0	1	7

Deer Lake	5,222	4	1,306	0	1	6
Wabana	3,136	0	N/A	2	3	6
Clarenville	5,335	5	1,067	0	0	6
Spaniard's Bay	2,771	0	N/A	1	3	6
Bishop's Falls	4,048	3	1,349	0	1	5
Pasadena	3,445	2	1,723	0	1	5
Grand Bank	3,328	2	1,664	0	1	5
Stephenville Crossing	2,283	0	N/A	1	2	5
Burin	2,682	1	2,682	0	2	4
Burgeo	2,098	0	N/A	1	2	4
Holyrood	2,090	0	N/A	1	2	4
Upper Island Cove	2,034	0	N/A	1	2	4
Wabush	2,018	0	N/A	1	2	4
St. Anthony	2,996	2	1,498	0	1	4
Springdale	3,381	3	1,127	0	0	4
Harbour Breton	2,290	1	2,290	0	1	4
Twillingate	2,954	3	985	0	0	3
Gambo	2,339	2	1,170	0	0	3
Glovertown	2,292	3	764	0	0	2
Lewisporte	3,709	6	618	0	0	1
Botwood	3,613	6	602	0	0	1

Prince Edward Island

City / Town	Actual 1996 Population	Reported Evangelical Churches	People per Evangelical Churches	New Evangelical Churches Needed to Have One Church for Every		
				2000 People	1000 People	500 People
Charlottetown	32,531	19	1,712	0	14	46
Summerside	14,525	9	1,614	0	6	20
Stratford	5,869	0	N/A	3	6	12
Cornwall	4,291	0	N/A	0	0	9
Montague	2,001	6	334	0	0	0

Nova Scotia

City / Town	Actual 1996 Population	Reported Evangelical Churches	People per Evangelical Churches	New Evangelical Churches Needed to Have One Church for Every		
				2000 People	1000 People	500 People
Halifax	113,910	34	3,350	23	80	194
Dartmouth	65,629	22	2,983	11	44	109
Bedford	13,638	4	3,410	3	10	23
Amherst	9,669	7	1,381	0	3	12
New Glasgow	9,812	9	1,090	0	1	11
Stellarton	4,968	1	4,968	1	4	9

Antigonish	4,860	2	2,430	0	3	8
Pictou	4,022	1	4,022	1	3	7
Westville	3,976	1	3,976	1	3	7
Springhill	4,193	2	2,097	0	2	6
Truro	11,938	18	663	0	0	6
Port Hawkesbury	3,809	2	1,905	0	2	6
Kentville	5,551	6	925	0	0	5
Trenton	2,952	1	2,952	0	2	5
Bridgewater	7,351	10	735	0	0	5
Wolfville	3,833	3	1,278	0	1	5
Lunenburg	2,599	1	2,599	0	2	4
Liverpool	3,048	3	1,016	0	0	3
Shelburne	2,132	2	1,066	0	0	2
Digby	2,199	7	314	0	0	0
Windsor	3,726	8	466	0	0	0
Berwick	2,195	5	439	0	0	0
Yarmouth	7,568	17	445	0	0	0

New Brunswick

City / Town	Actual 1996 Population	Reported Evangelical Churches	People per Evangelical Churches	New Evangelical Churches Needed to Have One Church for Every		
				2000 People	1000 People	500 People
Saint John	72,494	27	2,685	9	45	118
Moncton	59,313	37	1,603	0	22	82
Fredericton	46,507	44	1,057	0	3	49
Miramichi	19,241	9	2,138	1	10	29
Riverview	16,653	7	2,379	1	10	26
Dieppe	12,497	1	12,497	5	11	24
Bathurst	13,815	7	1,974	0	7	21
Edmundston	11,033	2	5,517	4	9	20
Quispamsis	8,839	3	2,946	1	6	15
Oromocto	9,194	5	1,839	0	4	13
Campbellton	8,404	5	1,681	0	3	12
Grand Falls	6,133	2	3,067	1	4	10
Fairvale	4,951	0	N/A	2	5	10
Caraquet	4,653	0	N/A	2	5	9
Gondola Point	4,324	0	N/A	2	4	9
Tracadie-Sheila	4,773	1	4,773	1	4	9
Beresford	4,720	1	4,720	1	4	8
Memramcook	4,904	2	2,452	0	3	8
Shediac	4,664	2	2,332	0	3	7

New Maryland	4,284	2	2,142	0	2	7
Dalhousie	4,500	3	1,500	0	2	6
Sackville	5,393	5	1,079	0	0	6
Shippagan	2,862	0	N/A	1	3	6
Saint-Jacques	2,767	0	N/A	1	3	6
Grand Manan	2,577	0	N/A	1	3	5
Bouctouche	2,459	0	N/A	1	2	5
Saint-Quentin	2,424	0	N/A	1	2	5
Saint-Basile	3,321	2	1,661	0	1	5
Cap-Pele	2,242	0	N/A	1	2	4
Grand Bay	3,713	3	1,238	0	1	4
Belledune	2,060	0	N/A	1	2	4
St. Stephen	4,961	6	827	0	0	4
Petit Rocher	2,078	1	2,078	0	1	3
Minto	3,056	5	611	0	0	1
Hampton	4,081	9	453	0	0	0
Sussex	4,293	10	429	0	0	0
Woodstock	5,092	13	392	0	0	0

Québec

City / Town	Actual 1996 Population	Reported Evangelical Churches	People per Evangelical Churches	New Evangelical Churches Needed to have One Church for Every		
				2000 People	1000 People	500 People
Montréal	1,016,376	148	6,867	360	868	1,885
Laval	330,393	21	15,733	144	309	640
Québec	167,264	10	16,726	74	157	325
Longueuil	127,977	8	15,997	56	120	248
Gatineau	100,702	5	20,140	45	96	196
Montréal-Nord	81,581	16	5,099	25	66	147
Sherbrooke	76,786	7	10,969	31	70	147
Saint-Hubert	77,042	8	9,630	31	69	146
Beauport	72,920	2	36,460	34	71	144
Charlesbourg	70,942	2	35,471	33	69	140
Sainte-Foy	72,330	6	12,055	30	66	139
Saint-Léonard	71,327	5	14,265	31	66	138
LaSalle	72,029	8	9,004	28	64	136
Saint-Laurent	74,240	16	4,640	21	58	132
Brossard	65,927	4	16,482	29	62	128
Chicoutimi	63,061	3	21,020	29	60	123
Hull	62,339	3	20,780	28	59	122
Verdun	59,714	8	7,464	22	52	111
Jonquière	56,503	3	18,834	25	54	110

Repentigny	53,824	3	17,941	24	51	105
Pierrefonds	52,986	5	10,597	21	48	101
Trois-Rivières	48,419	6	8,070	18	42	91
Dollard-des-Ormeaux	47,826	8	5,978	16	40	88
Drummondville	44,882	5	8,976	17	40	85
Terrebonne	42,214	3	14,071	18	39	81
Lévis	40,407	2	20,204	18	38	79
Saint-Eustache	39,848	1	39,848	19	39	79
Châteauguay	41,423	5	8,285	16	36	78
Granby	43,316	11	3,938	11	32	76
Saint-Hyacinthe	38,981	5	7,796	14	34	73
Anjou	37,308	2	18,654	17	35	73
Victoriaville	38,174	5	7,635	14	33	71
Boucherville	34,989	2	17,495	15	33	68
Saint-Jean-sur-Richelieu	36,435	5	7,287	13	31	68
Aylmer	34,901	3	11,634	14	32	67
Lachine	35,171	5	7,034	13	30	65
Cap-de-la-Madeleine	33,438	5	6,688	12	28	62
Rimouski	31,773	3	10,591	13	29	61
Côte-Saint-Luc	29,705	0	N/A	15	30	59
Blainville	29,603	0	N/A	15	30	59
Pointe-Claire	28,435	3	9,478	11	25	54
Rouyn-Noranda	28,819	4	7,205	10	25	54
Mascouche	28,097	3	9,366	11	25	53

Québec, Cont'd

City / Town	Actual 1996 Population	Reported Evangelical Churches	People per Evangelical Churches	New Evangelical Churches Needed to have One Church for Every		
				2000 People	1000 People	500 People
Salaberry-de-Valleyfield	26,600	2	13,300	11	25	51
Alma	26,127	2	13,064	11	24	50
Boisbriand	25,227	1	25,227	12	24	49
Sept-Îles	25,224	2	12,612	11	23	48
Baie-Comeau	25,554	3	8,518	10	23	48
Saint-Bruno-de-Montarville	23,714	0	N/A	12	24	47
Val-d'Or	24,285	2	12,143	10	22	47
Sainte-Julie	24,030	2	12,015	10	22	46
Sainte-Thérèse	23,477	1	23,477	11	22	46
Trois-Rivières-Ouest	22,886	0	N/A	11	23	46
Sorel	23,248	1	23,248	11	22	45
Mirabel	22,689	0	N/A	11	23	45
Saint-Jérôme	23,916	4	5,979	8	20	44
Outremont	22,571	2	11,286	9	21	43
La Baie	21,057	0	N/A	11	21	42
Saint-Constant	21,933	2	10,967	9	20	42
Val-Bélair	20,176	0	N/A	10	20	40
Saint-Lambert	20,971	2	10,486	8	19	40
Beaconsfield	19,414	0	N/A	10	19	39

Chambly	19,716	1	19,716	9	19	38
Kirkland	18,678	0	N/A	9	19	37
Lachenaie	18,489	0	N/A	9	18	37
Saint-Luc	18,371	0	N/A	9	18	37
Varennes	18,842	1	18,842	8	18	37
Beloeil	19,294	2	9,647	8	17	37
Westmount	20,420	5	4,084	5	15	36
Saint-Georges	20,057	5	4,011	5	15	35
Vaudreuil-Dorion	18,466	2	9,233	7	16	35
Mont-Royal	18,282	2	9,141	7	16	35
Le Gardeur	16,853	0	N/A	8	17	34
Shawinigan	18,678	4	4,670	5	15	33
La Prairie	17,128	1	17,128	8	16	33
Dorval	17,572	2	8,786	7	16	33
Joliette	17,541	2	8,771	7	16	33
Fleurimont	16,262	0	N/A	8	16	33
Thetford Mines	17,635	3	5,878	6	15	32
Gaspé	16,517	1	16,517	7	16	32
L'Ancienne-Lorette	15,895	0	N/A	8	16	32
Greenfield Park	17,337	3	5,779	6	14	32
Saint-Jean-Chrysostome	16,161	1	16,161	7	15	31
Rock Forest	16,604	2	8,302	6	15	31
Bernières-Saint-Nicolas	15,594	0	N/A	8	16	31

Québec, Cont'd

City / Town	Actual 1996 Population	Reported Evangelical Churches	People per Evangelical Churches	New Evangelical Churches Needed to have One Church for Every		
				2000 People	1000 People	500 People
Deux-Montagnes	15,953	2	7,977	6	14	30
La Plaine	14,413	0	N/A	7	14	29
Loretteville	14,168	0	N/A	7	14	28
Cap-Rouge	14,163	0	N/A	7	14	28
Sainte-Catherine	13,724	0	N/A	7	14	27
Grand-Mère	14,223	1	14,223	6	13	27
Rivière-du-Loup	14,721	3	4,907	4	12	26
Amos	13,632	1	13,632	6	13	26
Magog	14,050	2	7,025	5	12	26
L'île-Bizard	13,038	0	N/A	7	13	26
Sainte-Anne-des-Plaines	12,908	0	N/A	6	13	26
Mont-Saint-Hilaire	13,064	1	13,064	6	12	25
Tracy	12,773	1	12,773	5	12	25
Sillery	12,003	0	N/A	6	12	24
Candiac	11,805	0	N/A	6	12	24
Shawinigan-Sud	11,804	0	N/A	6	12	24
Saint-Basile-le-Grand	11,771	0	N/A	6	12	24
La Tuque	12,102	1	12,102	5	11	23
Cowansville	12,051	1	12,051	5	11	23

Bécancour	11,489	0	N/A	6	11	23
L'Assomption	11,366	0	N/A	6	11	23
Vanier	11,174	0	N/A	6	11	22
Rosemère	12,025	2	6,013	4	10	22
Montmagny	11,885	2	5,943	4	10	22
Saint-Antoine	10,806	0	N/A	5	11	22
Roberval	11,640	2	5,820	4	10	21
Matane	12,364	4	3,091	2	8	21
Buckingham	11,678	3	3,893	3	9	20
Charny	10,661	1	10,661	4	10	20
Sainte-Marie	10,966	2	5,483	3	9	20
Saint-Émile	9,889	0	N/A	5	10	20
Saint-Romuald	10,604	2	5,302	3	9	19
L'île-Perrot	9,178	0	N/A	5	9	18
Iberville	9,635	1	9,635	4	9	18
Saint-Félicien	9,599	1	9,599	4	9	18
Mercier	9,059	0	N/A	5	9	18
Pincourt	10,023	2	5,012	3	8	18
Lafontaine	9,008	0	N/A	5	9	18
Lorraine	8,876	0	N/A	4	9	18
Saint-Raymond	8,733	0	N/A	4	9	17
Saint-Timothée	8,495	0	N/A	4	8	17
Lachute	11,493	6	1,916	0	5	17

Québec, Cont'd

City / Town	Actual 1996 Population	Reported Evangelical Churches	People per Evangelical Churches	New Evangelical Churches Needed to have One Church for Every		
				2000 People	1000 People	500 People
Bois-des-Filion	7,124	0	N/A	4	7	14
Mont-Laurier	8,007	2	4,004	2	6	14
Mistassini	6,904	0	N/A	3	7	14
La Sarre	8,345	3	2,782	1	5	14
Saint-Louis-de-France	7,327	1	7,327	3	6	14
Otterburn Park	7,320	1	7,320	3	6	14
Delson	6,703	0	N/A	3	7	13
Chibougamau	8,664	4	2,166	0	5	13
Port-Cartier	7,070	1	7,070	3	6	13
Beauharnois	6,435	0	N/A	3	6	13
Saint-Rédempteur	6,358	0	N/A	3	6	13
Plessisville	6,810	1	6,810	2	6	13
Amqui	6,800	1	6,800	2	6	13
Asbestos	6,271	0	N/A	3	6	13
Mont-Joli	6,267	0	N/A	3	6	13
Coaticook	6,653	1	6,653	2	6	12
Hampstead	6,986	2	3,493	1	5	12
Lavaltrie	5,821	0	N/A	3	6	12
Donnacona	5,739	0	N/A	3	6	11

Charlemagne	5,739	0	N/A	3	6	11
Saint-Rémi	5,707	0	N/A	3	6	11
Carignan	5,614	0	N/A	3	6	11
Marieville	5,510	0	N/A	3	6	11
Pointe-Calumet	5,443	0	N/A	3	5	11
Lac-Mégantic	5,864	1	5,864	2	5	11
Montréal-Ouest	5,254	0	N/A	3	5	11
Lac-Brome	5,073	0	N/A	3	5	10
Farnham	6,044	2	3,022	1	4	10
Windsor	4,904	0	N/A	2	5	10
La Pocatière	4,887	0	N/A	2	5	10
Sainte-Adèle	5,837	2	2,919	1	4	10
Laterrière	4,815	0	N/A	2	5	10
Sainte-Anne-de-Bellevue	4,700	0	N/A	2	5	9
Pont-Rouge	4,676	0	N/A	2	5	9
Sainte-Agathe-des-Monts	5,669	2	2,835	1	4	9
Sainte-Anne-des-Monts	5,617	2	2,809	1	4	9
LeMoyne	5,052	1	5,052	2	4	9
Roxboro	5,950	3	1,983	0	3	9
La Malbaie-Pointe-au-Pic	4,918	1	4,918	1	4	9
Black Lake	4,408	0	N/A	2	4	9
Nicolet	4,352	0	N/A	2	4	9
Hudson	4,796	1	4,796	1	4	9

Québec, Cont'd

City / Town	Actual 1996 Population	Reported Evangelical Churches	People per Evangelical Churches	New Evangelical Churches Needed to have One Church for Every		
				2000 People	1000 People	500 People
Bromont	4,290	0	N/A	2	4	9
Acton Vale	4,685	1	4,685	1	4	8
Sainte-Rosalie	4,153	0	N/A	2	4	8
Pointe-au-Père	4,145	0	N/A	2	4	8
Saint-Jovite	4,609	1	4,609	1	4	8
Waterloo	4,040	0	N/A	2	4	8
Maniwaki	4,527	1	4,527	1	4	8
Saint-Boniface-de-Shawinigan	3,998	0	N/A	2	4	8
Princeville	3,997	0	N/A	2	4	8
Percé	3,993	0	N/A	2	4	8
Saint-Georges	3,929	0	N/A	2	4	8
Forestville	3,894	0	N/A	2	4	8
Normandin	3,873	0	N/A	2	4	8
Trois-Pistoles	3,807	0	N/A	2	4	8
Baie-d'Urfé	3,774	0	N/A	2	4	8
Beauceville	3,751	0	N/A	2	4	8
Saint-Pierre	4,739	2	2,370	0	3	7
Saint-Zotique	3,683	0	N/A	2	4	7
Malartic	4,154	1	4,154	1	3	7
L'Épiphanie	4,153	1	4,153	1	3	7

East Angus	3,642	0	N/A	2	4	7
Château-Richer	3,579	0	N/A	2	4	7
Métabetchouan	3,474	0	N/A	2	3	7
Berthierville	3,952	1	3,952	1	3	7
Dégelis	3,437	0	N/A	2	3	7
Bromptonville	3,426	0	N/A	2	3	7
Lebel-sur-Quévillon	3,416	0	N/A	2	3	7
Grande-Rivière	3,888	1	3,888	1	3	7
Dunham	3,370	0	N/A	2	3	7
Chandler	3,358	0	N/A	2	3	7
Rawdon	3,855	1	3,855	1	3	7
Sainte-Geneviève	3,339	0	N/A	2	3	7
Pohénégamook	3,259	0	N/A	2	3	7
Saint-Joseph-de-Beauce	3,240	0	N/A	2	3	6
Richelieu	3,195	0	N/A	2	3	6
Témiscaming	3,112	0	N/A	2	3	6
Cabano	3,086	0	N/A	2	3	6
Baie-Saint-Paul	3,569	1	3,569	1	3	6
Richmond	3,053	0	N/A	2	3	6
Sainte-Anne-de-Beaupré	3,023	0	N/A	2	3	6
Montréal-Est	3,523	1	3,523	1	3	6
Napierville	3,004	0	N/A	2	3	6
Saint-Pamphile	2,990	0	N/A	1	3	6
Saint-Césaire	2,990	0	N/A	1	3	6

Québec, Cont'd

City / Town	Actual 1996 Population	Reported Evangelical Churches	People per Evangelical Churches	New Evangelical Churches Needed to have One Church for Every		
				2000 People	1000 People	500 People
Val-David	3,473	1	3,473	1	2	6
Saint-Marc-des-Carrières	2,955	0	N/A	1	3	6
Warwick	2,904	0	N/A	1	3	6
Saint-Sauveur-des-Monts	2,904	0	N/A	1	3	6
Carleton	2,886	0	N/A	1	3	6
Mont-Rolland	2,882	0	N/A	1	3	6
Saint-Gabriel	2,862	0	N/A	1	3	6
Ville-Marie	2,855	0	N/A	1	3	6
Cap-Chat	2,847	0	N/A	1	3	6
Beaupré	2,799	0	N/A	1	3	6
Bedford	2,748	0	N/A	1	3	5
Huntingdon	2,746	0	N/A	1	3	5
Fermont	3,234	1	3,234	1	2	5
Clermont	3,225	1	3,225	1	2	5
Laurentides	2,703	0	N/A	1	3	5
Disraëli	2,657	0	N/A	1	3	5
Stanstead	3,112	1	3,112	1	2	5
Maple Grove	2,606	0	N/A	1	3	5
Deauville	2,599	0	N/A	1	3	5
Saint-Tite	2,555	0	N/A	1	3	5

Lac-Etchemin	2,488	0	N/A	1	2	5
Senneterre	3,488	2	1,744	0	1	5
Melocheville	2,486	0	N/A	1	2	5
New Richmond	3,941	3	1,314	0	1	5
Léry	2,410	0	N/A	1	2	5
Laurier-Station	2,399	0	N/A	1	2	5
Saint-Jacques	2,261	0	N/A	1	2	5
Saint-Pie	2,249	0	N/A	1	2	4
Matagami	2,243	0	N/A	1	2	4
Sainte-Agathe-Sud	2,209	0	N/A	1	2	4
Ferme-Neuve	2,178	0	N/A	1	2	4
Chute-aux-Outardes	2,155	0	N/A	1	2	4
Rimouski-Est	2,119	0	N/A	1	2	4
Causapscal	2,080	0	N/A	1	2	4
Omerville	2,068	0	N/A	1	2	4
Pointe-Lebel	2,011	0	N/A	1	2	4
Saint-Pascal	2,504	1	2,504	0	2	4
Valcourt	2,442	1	2,442	0	1	4
Notre-Dame-du-Lac	2,193	1	2,193	0	1	3
L'Annonciation	2,085	1	2,085	0	1	3
Lennoxville	4,036	5	807	0	0	3
Thurso	2,498	2	1,249	0	0	3
Chapais	2,030	2	1,015	0	0	2
Brownsburg	2,583	4	646	0	0	1

Ontario

City / Town	Actual 1996 Population	Reported Evangelical Churches	People per Evangelical Churches	New Evangelical Churches Needed to Have One Church for Every		
				2000 People	1000 People	500 People
Toronto	653,734	141	4,636	186	513	1,166
North York	589,653	120	4,914	175	470	1,059
Scarborough	558,960	100	5,590	179	459	1,018
Mississauga	544,382	74	7,357	198	470	1,015
Etobicoke	328,718	53	6,202	111	276	604
Ottawa	323,340	52	6,218	110	271	595
London	325,646	81	4,020	82	245	570
Hamilton	322,352	85	3,792	76	237	560
Brampton	268,251	40	6,706	94	228	497
Windsor	197,694	50	3,954	49	148	345
Markham	173,383	29	5,979	58	144	318
Kitchener	178,420	56	3,186	33	122	301
York	146,534	23	6,371	50	124	270
Vaughan	132,549	11	12,050	55	122	254
Burlington	136,976	27	5,073	41	110	247
Oshawa	134,364	25	5,375	42	109	244
Oakville	128,405	20	6,420	44	108	237
St. Catharines	130,926	48	2,728	17	83	214
Nepean	115,100	21	5,481	37	94	209

Thunder Bay	113,662	30	3,789	27	84	197
East York	107,822	19	5,675	35	89	197
Gloucester	104,022	15	6,935	37	89	193
Richmond Hill	101,725	17	5,984	34	85	186
Cambridge	101,429	31	3,272	20	70	172
Sudbury	92,059	16	5,754	30	76	168
Guelph	95,821	28	3,422	20	68	164
Pickering	78,989	9	8,777	30	70	149
Brantford	84,764	30	2,825	12	55	140
Whitby	73,794	10	7,379	27	64	138
Barrie	79,191	21	3,771	19	58	137
Sault Ste. Marie	80,054	24	3,336	16	56	136
Waterloo	77,949	27	2,887	12	51	129
Niagara Falls	76,917	25	3,077	13	52	129
Sarnia	72,738	26	2,798	10	47	119
Ajax	64,430	10	6,443	22	54	119
Peterborough	69,535	26	2,674	9	44	113
Clarington	60,615	11	5,510	19	50	110
Newmarket	57,125	18	3,174	11	39	96
North Bay	54,332	14	3,881	13	40	95
Stoney Creek	54,318	17	3,195	10	37	92
Kanata	47,909	7	6,844	17	41	89
Cornwall	47,403	10	4,740	14	37	85

Ontario, Cont'd

City / Town	Actual 1996 Population	Reported Evangelical Churches	People per Evangelical Churches	New Evangelical Churches Needed to Have One Church for Every		
				2000 People	1000 People	500 People
Kingston	55,947	31	1,805	0	25	81
Timmins	47,499	16	2,969	8	31	79
Welland	48,411	19	2,548	5	29	78
Halton Hills	42,390	10	4,239	11	32	75
Caledon	39,893	10	3,989	10	30	70
Chatham	43,409	22	1,973	0	21	65
Aurora	34,857	6	5,810	11	29	64
Georgina	34,777	7	4,968	10	28	63
Flamborough	34,037	10	3,404	7	24	58
Belleville	37,083	17	2,181	2	20	57
Milton	32,104	8	4,013	8	24	56
Woodstock	32,086	14	2,292	2	18	50
Stratford	28,987	11	2,635	3	18	47
Innisfil	24,711	3	8,237	9	22	46
Valley East	23,537	2	11,769	10	22	45
St. Thomas	32,275	21	1,537	0	11	44
Orillia	27,846	13	2,142	1	15	43
Fort Erie	27,183	12	2,265	2	15	42
New Tecumseth	22,902	6	3,817	5	17	40

Dundas	23,125	7	3,304	5	16	39
LaSalle	20,566	3	6,855	7	18	38
East Gwillimbury	19,770	3	6,590	7	17	37
Bradford West Gwillimbury	20,213	4	5,053	6	16	36
Ancaster	23,403	11	2,128	1	12	36
Brockville	21,752	8	2,719	3	14	36
Grimsby	19,585	6	3,264	4	14	33
Vanier	17,247	2	8,624	7	15	32
Rayside-Balfour	16,050	0	N/A	8	16	32
Whitchurch-Stouffville	19,835	8	2,479	2	12	32
Haldimand	22,128	13	1,702	0	9	31
Orangeville	21,498	12	1,792	0	9	31
Nanticoke	23,485	17	1,381	0	6	30
Thorold	17,883	6	2,981	3	12	30
Port Colborne	18,451	10	1,845	0	8	27
Owen Sound	21,390	16	1,337	0	5	27
Tecumseh	12,828	0	N/A	6	13	26
Trenton	17,179	9	1,909	0	8	25
Cobourg	16,027	7	2,290	1	9	25
Nickel Centre	13,017	1	13,017	6	12	25
Pelham	14,343	4	3,586	3	10	25
Lindsay	17,638	11	1,603	0	7	24
Midland	15,035	6	2,506	2	9	24

Ontario, Cont'd

City / Town	Actual 1996 Population	Reported Evangelical Churches	People per Evangelical Churches	New Evangelical Churches Needed to Have One Church for Every		
				2000 People	1000 People	500 People
Lincoln	18,801	15	1,253	0	4	23
Huntsville	15,918	10	1,592	0	6	22
Niagara-on-the-Lake	13,238	5	2,648	2	8	21
Bracebridge	13,223	6	2,204	1	7	20
Collingwood	15,596	11	1,418	0	5	20
Elliot Lake	13,588	7	1,941	0	7	20
Strathroy	11,852	5	2,370	1	7	19
Port Hope	11,698	5	2,340	1	7	18
Leamington	16,188	14	1,156	0	2	18
Amherstburg	10,245	3	3,415	2	7	17
Hawkesbury	10,162	3	3,387	2	7	17
Walden	10,292	4	2,573	1	6	17
Wallaceburg	11,772	7	1,682	0	5	17
Tillsonburg	13,211	10	1,321	0	3	16
Wasaga Beach	8,698	1	8,698	3	8	16
Pembroke	14,177	12	1,181	0	2	16
Kapuskasing	10,036	4	2,509	1	6	16
Gravenhurst	10,030	5	2,006	0	5	15
Fergus	8,884	3	2,961	1	6	15

Simcoe	15,380	16	961	0	0	15
Rockland	8,070	2	4,035	2	6	14
Dunnville	12,471	11	1,134	0	1	14
Kirkland Lake	9,905	6	1,651	0	4	14
Ingersoll	9,849	6	1,642	0	4	14
Penetanguishene	7,291	1	7,291	3	6	14
Petawawa	6,540	0	N/A	3	7	13
Carleton Place	8,450	4	2,113	0	4	13
Kenora	10,063	8	1,258	0	2	12
Paris	8,987	6	1,498	0	3	12
Fort Frances	8,790	6	1,465	0	3	12
Sturgeon Falls	6,162	1	6,162	2	5	11
Smiths Falls	9,131	7	1,304	0	2	11
Goderich	7,553	5	1,511	0	3	10
Hearst	6,049	2	3,025	1	4	10
Port Elgin	7,041	4	1,760	0	3	10
Onaping Falls	5,277	1	5,277	2	4	10
Iroquois Falls	5,714	2	2,857	1	4	9
Renfrew	8,125	7	1,161	0	1	9
Kincardine	6,620	4	1,655	0	3	9
Arnprior	7,113	5	1,423	0	2	9
Espanola	5,454	2	2,727	1	3	9
Essex	6,785	5	1,357	0	2	9

Ontario, Cont'd

City / Town	Actual 1996 Population	Reported Evangelical Churches	People per Evangelical Churches	New Evangelical Churches Needed to Have One Church for Every		
				2000 People	1000 People	500 People
Wainfleet	6,253	4	1,563	0	2	9
Jaffray and Melick	4,244	0	N/A	2	4	8
Almonte	4,611	1	4,611	1	4	8
Belle River	4,531	1	4,531	1	4	8
Tilbury	4,448	1	4,448	1	3	8
Gananoque	5,219	3	1,740	0	2	7
Dryden	6,711	6	1,119	0	1	7
St. Clair Beach	3,705	0	N/A	2	4	7
Walkerton	5,036	3	1,679	0	2	7
Kingsville	5,991	5	1,198	0	1	7
Petrolia	4,908	3	1,636	0	2	7
Haileybury	4,875	3	1,625	0	2	7
Capreol	3,817	1	3,817	1	3	7
Marathon	4,791	3	1,597	0	2	7
Southampton	3,151	0	N/A	2	3	6
Brighton	4,584	3	1,528	0	2	6
Mount Forest	4,530	3	1,510	0	2	6
Deep River	4,491	3	1,497	0	1	6
Perth	5,886	6	981	0	0	6

Hanover	6,844	8	856	0	0	6
Parry Sound	6,326	7	904	0	0	6
Shelburne	3,790	2	1,895	0	2	6
Mitchell	3,670	2	1,835	0	2	5
Geraldton	2,627	0	N/A	1	3	5
Alexandria	3,531	2	1,766	0	2	5
Prescott	4,480	4	1,120	0	0	5
St. Marys	5,952	7	850	0	0	5
Cochrane	4,443	4	1,111	0	0	5
Seaforth	2,302	0	N/A	1	2	5
Keewatin	2,058	0	N/A	1	2	4
Morrisburg	2,538	1	2,538	0	2	4
Port Stanley	2,499	1	2,499	0	1	4
Casselman	2,877	2	1,439	0	1	4
Blenheim	4,873	6	812	0	0	4
Elora	3,346	3	1,115	0	0	4
Bobcaygeon	2,753	2	1,377	0	1	4
Blind River	3,152	3	1,051	0	0	3
Vankleek Hill	2,030	1	2,030	0	1	3
Aylmer	7,018	11	638	0	0	3
Ridgetown	3,454	4	864	0	0	3
Wingham	2,941	3	980	0	0	3
Mattawa	2,281	2	1,141	0	0	3

Ontario, Cont'd

City / Town	Actual 1996 Population	Reported Evangelical Churches	People per Evangelical Churches	New Evangelical Churches Needed to Have One Church for Every		
				2000 People	1000 People	500 People
Glencoe	2,178	2	1,089	0	0	2
Picton	4,673	7	668	0	0	2
Durham	2,641	3	880	0	0	2
Arthur	2,139	2	1,070	0	0	2
New Liskeard	5,112	8	639	0	0	2
Longlac	2,074	2	1,037	0	0	2
Exeter	4,472	7	639	0	0	2
Sioux Lookout	3,469	5	694	0	0	2
Palmerston	2,468	3	823	0	0	2
Listowel	5,467	9	607	0	0	2
Napanee	5,450	9	606	0	0	2
Lakefield	2,444	3	815	0	0	2
Wiarton	2,400	3	800	0	0	2
Kemptville	3,272	5	654	0	0	2
Clinton	3,216	5	643	0	0	1
Stirling	2,173	3	724	0	0	1
Campbellford	3,647	6	608	0	0	1
Wyoming	2,131	3	710	0	0	1
Frankford	2,096	3	699	0	0	1

Colborne	2,054	3	685	0	0	1
Forest	3,020	5	604	0	0	1
Harrow	2,806	5	561	0	0	1
Bancroft	2,554	5	511	0	0	0
Fenelon Falls	2,040	4	510	0	0	0
Winchester	2,334	6	389	0	0	0
Harriston	2,008	5	402	0	0	0
Dresden	2,589	7	370	0	0	0

Manitoba

City / Town	Actual 1996 Population	Reported Evangelical Churches	People per Evangelical Churches	New Evangelical Churches Needed to Have One Church for Every		
				2000 People	1000 People	500 People
Winnipeg	618,477	175	3,534	134	443	1,062
Brandon	39,175	20	1,959	0	19	58
Thompson	14,385	5	2,877	2	9	24
Selkirk	9,881	6	1,647	0	4	14
Portage la Prairie	13,077	17	769	0	0	9
Dauphin	8,266	8	1,033	0	0	9
The Pas	5,945	5	1,189	0	1	7
Stonewall	3,689	2	1,845	0	2	5
Flin Flon	6,572	8	822	0	0	5
Virden	2,956	3	985	0	0	3
Winkler	7,241	12	603	0	0	2
Steinbach	8,478	15	565	0	0	2
Neepawa	3,301	5	660	0	0	2
Beausejour	2,712	4	678	0	0	1
Swan River	3,986	7	569	0	0	1
Minnedosa	2,443	4	611	0	0	1
Morden	5,689	11	517	0	0	0
Altona	3,286	8	411	0	0	0
Carman	2,704	6	451	0	0	0
Killarney	2,208	7	315	0	0	0

Saskatchewan

City / Town	Actual 1996 Population	Reported Evangelical Churches	People per Evangelical Church	New Evangelical Churches Needed to Have One Church for Every		
				2000 People	1000 People	500 People
Saskatoon	193,647	70	2,766	27	124	317
Regina	180,400	52	3,469	38	128	309
Moose Jaw	32,973	17	1,940	0	16	49
Prince Albert	34,777	22	1,581	0	13	48
Yorkton	15,154	13	1,166	0	2	17
North Battleford	14,051	11	1,277	0	3	17
Weyburn	9,723	9	1,080	0	1	10
Swift Current	14,890	20	745	0	0	10
Estevan	10,752	12	896	0	0	10
Lloydminster (Part)	7,636	6	1,273	0	2	9
Humboldt	5,074	1	5,074	2	4	9
Battleford	3,936	1	3,936	1	3	7
Melville	4,646	4	1,162	0	1	5
Martensville	3,477	3	1,159	0	0	4
La Ronge	2,964	2	1,482	0	1	4
Moosomin	2,420	1	2,420	0	1	4
Meadow Lake	4,813	6	802	0	0	4
Kindersley	4,679	6	780	0	0	3
Esterhazy	2,602	2	1,301	0	1	3

Saskatchewan, Cont'd

City / Town	Actual 1996 Population	Reported Evangelical Churches	People per Evangelical Church	New Evangelical Churches Needed to Have One Church for Every		
				2000 People	1000 People	500 People
Kamsack	2,264	2	1,132	0	0	3
Unity	2,200	2	1,100	0	0	2
Rosetown	2,496	3	832	0	0	2
Tisdale	2,966	4	742	0	0	2
Canora	2,208	3	736	0	0	1
Assiniboia	2,653	4	663	0	0	1
Outlook	2,116	3	705	0	0	1
Warman	2,839	5	568	0	0	1
Nipawin	4,318	8	540	0	0	1
Melfort	5,759	11	524	0	0	1
Maple Creek	2,307	7	330	0	0	0
Biggar	2,351	5	470	0	0	0

Alberta

City / Town	Actual 1996 Population	Reported Evangelical Churches	People per Evangelical Church	New Evangelical Churches Needed to Have One Church for Every		
				2000 People	1000 People	500 People
Calgary	768,082	211	3,640	173	557	1,325
Edmonton	616,306	174	3,542	134	442	1,059
Sherwood Park	64,176	11	5,834	21	53	117
Lethbridge	63,053	27	2,335	5	36	99
Red Deer	60,075	30	2,003	0	30	90
St. Albert	46,888	12	3,907	11	35	82
Medicine Hat	46,783	24	1,949	0	23	70
Fort McMurray	35,213	13	2,709	5	22	57
Grande Prairie	31,140	19	1,639	0	12	43
Airdrie	15,946	7	2,278	1	9	25
Spruce Grove	14,271	4	3,568	3	10	25
Leduc	14,305	8	1,788	0	6	21
Fort Saskatchewan	12,408	6	2,068	0	6	19
Lloydminster (Part)	11,317	6	1,886	0	5	17
Hinton	9,961	4	2,490	1	6	16
Camrose	13,728	12	1,144	0	2	15
Okotoks	8,510	3	2,837	1	6	14
Whitecourt	7,783	3	2,594	1	5	13
Brooks	10,093	8	1,262	0	2	12

Alberta, Cont'd

City / Town	Actual 1996 Population	Reported Evangelical Churches	People per Evangelical Church	New Evangelical Churches Needed to Have One Church for Every		
				2000 People	1000 People	500 People
Cochrane	7,424	4	1,856	0	3	11
Canmore	8,354	6	1,392	0	2	11
Banff	6,098	2	3,049	1	4	10
Crowsnest Pass	6,356	3	2,119	0	3	10
Stony Plain	8,274	7	1,182	0	1	10
Morinville	6,226	3	2,075	0	3	9
Slave Lake	6,553	4	1,638	0	3	9
Wetaskiwin	10,959	13	843	0	0	9
Edson	7,399	6	1,233	0	1	9
Beaumont	5,810	3	1,937	0	3	9
Peace River	6,536	5	1,307	0	2	8
Lacombe	8,018	8	1,002	0	0	8
Drayton Valley	5,883	4	1,471	0	2	8
St. Paul	4,861	2	2,431	0	3	8
Redcliff	4,104	1	4,104	1	3	7
Wainwright	5,079	3	1,693	0	2	7
Grande Cache	4,441	2	2,221	0	2	7
High River	7,359	8	920	0	0	7
Vegreville	5,337	4	1,334	0	1	7

Jasper	4,301	2	2,151	0	2	7
Strathmore	5,282	4	1,321	0	1	7
Sylvan Lake	5,178	4	1,295	0	1	6
Grand Centre	4,176	2	2,088	0	2	6
Ponoka	6,149	6	1,025	0	0	6
Innisfail	6,116	6	1,019	0	0	6
Devon	4,496	3	1,499	0	1	6
Bonnyville	5,100	5	1,020	0	0	5
Cold Lake	4,089	3	1,363	0	1	5
Gibbons	2,748	1	2,748	0	2	4
Vermilion	3,744	3	1,248	0	1	4
Taber	7,214	10	721	0	0	4
Olds	5,815	8	727	0	0	4
High Level	3,093	3	1,031	0	0	3
Didsbury	3,553	4	888	0	0	3
Three Hills	3,022	3	1,007	0	0	3
Blackfalds	2,001	1	2,001	0	1	3
High Prairie	2,907	3	969	0	0	3
Fox Creek	2,321	2	1,161	0	0	3
Rocky Mountain House	5,805	9	645	0	0	3
Grimshaw	2,661	3	887	0	0	2
Drumheller	6,587	11	599	0	0	2
Raymond	3,056	4	764	0	0	2

Alberta, Cont'd

City / Town	Actual 1996 Population	Reported Evangelical Churches	People per Evangelical Church	New Evangelical Churches Needed to Have One Church for Every		
				2000 People	1000 People	500 People
Redwater	2,053	2	1,027	0	0	2
Swan Hills	2,030	2	1,015	0	0	2
Claresholm	3,427	5	685	0	0	2
Cardston	3,417	5	683	0	0	2
Fairview	3,316	5	663	0	0	2
Barrhead	4,239	7	606	0	0	1
Coaldale	5,731	10	573	0	0	1
Stettler	5,220	9	580	0	0	1
Lac la Biche	2,611	4	653	0	0	1
Westlock	4,817	9	535	0	0	1
Pincher Creek	3,659	8	457	0	0	0
Sundre	2,028	4	507	0	0	0
Hanna	3,001	7	429	0	0	0
Athabasca	2,313	6	386	0	0	0
Rimbey	2,106	7	301	0	0	0
Fort MacLeod	3,034	9	337	0	0	0

British Columbia

City / Town	Actual 1996 Population	Reported Evangelical Churches	People per Evangelical Church	New Evangelical Churches Needed to Have One Church for Every		
				2000 People	1000 People	500 People
Vancouver	520,841	167	3,119	93	354	875
Surrey	304,477	91	3,346	61	213	518
Burnaby	179,209	57	3,144	33	122	301
Richmond	148,867	41	3,631	33	108	257
Coquitlam	101,820	17	5,989	34	85	187
Saanich	101,388	20	5,069	31	81	183
Delta	95,411	23	4,148	25	72	168
N. Vancouver District	80,418	13	6,186	27	67	148
Abbotsford	105,403	68	1,550	0	37	143
Kelowna	89,442	44	2,033	0	45	135
Langley District	80,179	33	2,430	7	47	127
Victoria	73,504	24	3,063	13	50	123
Kamloops	76,394	32	2,387	6	44	121
Nanaimo	70,130	20	3,507	15	50	120
Prince George	75,150	32	2,348	6	43	118
Maple Ridge	56,173	15	3,745	13	41	97
Chilliwack	60,186	33	1,824	0	27	87
New Westminster	49,350	18	2,742	7	31	81
Port Coquitlam	46,682	14	3,334	9	33	79

British Columbia, Cont'd

City / Town	Actual 1996 Population	Reported Evangelical Churches	People per Evangelical Church	New Evangelical Churches Needed to Have One Church for Every		
				2000 People	1000 People	500 People
W. Vancouver	40,882	4	10,221	16	37	78
N. Vancouver City	41,475	8	5,184	13	33	75
Campbell River	28,851	10	2,885	4	19	48
Penticton	30,987	15	2,066	0	16	47
Mission	30,519	17	1,795	0	14	44
Port Moody	20,847	4	5,212	6	17	38
Vernon	31,817	26	1,224	0	6	38
Oak Bay	17,865	2	8,933	7	16	34
Langford	17,484	4	4,371	5	13	31
Esquimalt	16,151	3	5,384	5	13	29
Langley City	22,523	17	1,325	0	6	28
White Rock	17,210	7	2,459	2	10	27
Pitt Meadows	13,436	2	6,718	5	11	25
Colwood	13,848	3	4,616	4	11	25
Squamish	13,994	4	3,499	3	10	24
Port Alberni	18,468	13	1,421	0	5	24
Cranbrook	18,131	13	1,395	0	5	23
Courtenay	17,335	12	1,445	0	5	23
Central Saanich	14,611	7	2,087	0	8	22

Prince Rupert	16,741	13	1,288	0	4	20
Comox	11,069	3	3,690	3	8	19
Fort St. John	15,021	11	1,366	0	4	19
North Saanich	10,411	2	5,206	3	8	19
Sidney	10,701	3	3,567	2	8	18
Powell River	13,131	8	1,641	0	5	18
Kitimat	11,136	5	2,227	1	6	17
Summerland	10,584	4	2,646	1	7	17
Coldstream	8,975	2	4,488	2	7	16
Salmon Arm	14,664	14	1,047	0	1	15
Parksville	9,472	4	2,368	0	5	15
Whistler	7,172	1	7,172	3	6	13
View Royal	6,441	0	N/A	3	6	13
Nelson	9,585	7	1,369	0	3	12
Revelstoke	8,047	4	2,012	0	4	12
Terrace	12,779	14	913	0	0	12
Kimberley	6,738	2	3,369	1	5	11
Qualicum Beach	6,728	2	3,364	1	5	11
Merritt	7,631	4	1,908	0	4	11
Ladysmith	6,456	2	3,228	1	4	11
Spallumcheen	5,322	0	N/A	3	5	11
Quesnel	8,468	7	1,210	0	1	10
Sechelt	7,343	5	1,469	0	2	10

British Columbia, Cont'd

City / Town	Actual 1996 Population	Reported Evangelical Churches	People per Evangelical Church	New Evangelical Churches Needed to Have One Church for Every		
				2000 People	1000 People	500 People
Metchosin	4,709	0	N/A	2	5	9
Williams Lake	10,472	12	873	0	0	9
Hope	6,247	4	1,562	0	2	8
Rossland	3,802	0	N/A	2	4	8
Peachland	4,524	2	2,262	0	3	7
Fort Nelson	4,401	2	2,201	0	2	7
Sparwood	3,982	2	1,991	0	2	6
Fernie	4,877	4	1,219	0	1	6
Port Hardy	5,283	6	881	0	0	5
Osoyoos	4,021	4	1,005	0	0	4
Houston	3,934	4	984	0	0	4
Port McNeill	2,925	2	1,463	0	1	4
Lake Cowichan	2,856	2	1,428	0	1	4
Tumbler Ridge	3,775	4	944	0	0	4
Gibsons	3,732	4	933	0	0	3
Invermere	2,687	2	1,344	0	1	3
Smithers	5,624	8	703	0	0	3
Fruitvale	2,117	1	2,117	0	1	3
Duncan	4,583	6	764	0	0	3

Cumberland	2,548	2	1,274	0	1	3
Gold River	2,041	1	2,041	0	1	3
Logan Lake	2,492	2	1,246	0	0	3
Armstrong	3,906	5	781	0	0	3
Sicamous	2,827	3	942	0	0	3
Princeton	2,826	3	942	0	0	3
Oliver	4,285	6	714	0	0	3
Elkford	2,729	3	910	0	0	2
Grand Forks	3,994	6	666	0	0	2
Creston	4,816	8	602	0	0	2
Enderby	2,754	4	689	0	0	2
Fort St. James	2,046	3	682	0	0	1
Chetwynd	2,980	5	596	0	0	1
Golden	3,968	7	567	0	0	1
Chase	2,460	4	615	0	0	1
Vanderhoof	4,401	10	440	0	0	0

Yukon

City / Town	Actual 1996 Population	Reported Evangelical Churches	People per Evangelical Churches	New Evangelical Churches Needed to Have One Church for Every		
				2000 People	1000 People	500 People
Whitehorse	19,157	10	1,916	0	9	28

Northwest Territories

City / Town	Actual 1996 Population	Reported Evangelical Churches	People per Evangelical Churches	New Evangelical Churches Needed to Have One Church for Every		
				2000 People	1000 People	500 People
Yellowknife	17,275	7	2,468	2	10	28
Iqaluit	4,220	1	4,220	1	3	7
Inuvik	3,296	2	1,648	0	1	5
Fort Smith	2,441	1	2,441	0	1	4
Hay River	3,611	4	903	0	0	3

Appendix Four
Maps

"Every new church robs Satan of turf. Every new fellowship of believers takes away his power."

*- Elijah Khoza
former witch doctor,
Zululand, South Africa*

**GREATER TORONTO CENSUS TRACTS
INDICATING PERCENT CAUCASION**

% Caucasion
1 - 10
11 - 20
21 - 30
31 - 40
41 - 50
51 - 60
61 - 70
71 - 80
81 - 90
91 - 100
None

OUTREACH CANADA (AUGUST 1998)

GREATER MONTREAL CENSUS TRACTS
INDICATING HOME LANGUAGE - ITALIAN

% Italian
1 - 2
3 - 4
5 - 6
7 - 8
9 - 10
11 - 15
16 - 20
21 - 25
26 - 30
31 - 40
None

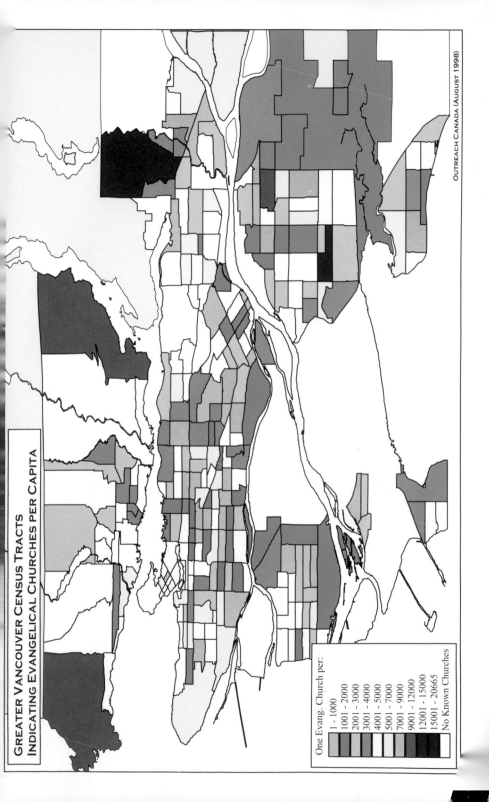

GREATER VANCOUVER CENSUS TRACTS
INDICATING EVANGELICAL CHURCHES PER CAPITA

One Evang. Church per:

1 - 1000
1001 - 2000
2001 - 3000
3001 - 4000
4001 - 5000
5001 - 7000
7001 - 9000
9001 - 12000
12001 - 15000
15001 - 20665
No Known Churches

OUTREACH CANADA (AUGUST 1998)

GREATER OTTAWA-HULL CENSUS TRACTS
INDICATING ETHNIC ORIGIN - GERMAN

% German
1 - 2
3 - 4
5 - 6
7 - 8
9 - 10
11 - 15
16 - 20
21 - 25
26 - 30
31 - 55
None

OUTREACH CANADA (AUGUST 1998)